CICERO
Pro Caelio

— Third Edition —

Stephen Ciraolo
Foreword by Steven Cerutti

Bolchazy-Carducci Publishers, Inc.
Mundelein, Illinois USA

Contributing Editors: Aaron Baker, Gaby Huebner
General Editor: Laurie Haight Keenan
Cover Design & Typography: Adam Phillip Velez
Cover Illustration: Bust of Cicero, Capitoline Museum
Latin text of Cicero's PRO CAELIO: M. T. Ciceronis, *Orationes,* ed. Albert Curtis Clark
 Oxford University Press, 1905

Cicero: Pro Caelio

Stephen Ciraolo

Bolchazy-Carducci Publishers, Inc.
1570 Baskin Road
Mundelein, Illinois 60060
www.bolchazy.com

Printed in the United States of America
2017
by Publishers' Graphics

ISBN 978-0-86516-559-5

Library of Congress Cataloging-in-Publication Data

Cicero, Marcus Tullius.
 Pro Caelio / Cicero ; [edited by] Stephen Ciraolo ; foreword Steven M. Cerutti.-- 3rd ed.
 p. cm.
Includes bibliographical references.
Text in Latin; foreword, introd., and notes in English.
 ISBN 0-86516-559-9 (pbk. : alk. paper)
 1. Caelius Rufus, Marcus. 2. Rome--Politics and government--265-30 B.C. 3. Speeches, addresses, etc., Latin.
I. Ciraolo, Stephen, 1968-
II. Title.

PA6279.C18 2003
875'.01--dc21

2003011047

matri optimae

CONTENTS

FOREWORD

This edition was written for the beginning student of Latin who wishes to translate the speech Cicero delivered in 56 B.C. for the defense of M. Caelius Rufus. Yet nearly everyone who has survived the often tedious process of learning Latin has at one time or another asked: "Why translate at all?" Indeed, if one wishes to read Cicero's *pro Caelio* he need not even know Latin, as all of Cicero's surviving speeches have already been translated into virtually every modern language. Why, then, do students the world over, year in and year out, take lexicon in hand in almost ritualistic fashion to render the same two thousand-year-old sentences into the modern syntax of their own vernaculars?

The answer must be that the process of translation—the observation of nouns and verbs, the determination of semantic function through analysis of morphology and syntax, the marshaling of clauses independent and dependent—is of itself a process through which the mind learns to think rationally. In his statement to the American Council of Learned Societies in 1996, Martin Ostwald addressed this very question: "We must take the training of the mind seriously enough to recognize that each language has its own built-in logic and its own idioms, immersion in which expands our horizons in that it familiarizes us with hitherto unaccustomed ways of thought and expression. The more languages we know the more thoughts we can think and the wider the range of thoughts we are capable of, and the more likely we are to understand patterns of conduct other than our own." Ostwald also recognized that the study of so-called 'dead' languages, such as Latin and Greek, "is of especial importance here in that it compels the student to think in terms that presuppose an entirely different ambience than that to which we are accustomed, highlighting our own peculiarities and bringing before our minds cultural differences side by side with similarities and affinities." If we mean, as we do, to take the training of the mind as the primary objective of the liberal arts education, then we must equip our students with the means to access the texts that form the core of that experience, namely those of the classical authors. Certainly no author better represents the tenets of classical thought than Cicero, and no commentary to date empowers the beginning student with the means to read and enjoy Cicero's *pro Caelio* as does this one.

The *pro Caelio* is a speech that has great appeal for both the neophyte and the advanced student alike. Perhaps more than any other speech in the corpus, the *pro Caelio* stands out as a *tour de force* of Ciceronian persuasion, but in addition it affords us a privileged view into the social circles haunted by Clodia Metelli, generally assumed to be the notorious Lesbia celebrated in the poetry of Catullus. Although the speech was admired in antiquity as one of Cicero's masterpieces, it was generally neglected in modern times before the appearance of R. G. Austin's excellent Oxford edition of 1933. Thereafter it began to be used in college courses, although it was admitted to be very difficult Latin and a test of a student's proficiency. Because of its illumination of the Roman society in which Catullus lived and wrote, his friends and their politics and love affairs, it is best read side by side with the poetry of Catullus and when a student first encounters Catullus. Since the committee for the Advanced Placement* program in Latin has perceived this and included the *pro Caelio* in the curriculum, a new edition of the speech designed especially for AP* students has been badly needed. It is to meet this need that the present edition was undertaken, tested extensively in secondary school and college classes, and now offered to a wider public.

Steven M. Cerutti
East Carolina University

---

* AP is a registered trademark of the College Entrance Examination Board, which was not involved in the production of, and does not endorse, this product.

PREFACE

The third edition of Bolchazy-Carducci's *pro Caelio* has been prepared for at least two and possibly three audiences. It is suitable for third- and fourth-year secondary school students in Advanced Placement* Latin or as one component of undergraduate courses in Roman rhetoric. Additionally, some graduate students in classics approach the literature with less language preparation than in earlier days, and I hope that the volume can answer some of their needs, particularly through its bibliography and its notes on grammatical constructions, textual problems, classical philosophy, Roman history, Latin literary history, and the like. The new edition includes the entire Latin text of *pro Caelio* (80 "chapters" in the Oxford text, 991 lines in this text), plus vocabulary and running notes on pertinent grammatical, stylistic, and historical matters.

The student will note that every word is glossed, in dictionary form, the first time it appears. Vocabulary that first appears in chs. 10–30.15 (lines 102–353) is glossed a second time if it recurs, so that AP* students (who may omit much of this section) will not find themselves working without vocabulary help. Within a given entry, synonyms are separated by commas, while distinctions between meanings are indicated by semicolons. Along with basic definitions I have given basic derivations in square brackets, where the components of a word or their meanings might cause difficulty. These derivations have intrinsic interest and are a pedagogical device designed to help cement the word in the student's mind. Because common words are not glossed the second time they appear, the students are advised to maintain and regularly review their own list of words to be memorized.

In addition to vocabulary help, this manual provides a running grammatical and stylistic commentary. Each difficult grammatical or stylistic concept is fully explained the first time it appears[1], with later references to those sections or to Bennett's *New Latin Grammar,* available from Bolchazy-Carducci Publishers. If the vocabulary and commentary appear dauntingly full in the first few pages, it is partly because they contain the bulk of these grammatical descriptions, partly because much elementary vocabulary is glossed there, and partly because the first two chapters of *pro Caelio* contain rather difficult Latin. (The Romans considered a formal, periodic style appropriate to the exordium of a forensic oration.) The student should not be discouraged by any of

---

* AP is a registered trademark of the College Entrance Examination Board, which was not involved in the production of, and does not endorse, this product.

[1] Please note that prompts like "case?" and "mood?" mean "case and reason?" and "mood and reason?", and reason usually is the most intellectually significant part of the question.

this. Cicero's language may be ornate, but it is natural and never forced. Most sections from ch. 3 on will be considerably easier to translate than (say) many portions of the first book of Caesar's *de bello Gallico*.

Some explanation is also needed on other features of this text. It is hoped that the large amount of vocabulary and grammatical help will reduce unproductive page-flipping through dictionaries to a minimum and so allow students to progress as rapidly through the text as possible. At the same time, the vocabulary entries are full, and respectful of the larger meanings of the words, in order to force students to make their own discoveries and judgments about the meanings of words in context and, ultimately, about the meaning of the text; and, because dictionary skills are important, I have suggested some words worth looking up in a comprehensive lexicon. An hour spent looking up a hundred words in a paperback dictionary is very nearly useless. An hour examining the uses of *mulier, femina, domina, era,* and *matrona*[2] is quite productive indeed. Students of pedagogy may be interested to know that my principal model for this commentary is Arthur Tappan Walker's 1926 edition of Caesar's *de bello Gallico*.

The bibliography will indicate major debts to scholars and sources for further study. I feel it necessary here to point out the immense debt anyone doing serious work on *pro Caelio* owes to Albert Curtis Clark, with whose 1905 Oxford text modern philological scholarship on more than half a dozen speeches of Cicero begins, and to R. G. Austin, whose Oxford commentary is invaluable, particularly in its 1960 incarnation (despite overemphasis, in my view, on reading the speech as a society trial). My debt to these and other scholars goes far beyond the citations in my commentary. Clark's 1905 Oxford text is used here (but with a different typeface and consecutive line numbering), except (1) at line 51 (my numbering), where Austin was permitted to admit *Praetuttiani* to the Oxford text in place of Clark's *Praestutiani* (the reading of S), and (2) at 961, where Shackleton Bailey (1960) would emend *Clodius* to *Cloelius*. In the first case, students should not be bothered with daggers and an incomprehensible corruption for which an obvious emendation has long been recognized; in the second, the emendation seems certainly correct (and is accepted by all commentators I have seen and by Maslowski in his Teubner edition). In general, I have avoided extensive discussion of textual issues in this volume, except where of particular thematic, historical, or grammatical interest.

Lou Bolchazy, Ph.D., took a personal interest in this project from the very start, and I am grateful for his advice, encouragement, and prodding. The principal editor of the first and second edition, Aaron Baker, Ph.D., Esq., formerly of Bolchazy-Carducci, provided a wealth of helpful comments for the first two

---

[2] Buller, p. 124.

editions: his ministrations helped turn word lists, notes, and scrawled margi-
nalia into publishable notes. My sincere thanks for the third edition go to the
editorial and production staff of Bolchazy-Carducci Publishers, and especially to Laurie Haight Keenan, General Editor, whose guidance and extraordinary patience I appreciate more than she knows; to the Classics Departments
of Tabor Academy, The Baldwin School, St. Joseph's Preparatory School, and
Villanova University; and especially to Mr. Bruce Cobbold and Mrs. Jeannette
Keshishian, and to Henry V. Bender, Ph.D., whose friendship, useful information, and unerring advice are a constant source of inspiration.

STEPHEN N. CIRAOLO
Tabor Academy
Marion, Massachusetts
April, 2003

GENERAL ABBREVIATIONS

abl.	ablative	fig.	figuratively
abs.	absolute	fr.	from
acc.	accusative	Fr.	French
act.	active	freq.	frequentative
adj.	adjective	fut.	future
adv.	adverb	gen.	genitive
app.	appendix	Gk.	Greek
b.	born	i.e.	id est,
ca.	circa, "about"		"that is"
card.	cardinal	imp.	imperative
cf.	confer,	impf.	imperfect
	"compare"	indecl.	indeclinable
ch.	chapter	indef.	indefinite
colloq.	colloquial	indic.	indicative
compar.	comparative	indir.	indirect
conj.	conjugation;	inf.	infinitive
	conjunction	interrog.	interrogative
constr.	construction	intrans.	intransitive
correl.	correlative	intro.	introduction
d.	died	irreg.	irregular
dat.	dative	Lat.	Latin
decl.	declension	lit.	literal(ly)
dem.	demonstrative	m.	masculine
dim.	diminutive	MS	manuscript
dir.	direct	n.	neuter; note
ed.	editor, edition	n. s.	new series
e.g.	exempli gratia,	nom.	nominative
	"for example"	num.	numer(ic)al
encl.	enclitic	obj.	object
Engl.	English	p.	page
esp.	especially	pass.	passive
et al.	et alii/alia,	part.	participle
	"and other	perf.	perfect
	people/things"	pers.	person(al)
etc.	et cetera, "and the rest"	pert.	pertaining
ex.	example	pl.	plural
expr.	expressing	plupf.	pluperfect
f.	feminine	poss.	possessive
fasc.	fascicle	postpos.	postpositive

prep.	preposition
pres.	present
priv.	privative
prob.	probably
pron.	pronoun
reflex.	reflexive
rel.	related, relative
repr.	reprinted
sec.	section (of the introduction)
signif.	signifying
sim.	similar
sg.	singular
subj.	subjunctive
subst.	substantive (noun)
suff.	suffix
superl.	superlative
supra	"above"
s.v.	sub voce, "under the heading"
trans.	transitive
transl.	translate; translation; translator
usu.	usually
v.	vide, "see"
var.	various
voc.	vocative
vol.	volume
vs.	versus
w.	with
x	times, occurences
[ ]	material to be supplied
*	hypothetical or unattested form

Praenomina:

C.	Gaius
Cn.	Gnaeus
L.	Lucius
M.	Marcus
M'.	Manius
P.	Publius
Q.	Quintus
Sex.	Sextus
T.	Titus

Other abbreviations as reported in *Oxford Latin Dictionary*.

Italicized text indicates Clark's conjectural insertions.

INTRODUCTION
LIFE AND TIMES OF CICERO

1. Family and Birthplace. M. (Marcus) Tullius Cicero was born on 3 January 106 B.C. to a wealthy equestrian family of Arpinum, a town in the Volscian district of Italy, about seventy miles southeast of Rome. "Equestrian" *(equester)* was originally a military classification, designating individuals of sufficient means to maintain a horse *(equus)* for the cavalry,[3] but in Cicero's day its signification was more economic and political than military: the equestrians formed the Roman upper-middle class, or, to put it less traditionally but more accurately, the non-senatorial branch of the Roman aristocracy.[4]

Rome had conquered Arpinum in 305 B.C., at the conclusion of the Second Samnite War, during the period in which Rome was unifying Italy. The developing Roman organization of Italy might best be described as a federation of states in alliance with Rome *(foedus,* treaty), with varying degrees of rights and obligations vis-à-vis the capital city. Rome had given the residents of Arpinum *cīvitās sine suffrāgiō* (citizenship without the franchise) in 303 B.C., and full citizenship sometime just after 188 B.C., so that by the time of Cicero's birth the area was thoroughly Romanized.

2. Early Education and Tīrōcinium Forī. At some point during Cicero's youth, his father moved the family to Rome, doubtless in part to provide precocious Marcus and his younger brother Quintus, born in 102 B.C., with the best education then available in Italy. Indeed, upon receiving the *toga virīlis* (toga of adulthood) at the age of 15 or 16 in 91 B.C. or 90 B.C., Cicero was entrusted to Q. (Quintus) Mucius Scaevola ("Scaevola the Augur"), one of the foremost lawyers of the day, for his *tīrōcinium forī,* or apprenticeship (*tīrō,* beginner) in law and public life. There were no law schools in the Roman Republic, nor for that matter in most of the United States and Britain, until the end of the nineteenth century. "Studying in chambers" with a prominent lawyer was the normal method of training young lawyers.

---

[3] Throughout this volume I deliberately avoid translating *eques* and *equester* as "knight," since this conjures up inappropriate images of medieval jousts! "Equestrian" presents fewer possibilities for confusion, and possesses the merit of retaining the equus root. If the student or teacher prefers "knight," and if he or she must have a modern parallel, the closest one is probably the English gentry of the eighteenth and nineteenth centuries. See Stockton, p. 1.

[4] "Roman" is a tricky term. In a legal sense, it means a citizen of Rome, whether living in the city or not, and it often excludes residents of the city who were not citizens. Cicero was "Roman" because he was a Roman citizen. However, in a social sense, Roman citizens who did not hail from Rome proper were not as "Roman" as citizens residing in the city itself. Roman aristocrats redefine the meaning of "snobby."

Law at Rome was inextricably intertwined with politics. A young and as-
piring Roman like Cicero would accompany his mentor to the forum to learn
about practical politics, to see how the older man dealt with his political allies
(*amīcī*) in the Senate, and to watch him network with his wider circle of supporters, his *clientēla* (*clientēs,* followers), who in return for their votes and other
services depended upon him as their *patrōnus* for legal representation and
protection. Yet even while diligently drinking in the technical points of law
and rhetoric (public speaking, oratory) from Scaevola and others in his circle,
Cicero was studying hard to master the liberal arts. A well-rounded education
in literature, rhetoric, philosophy, the natural sciences, and mathematics was
considered essential to the development of the sharp mind needed by a first-
class lawyer-statesman.

3. Military Service and Further Studies. In 90–89 B.C. Cicero served briefly under Cn. (Gnaeus) Pompeius Strabo, and later, probably in 88 B.C., under
L. (Lucius) Cornelius Sulla in the Social War, an Italian civil war pitting Rome
and the Roman governing aristocracy against the Italian towns who were al-
lied (*sociī* = "allies") with Rome and were seeking the full political rights of
Roman citizenship. At terrible cost in men and resources, Rome emerged victorious, but a complicated political settlement gave the allies most of what
they had been seeking in the first place. After the war, Cicero spent his late
teens and early twenties furthering his education and even wrote his first
treatise on rhetoric, the *dē inventiōne rhētoricā* ("On Rhetorical Composition").

4. Dictatorship of Sulla. The 80s B.C. were marked by political, social, and
military upheavals between the self-proclaimed "populist" C. (Gaius) Marius
and his followers and the aristocratic Sulla, in which civil government broke
down before military leaders who, returning with victorious armies from cam-
paigns abroad, were capable of imposing their will upon the state. Studying
hard, Cicero himself passed unharmed through this dreadful period, but he
never forgot the terrible experience of this decade of civil war, armed marches
upon Rome, and murder legalized through proscriptions. Sulla was firmly in
control as a despotic *dictātor*[5] and was modifying the constitution so as to give
the Roman senatorial aristocracy full and unchecked power over legislation

---

[5] In the early days of the Roman Republic, the *dictātor* was a magistrate of virtually unlimited authority, appointed by a consul upon senatorial request in order to meet a grave, usually foreign, threat or emergency. The last such dictator was appointed in 216 B.C., during
the Hannibalic invasion. The office was replaced to some extent by the quasi-legal senatorial
decree, the *senātūs cōnsultum ultimum,* which vested the consuls with near-dictatorial power.
Far from saving the state from a foreign incursion, the Sullan assumption of the title in 81 B.C.
was a naked grab for political power.

and the courts,[6] when Cicero began arguing cases before the courts at about the age of 25. In fact, Cicero's first big case, the *prō Rosciō Amerīnō,* won him considerable fame because he successfully opposed Roscius's prosecution by a partisan of Sulla without incurring the dangerous dictator's open disfavor.

5. Weakness of the Republican Constitution. The history of the 80s B.C. illustrates the decline of the Republican political system. A structure erected on a foundation designed when Rome was a mere city-state, the Republican political apparatus, although it had been capable of conquering the entire Mediterranean, was proving insufficient at adapting to governing the world-empire it had created. Ultimately, rule by emperors would at least put an end to the aristocratic rivalries and instability of the late Republic and would provide it with some measure of political and social stability. The price would be *lībertās,* the political freedom of the senatorial class.

6. Further Education and Pleading. Either to make himself scarce after his opposition to Sulla's henchman or, his stated reason, to restore health shattered by overwork, Cicero next spent two years in Greece and Asia Minor, where he attended lectures on philosophy, improved his oratorical style, and otherwise rounded out his education. Upon his return to Rome in 77 B.C., he continued his legal practice and married his first wife, Terentia, who bore him a daughter, Tullia, and a son, Marcus.

7. Election to the Quaestorship and Membership in the Senate. At the minimum age of thirty in 76 B.C., Cicero successfully stood for election to the office of *quaestor,* or finance officer. This was the first magistracy in the *cursus honōrum,* the series of one-year elective offices *(honōrēs)* culminating, for a lucky few, in the consulship. Cicero served his quaestorship in the province of Lilybaeum in western Sicily, where he was an able and honest member of the governor's staff—not very common attributes of provincial officials at this period. Most important, the quaestorship also conferred upon him life membership in the 600-member Senate *(senātus).*

In constitutional theory, the Roman Senate existed merely to advise magistrates when they requested such advice. Moreover, in theory senatorial opinions *(senātūs cōnsulta)* were not binding on magistrates and were not considered "law"; strictly speaking, only a vote taken in a popular assembly of all adult male citizens could make law. But in practice, its accumulation

---

[6] Specifically, the Sullan reforms (1) stripped the tribunes of their right to veto acts of the Senate; (2) deprived the censors of their ability to enrole and remove senators; (3) excluded the equestrians from the juries of the *quaestiōnēs perpetuae* ("standing criminal courts," like the one in which Caelius was later prosecuted), thus leaving them entirely to the senators; and (4) disenfranchised certain Italian towns.

of political clout[7] and its experience in directing Rome's ever more complicated foreign and financial policies gave the Senate a paramount position in
the Roman state for almost two centuries. A magistrate would have been extremely shortsighted to ignore the wishes of the Senate, particularly when
such wishes were given formally as a *senātūs consultum*.

8. Weakening of Senatorial Control. Yet by Cicero's day the Senate's grip
was weakening. Within Rome, its authority was challenged in the name of the
sovereign people by dissatisfied politicians ranging from honest reformers to
scheming demagogues. "The sovereign people," it must be remembered, were
no longer an assembly of hardy country folk from the territory surrounding
Rome, but now an underemployed urban mob. The growth of the empire, the
economic dislocation caused by growing overseas trade, and the importation
of large numbers of foreign slaves had long before ruined the Italian farmer
on whose industry the empire had been built. Moreover, overseas conquest
and administration required powerful military commanders (usually proconsuls [*prō cōnsule*, "in the capacity of a consul"]), who, with an army behind
them, were able to bring their own pressure to bear upon the civil government, or, failing that, to march upon Rome outright as Marius and Sulla had.
This development is the great irony of the history of the Roman Republic. The
early founders of the Republic were said to have feared the concentration of
power in the hands of one man and so had carefully vested supreme authority
in the hands of *two* magistrates *(cōnsulēs)*, each as a check on the other; yet the
late Republic did not need to fear the power of consuls so much as that of the
proconsuls who controlled armies in overseas provinces.

9. Crassus and Pompey Undo the Sullan Constitution. The same age as
Cicero, Cn. Pompeius Magnus ("Pompey the Great"), son of Cn. Pompeius
Strabo, under whom Cicero had served in the Social War, had become a mili-
tary commander under Sulla while still in his early twenties. From 76 B.C. to 73
B.C., he had helped suppress Sertorius, the renegade propraetor of Spain, then
returned to Italy to help M. Licinius Crassus finish off a slave revolt under
Spartacus. As consul (illegally, as he was well below the minimum age) in 70
B.C., Pompey, with M. Licinius Crassus as his colleague, had the bulk of Sulla's
Senate-centered enactments repealed.

10. Prosecution of Verres and Election to the Aedileship. On his return
from Sicily, Cicero continued his tireless efforts at the bar for some years.
Particularly noteworthy was his successful prosecution in 70 B.C. of C. Verres,
a rapacious governor of Sicily, which pitted Cicero against Q. Hortensius

---

[7] Such a collection of leading figures would be powerful in any nation, but was especially so in
Rome because of the enormous importance of the social hierarchy in every area of society.

Hortalus, leader of the Roman bar, and against a senatorial jury far more sympathetic to Verres, a fellow Roman senator, than to a group of Sicilian provincials. Like so many Roman trials, the case had widespread political ramifications, for part of the Senate's legislative agenda that year was reform of the courts, a theme Cicero stresses.

In this year Cicero, now thirty-six years of age, was elected *aedīlis*, or commissioner of public works.[8] Among other duties, aediles were expected, at their own expense, to provide the public with extravagant games and other diversions. In short, the officeholder had to ingratiate himself with the electorate through free entertainment, if he ever wanted to win election to a higher office. Cicero found the whole thing distasteful, and his games were not particularly lavish, but he was able to supply the plebeians of Rome with free meat, procured from the grateful Sicilians for his work against Verres.

11. Election to the Praetorship and Support of Pompey. By a large majority, Cicero was elected *praetor*, or judge, in 67 B.C. at the age of thirty-nine. The praetorship was the next-to-last rung on the Roman political ladder. Just as important, during his praetorship in 66 B.C., Cicero delivered before the people the speech *dē imperiō Cn. Pompeī* ("On Pompey's Command"), supporting, in the teeth of severe conservative opposition, a grant of extraordinary military powers to Pompey. In 67 B.C. Pompey had been given an unprecedented three-year commission to subdue the Mediterranean pirates, whom he supressed in just three months. *Dē imperiō Cn. Pompeī* persuaded the people to give Pompey an enormous extension of his *imperium* ("command"), making him governor of Asia Minor as well as director of the ongoing war against Mithridates, king of Pontus (in northern Asia Minor). After subduing Mithridates, Pompey extended Roman control to most of Asia Minor, as well as to Syria, Judaea, and other parts of the eastern Mediterranean. He amassed vast wealth and *auctōritās* ("political prestige") along the way, a veritable Roman Alexander. Despite some moments of friction and doubt on the part of both Pompey and Cicero, from this point until the Civil War and his death nearly two decades later (48 B.C.), Pompey would be the usual focus of Cicero's political allegiance (though certainly not vice-versa).

During this period begins the extant correspondence between Cicero and his friend Atticus *(epistulae ad Atticum)*. Along with his letters to his friends and family *(epistulae ad familiārēs* and *epistulae ad Quintum frātrem)*, these

---

[8] We do not know whether Cicero was curule (patrician) or plebeian aedile. It might be noted in passing here that the well-known and overemphasized social and legal distinction between patricians and plebeians (lords and commons, so to speak), though important during the first two centuries of the Republic, had actually ceased to be of much legal importance by this period in Roman history. A new nobility had grown up, based upon wealth and attainment of office (see n. 11).

remarkable letters give us a glimpse of Cicero's inner thoughts about the events in which he was an important part and about more private matters, and are important social and historical documents.

12. Character of Roman Political Parties. We have used the terms "populist" in connection with Marius, and "aristocratic" to describe Sulla, and have spoken of "conservative opposition" to Pompey. Loosely speaking, the *populārēs* ("popular party") championed the rights and privileges of the sovereign people, while *optimātēs* ("party of the best men") or *bonī* ("the good men") tended to favor senatorial power and the settled rights of property. But it must be borne in mind that Roman politics had always centered on personalities and personal alliances far more than on policies, programs, or parties in the modern sense. And in many cases scheming aristocrats toed a "popular" line not out of any deep political convictions, but merely in order to get elected. Although some consistent and concrete "policies" had been espoused by *populārēs* during the period of the Gracchi (130s and 120s B.C.), the Roman inclination toward government by personality was increasing in the first century B.C., especially with the rise of "personal" armies and with the glory associated with overseas conquest. Cicero himself drew a distinction between "good" *populārēs* and "bad" *populārēs* (= *furentēs* or *turbulentī*), usually according to whether or not they agreed with him.[9] At any rate, bonds of *amīcitia* (political friendship) trumped any nascent ties of *partēs* (political party). Cicero could therefore consider himself an "optimate," yet support Pompey, a *populāris*, through much of his career.[10]

13. Difficulties of Election to the Consulship. Thus far, to 66 B.C., Cicero had attained each of the offices of the *cursus honōrum* at the minimum legal age, and had shown honorable distinction as well as political savvy in his administration of those offices. But there remained the office of *cōnsul*, chief executive magistrate of the Roman Republic, to some extent less important for the innate power of the office (great though it was) than for its ennoblement[11] of the officeholder and his family forever. Yet the difficulties attendant to a bid for the consulship by a man from Cicero's class, the equestrians, cannot be overstated. With only two consuls elected each year, competition was keen. Moreover, this crown jewel of Roman politics was jealously guarded by

---

[9] For more information on these and other political catchwords, see the notes *ad locc.* (esp. 105n.).

[10] Here indeed lies one of the conspicuous failings of the Roman Republic: dominated by personalities and shifting factions, it never evolved parties capable of proposing to the voters any true and consistent policies.

[11] In the first century B.C., *nōbilitās* meant, in the strictest sense, that a person or his ancestors had attained the consulship.

a small circle of aristocratic houses who regarded it as their personal property. They controlled sufficient resources of money and connections to prevent the election of what they sneered at as a *novus homō*, a "new man."[12]

14. Aristocratic Fear of the Upstart Catiline Helps Cicero into Office. However, political realities surrounding the election of 64 B.C. conspired in such a way as to ensure Cicero's election. The most serious contenders included Cicero, L. Sergius Catilina, commonly known in English as Catiline, a Roman of the noblest birth but also a populist demagogue, and C. Antonius Hybrida, an erratic partisan of Catiline. It is impossible to get an accurate picture of Catiline, because all the literary sources we have are hostile to him. But his rhetoric about debt relief and land reorganization was altogether too much for his fellow aristocrats. In Cicero they had a viable alternative: despite his sometimes "reformist" bent and his leanings toward the populist Pompey, he was essentially a conservative, a bedrock member of the *bonī*, and an advocate of the authority of the Senate. The aristocrats no doubt swallowed their pride and, with Antonius as his colleague, Cicero squeaked into office, the first *novus homō* since 94 B.C.

15. Cicero's Political Position and the Conspiracy of Catiline. Cicero's political program as consul centered on formation of a so-called *concordia ordinum*, a "union of the political orders," namely, of aristocratic and equestrian families. By such an alliance of the wealthy classes he hoped to avert any populist groundswells. But Cicero's activities in the first half of his consulship are overshadowed by Catiline's next moves. Catiline presented himself for election a second time in July of 63 B.C.; when he failed to be elected he hatched a plot to overthrow the government. In Cicero's four famous speeches *in Catilīnam* ("Against Catiline"), delivered in the fall of 63 B.C., Cicero roused the Senate to the severity of the situation and to passage of a *senātūs cōnsultum ultimum* ("final decree of the senate"), a virtual declaration of martial law that granted the consuls full powers to deal with the emergency. With the Senate's advice and consent, five conspirators, who had been nabbed with evidence implicating them, were executed by Cicero without trial or appeal to the people, and therefore in violation of Roman law. Cicero argued that the demands of the moment and the heinousness of the conspirators' crimes gave him authority to do this, but he was on dubious legal grounds to say the least, and, in litigious late-Republican Rome, he became politically vulnerable. Moreover, the suppression of the conspiracy did nothing to solve the underlying social problems which gave life to insurrections such as Catiline's.

---

[12] It is worth mentioning that the conservative tendencies of the Roman voter contributed to the difficulties a man like Cicero would have. In American politics modest or disadvantaged parentage is virtually a badge of distinction; the Romans felt the exact opposite. And so the Republic of Cicero's day, in which theoretically any citizen could be elected to almost any office, generally secured the election of individuals from a tiny number of aristocratic families.

16. Clodius and the Bona Dea Scandal. The year after Cicero's consulship saw the destruction in battle of Catiline and a ragtag collection of his followers, as well as a major religious and political scandal. Each year the Vestal Virgins and other noble women carried out the secret and mysterious rites of the *Bona Dea* ("Good Goddess") in the house of the *pontifex maximus* (chief priest, then C. Julius Caesar; practically speaking, the office was more political than religious). All males, even male animals, were rigorously excluded from the ceremony. P. Clodius Pulcher, a young, brilliant, but thoroughly depraved aristocrat,[13] and a loose cannon[14] in Roman politics, disguised himself as a woman and secretly infiltrated the house. Explanations of this bizarre behavior range from a wild prank to a liaison planned with Caesar's wife Pompeia. At any rate, Clodius was recognized by a servant girl. A cry went up; and though he managed to escape, the damage was done. An impiety had been committed, Roman conservative opinion was scandalized, and Clodius's political enemies saw an opportunity to ruin him. At his trial in 61 B.C., Clodius claimed he was out of town the night of the alleged sacrilege. Cicero himself imprudently took the witness stand and demolished Clodius's alibi, but what is said to have been a heavily bribed jury acquitted Clodius. Cicero had thus acquired a powerful and dangerous enemy.

17. The "First Triumvirate" and Caesar's Gallic Command. In 60 B.C., frustrated by optimate opposition to their political desires, Pompey, Rome's most prominent commander, Crassus, a shrewd aristocrat and businessman said to be the richest man in Rome, and the bold and rapidly rising Caesar formed the so-called "first triumvirate."[15] In this compact, secret at first, but open as time went on, the three men pooled their resources of money and *auctōritās* to control the political and legislative agenda. The most important outcome of this political alliance was Caesar's acquisition of an extraordinary five-year command in Cisalpine and Transalpine Gaul (Gaul this side of [*cis*] the Alps and Gaul beyond [*trāns*] the Alps). Through this command Caesar would hone his military skills and create an army enthusiastically devoted to him.

---

[13] Clodius was one of the *Claudiī Pulchrī*, a very old and influential clan at Rome. Instead of "Claudius," however, he spelled his name "Clodius," in imitation of a plebeian branch of the clan. He was adopted into the plebeian Clōdiī in 59 B.C., in order to become *tribūnus plēbis* (tribune of the plebeians).

Ten *tribūnī plēbis* were elected annually from and by the plebeians, in order to prevent patrician encroachment on their rights. Any tribune could veto virtually any act of an ordinary Roman magistrate, and he had certain advantages in formulating and passing legislation. The tribuneship was therefore an office through which Clodius could carry out his flamboyant activities, including the harassment and attempted political destruction of Cicero.

[14] A loose catapult?

[15] The "first triumvirate" was a purely private arrangement, at first secret and never with any legal standing; it therefore differs greatly from the Second Triumvirate of 43 B.C. (sec. 26).

18. Significance of the "First Triumvirate." The "first triumvirate" was the historical root of the Civil War ten years later and, therefore, of the dictatorship of Julius Caesar and of the monarchy of his successors, the emperors. The monopoly of political power enjoyed by the "triumvirs" rested on military supremacy, overwhelming *auctōritās,* and vast resources of money for patronage and electoral bribery; this formula would not change when three had been whittled down to one.

19. Exile and Recall of Cicero. Irritated by Cicero's independent ways, the "triumvirs" (including, of course, Pompey) were indifferent when, in March of 58 B.C., Clodius passed a bill that stated that anyone who had executed a Roman citizen without trial should be banished from Rome. If there was any doubt that this bill was aimed at Cicero for his execution in 63 B.C. of five Catilinarian conspirators, a second bill naming Cicero specifically and confiscating his property soon clarified matters. Cicero withdrew miserably from Rome. Clodius and his gangs burned down Cicero's house on the Palatine, and, with typical Claudian flair for the dramatic, began erecting a temple to *Lībertās* on the spot.

Almost as soon as Cicero was exiled, his friends and political allies began maneuvering to get him returned, and in August of 57 B.C. he was formally recalled. But despite the restoration of his property and his reinstatement as a senator and *cōnsulāris* (former consul or noble), there was in fact little for him to do: the "triumvirs" were firmly in control of the political process. Indeed, one of the reasons they themselves seem to have wanted his return was the usefulness to them of his silver tongue. Though Cicero had tried to stake out an independent position upon his return (when the grip of the "triumvirate" seemed to be weakening), he was forced to modify his stance after Pompey, Crassus, and Caesar conferred and extended their alliance in 56 B.C. at Luca. Thus, under pressure from Pompey and Caesar, he delivered an oration *dē prōvinciīs cōnsulāribus* ("On the Consular Provinces"), which argued for an extension of Caesar's command in Gaul.

20. Political and Legal Life in the 50s B.C. Cicero continued his work in the law courts through the rest of the 50s B.C. It was during this period, in April of 56 B.C., that he delivered the *prō Caeliō* ("On Behalf of Caelius"), perhaps his greatest private oration. But even here in the courts his activities were throttled by the power of the "triumvirs," and he found himself pressured into arguing cases he personally had no interest in, into supporting positions he opposed, and into defending men he loathed, as in the *prō Balbō* in 56 B.C., and in the defences of Vatinius and Gabinius in 54 B.C. While Cicero sometimes argued cases, like the *prō Sestiō,* for his friends and staked out his own positions, his independence was severely compromised. The pall that hung over the Senate and the courts during this period prefigured the atrophy which would set in during the Empire.[16]

---

[16] However, despite the coming decline in political and forensic oratory, it must be noted that the fullest development of Roman law and jurisprudence per se was achieved under the emperors.

21. Writings. But the world of learning and letters reaped a great harvest from the nadir of Cicero's political life. Now in middle age, he finally had time to turn to writing treatises on a variety of topics in oratory and philosophy: *dē ōrātōre* ("On the Orator") in 55 B.C.; *partītiōnēs ōrātōriae* ("The Kinds of Oratory"), probably in 53 B.C.; *dē rē pūblicā* ("On the Commonwealth") in 51 B.C.; *dē lēgibus* ("On the Laws") in 50 B.C. all belong to this period of his life. Coupled with the voluminous writings of the similar period 46–44 B.C., these essays, though derivative rather than original, helped to transmit Greek philosophical thought to the Roman world. Along with the speeches they helped refine the Latin language into a true literary language. They would be read for centuries by Cicero's fellow Romans, and would contribute to the revival of learning in the late Middle Ages and Renaissance, as well as to the eighteenth-century Enlightenment.

22. Proconsulship of Cilicia. Because of a change in the law affecting consular provinces, Cicero was named governor of Cilicia in Asia Minor in 52 B.C., and began his governorship in July of 51 B.C. Though he regarded this assignment as amounting nearly to another exile, he was again an honest and able administrator. During this period Caelius served as his correspondent, keeping him in touch with affairs in Rome, and the letters Cicero exchanged with Caelius are an excellent source of information about the complicated political situation unfolding in the capital during this crucial time. Indeed, when Cicero arrived back in Italy in late November of 50 B.C., the capital was in the throes of a political crisis of the first magnitude.

23. Weakening of the "First Triumvirate" and the Coming of the Civil War. Caesar's conquest of Gaul was nearing completion, and his proconsulship there was to expire legally in 50 B.C. From the summer of 51 B.C. on, Caesar, Pompey, the optimates, and various other senatorial factions and cliques had begun to worry about what would happen next. The optimates wanted to haul Caesar back to Rome and dispose of him through legal prosecutions. Caesar himself wanted to run for the consulship *in absentia.* If he were victorious (and he had every reason to believe he would be), he would pass directly from the legal immunity of his proconsular *imperium* to the legal immunity of consular *imperium,* and so avoid any chance for such potentially career-wrecking prosecutions. Meanwhile, the "triumvirate" had become a duumvirate: Crassus had been killed and his army annihilated by the Parthians at Carrhae in 53 B.C. Although the *amīcitia* between Caesar and Pompey had remained firm because of Pompey's happy marriage to Caesar's daughter Julia in 59 B.C., this link was severed when Julia died in 54 B.C. Pompey was increasingly jealous of and nervous about Caesar's growing military power.

The evidence seems to show that neither Caesar nor Pompey, and still less the Senate, wanted a showdown. But a small, determined war party proceeded to box Caesar in and so foist war upon the Republic. During the first week of January 49 B.C., the Senate decreed that Caesar must lay down his command or be considered a public outlaw. Feeling he had no alternative except political ruin, on the tenth or eleventh of January Caesar crossed the Rubicon River, the small tributary that formed the boundary between his province and Roman Italy, and the Civil War was on.

24. The Civil War. Having brought war on, the Senate had done little to prepare for it except to name Pompey commander. Unprepared and unwilling to face crack Caesarian troops, whose skills were sharp from years of fighting in Gaul and whose enthusiasm for Caesar was at a high pitch, Pompey, his army, and most of the Senate retired to Greece in March 49 B.C., trading space for time and leaving Caesar the master of Italy. Less than two weeks after Pompey's departure, Caesar met with Cicero at Formiae and encouraged him to return to Rome, but Cicero refused. Cicero was still uncertain about what to do, but in the summer of 49 B.C. he went to Greece and joined the forces of Pompey and the Senate. He was quite dejected by what he found there: most of the Republicans were not particularly worried about the Republican constitution, and Cicero more than anyone came to realize that this Civil War amounted not so much to a choice between Caesar and the legal government as a choice of dictators.

Meanwhile, Caesar did not directly attack Pompey. He turned to Spain, where he crushed a Pompeian army at Ilerda on August 2, 49 B.C. After a year of other operations, on August 9, 48 B.C., at Pharsalus in Greece, Caesar decisively defeated Pompey's forces; and although Caesar spent the next two years mopping up remnants of the Pompeian forces in Africa (at Thapsus in the winter of 47/46 B.C.) and in Spain (at Munda in 45 B.C.), and was personally in Rome only at intervals, he was now master of the Roman world.

25. Cicero's Activities During Caesar's Dictatorship. After the Battle of Pharsalus, Cicero crossed the Adriatic to Brundisium, and in a kind of semi-exile from Rome awkwardly awaited a pardon from Caesar. In September of 47 B.C. Caesar finally arrived in Brundisium, where he personally pardoned Cicero, and the latter returned to Rome the following month. Unable to warm to Caesar's repeated overtures, Cicero took virtually no part in public life. But the tacit price of political reinstatement was at least compliance: the speeches *prō Marcellō, prō Ligāriō,* and *dē rēge Dēiotarō* ("On King Deiotarus"), for instance, delivered in this period, are aptly named "Caesarian" because they betray the fact that they were argued before a dictator. Once again, Cicero turned to writing treatises: among others, *dē clārīs ōrātōribus* ("On

Distinguished Orators"), *dē fīnibus* ("On Ethics"), *Tusculānae disputātiōnēs* ("Debates at Tusculum"), *dē senectūte* ("On Old Age"), *dē amīcitiā* ("On Friendship"), and *dē officiīs* ("On Moral Duties") were all written from 46 B.C. on. These years were among the most depressing in Cicero's life. Domestic problems were piled atop his political troubles: he divorced Terentia in 46 B.C. His depression deepened with the death of his beloved daughter Tullia in February of 45 B.C., and when his second wife Publilia seemed insufficiently upset with Tullia's death, he divorced her.

Cicero looked on with despair as Caesar's regime slid into open autocracy. Forty years earlier, Sulla, having marched on Rome, had bloodily proscribed his enemies, but had eventually laid down his dictatorship. Now, though there were no proscriptions or other retaliations against his enemies, Caesar was given repeated extensions of the dictatorship, culminating in his appointment as *dictātor perpetuō* (dictator for life) in February of 44 B.C. Cicero was not privy to the assassination of Caesar on 15 March 44 B.C., although the Republican patriot M. Junius Brutus is said to have cried out "Cicero!" as he stood above Caesar's lifeless body; and indeed Cicero approved of the murder.

26. The Philippics and the Second Triumvirate. For some time Cicero looked upon Caesar's eighteen-year-old great nephew and adopted heir Octavian as a potential rehabilitator of the Republic. Cicero himself plunged back into politics with all his consular *auctōritās*—in fact, he was one of the few *cōnsulārēs* remaining alive and politically active after the Civil War. Between September of 44 B.C. and April of 43 B.C. Cicero authored an especially virulent series of speeches and pamphlets against M. Antonius, commonly known in English as Mark Antony, who had been one of Caesar's generals and to whom much of Caesar's power had devolved. These works were called the *Philippics,* recalling the fourth century B.C. Greek orator Demosthenes' attempt to rally his fellow Greeks against Philip of Macedon. But Octavian could not become a Republican—to do so would be to join his adoptive father's murderers—and he struck an accord with Mark Antony and M. Aemilius Lepidus, known as the Second Triumvirate, to take over the government. Their plans embraced widespread proscriptions of their enemies, including, at Antony's insistence, Cicero. After a halfhearted attempt to escape from Italy at Brundisium, apparently lacking the will to live any longer, Cicero was killed by henchmen of Antony on 7 December 43 B.C. His head and hands, with which he had written the *Philippics,* were brought to Rome and affixed to the orators' *rostra* (the speakers' platform in the Forum).

27. Postscript: the Augustan Settlement and the Founding of the Principate. Since Cicero died in the midst of a political, social, and economic revolution, a brief postscript on the final settlement of that revolution is in order. The Triumvirate made short work of the conspirators: in 42 B.C. the Republican forces led by Brutus and Cassius were decisively defeated at Philippi in eastern Macedonia. During the next decade Octavian pushed Lepidus into virtual retirement and maneuvered the Senate into declaring Antony, who had lingered too long with Cleopatra in Egypt, a public enemy. The forces of Antony and Cleopatra were decisively defeated in the naval battle of Actium in September of 31 B.C., and the two killed themselves to escape capture in the following year.

Octavian was master of the Roman world. Although he held back-to-back consulships until 23 B.C., he steered clear of overt dictatorship, no doubt mindful of his adoptive uncle's fate. Nonetheless, he was gathering the reins of legal power in his hands. On 13 January 27 B.C., he announced to much fanfare his resignation of all extraordinary powers and the restoration of free Republican institutions, but he was given proconsular *imperium* over Spain, Gaul, and Syria. As these were the most militarized regions of the empire, he thus retained unchallengeable control over the army. He was saluted as *Augustus* by the Senate, an adjective often applied to gods, and it is under that title we know him today. Capping this legal and military power were his *auctōritās* and his vast private fortune, including all Egypt, which he administered without reference to the senatorial government.

In 23 B.C. Augustus's legal position was further modified: he laid down the consulship but acquired *imperium prōcōnsulāre māius* ("greater proconsular *imperium*," superior to that of any other magistrate) over all provinces of the empire. This power, coupled with *tribūnicia potestās,* a permanent and conveniently amorphous grant of tribunician power to act in the name of the people, made his legal position unassailable. There would be other modifications of his powers as need arose and expediency demanded, but the settlement of 23 B.C. gave Augustus enough power to carry out his will, and can fairly be called the final nail in the Republic's coffin. By the time of Augustus's death in A.D. 14, after a "reign" of some forty years, it was almost impossible for the Senate and People of Rome to imagine government without a *princeps* ("first man") at the helm, and *imperātor,* once only the respectful salute of the army for a victorious general, gradually began to acquire the overtones that its English descendant, "emperor," has for us today.

LIFE OF CAELIUS AND THE *PRO CAELIO*

28. Family and Education. M. Caelius Rufus was born into an equestrian family on 28 May 82 B.C.,[17] at Interamnia, modern Teramo, in southern
Picenum, about eighty miles northeast of Rome across the rugged Apennine
range, which forms the backbone of Italy. After Caelius received the *toga virīlis*
at sixteen years of age in 66 B.C., his father entrusted him to Crassus, one of
Rome's shrewdest and wealthiest men, and to Cicero, in that year a praetor,
for his *tīrōcinium forī*. Caelius dutifully attended on Cicero during Cicero's
praetorship and campaign for the consulship, but, like many other young
men, was enticed into Catiline's circle when Catiline stood again for election
to the consulship in 63 B.C. Caelius's keen sense of politics and timing must
have led him to extricate himself from Catiline's spell before the latter began
spinning revolutionary designs, but not without damage to his reputation. He
went to Africa as a *contubernālis* or *aide-de-camp* in the train of the proconsul
Q. Pompeius Rufus in late 62 or early 61 B.C. Such service in a province was a
normal part of the education of an upper-middle-class or aristocratic young
man with political aspirations; when able, the young man would be relied
upon heavily by the proconsul or propraetor, and Caelius seems to have been
highly regarded by Pompeius.

    29. Successful Prosecution of Antonius. Caelius's education was com-
plete. Upon his return to Rome in 59 B.C., he formally entered public life with an
ambitious prosecution of C. Antonius Hybrida for *repetundae* (extortion) and/
or *māiestās* ("treason," defined far more broadly than in modern law); Caelius
accused him of scandalous mismanagement of his province of Macedonia the
previous year and of involvement in the Catilinarian conspiracy. A prosecution of this kind was a common method of entry into public life, in theory
considered a public service. If it seems strange to us that a private individual
undertook an endeavor which would so clearly be left to government prosecutors today, we must remember that there were no "public" prosecutors, no
attorneys general or district attorneys, and for that matter no police in Rome
at this period who could carry out such activities. Cicero defended Antonius,
who had been his colleague in the consulship in 63 B.C. But Caelius was ruth-
less and formidable in oratorical attack;[18] and as the weight of evidence and
sympathy was against Antonius, he was convicted in 59 B.C. and went into
exile. Cicero was quite disappointed by the result.

---

[17] I accept Austin's arguments for the date of Caelius's birth, pp. 144–146, and do not understand
Wiseman's casual acceptance of 87 or 88 B.C. (see Wiseman, p. 62).

[18] See an example of Caelio's vigorous oratory at 178n. and in Appendix B.

30. Love Affair With Clodia. With this spectacular victory Caelius moved from his father's house to an apartment he rented from Clodius (Cicero's political nemesis), on the fashionable Palatine Hill. There he met Clodius's sister Clodia, a woman of vast wealth, power, beauty, and caprice. Caelius fell under her spell, and seems to have been her lover for most of the period 59–57 B.C. At the end of 57 or very early in 56 he left her; but one could expect retaliation for such disrespect for a member of the powerful and arrogant Claudian clan. This doubly will have been the case if the reason for the breakup was a revelation that Caelius had been secretly working in the interests of Pompey, her brother Clodius's enemy at this time.[19]

31. Prosecution for vīs. Early in 56 B.C., Caelius unsuccessfully prosecuted L. Calpurnius Bestia for *ambitus* (electoral bribery). When Caelius began a second round of proceedings against Bestia, his son L. Sempronius Atratinus fought back, prosecuting Caelius on five counts of *vīs* (political violence). The charges were: (1) involvement in rioting at Naples; (2) the roughing up at Puteoli (near Naples) of ambassadors from Alexandria; (3) the murder of the philosopher Dio, one of the ambassadors; (4) some kind of affront by Caelius to the property of a certain Palla, about which we have no details; (5) an attempt to poison Clodia.

Later, in the *prō Caeliō,* Cicero would assert that Clodia was the real instigator and power behind this prosecution, and that in Atratinus she had simply found someone with a common interest in destroying Caelius. But we cannot trust Cicero on this point. Some of Atratinus's accusations probably had some truth to them: indeed, in the first three counts one can discern perhaps the outlines of a botched attempt by Caelius to ingratiate himself with Pompey, whose Egyptian policy was what Dio and his deputation were upset about. Moreover, it was to Cicero's advantage, indeed a part of his strategy, to leapfrog right over these possibly substantive charges and focus on Clodia. We have to treat the evidence carefully, and we will never know the extent to which Clodia was manipulating the prosecutors. Caelius turned to his old mentors Cicero and Crassus to defend him. And defend him they did (3–4 April 56 B.C.): Caelius was acquitted.

32. Later Career. At the end of the *prō Caeliō* (ch. 80) Cicero promised that Caelius's future efforts on behalf of the body politic would be great. It is, however, very hard to see in Caelius any really constructive long-term political vision. Caelius seems to have held the quaestorship sometime soon after his trial; he was tribune in 52 B.C., and curule aedile in 50 B.C., as the Roman senate was trying to navigate a course between Caesar and Pompey. In 51–50 B.C. he reported on events at Rome for Cicero during the latter's governorship of

---

19 Wiseman, p. 67.

Cilicia. His letters reveal a nimble political mind, which, among other things, did not fail to foresee Caesar victorious in the coming contest with Pompey.

Caesar made Caelius *praetor peregrīnus* (judge in suits involving non-citizens [*peregrīnī*]) in 48 b.c.; he bitterly resented that another man, Trebonius, a loyal and competent Caesarian, held the more important office of *praetor urbānus,* and he interfered violently with Trebonius's administration of Caesar's moderate debt-relief policy. When a *senātūs cōnsultum ultimum* stripped him of his office, he left Rome and attempted to stir up a rebellion in southern Italy. He was killed in a fracas at Thurii by Caesarian adherents whom he was trying to bribe.

STRUCTURE OF THE *PRO CAELIO*

It is not possible here to discuss in detail the history and role of oratory in the ancient world, except to note a few differences between ancient and modern speechmaking. First, as Americans living in an advanced, technological society, we are made almost indifferent to oratory by the constant bombardment of the written word and by our focus on the "bottom line" and "the point." It is, then, a stretch of our imagination to realize that the orator's talent was looked upon as an art, and, in a less scientifically advanced world, which lacked most of the diversions we have, public speaking was a form of entertainment, a spectacle not to be missed. The Roman orator spoke not in a paneled courtroom, but outside in the open air, with the forum crowd listening attentively in a corōna or ring around the proceedings.

Second, oratory held a privileged, almost monopolistic position in the ancient world. Our "best" minds today spend their careers in a hundred different fields ranging from chemistry to computers to law to journalism. There is no social pressure on any of these people to spend any part of their careers in public service. In the ancient world the elite were trained in oratory; and the upper-class man who remained aloof from public affairs was considered very nearly useless.

Third, the political structure of ancient societies made the orator's power immense: decisions in the public assemblies and law courts were taken not so much after careful deliberation and scrupulous attention to the issues as under the immediate impact of an orator's perfectly-honed ability to sway an audience. Interestingly, in the last few decades here in the United States and other Western democracies there has been a shift in public discourse from the written back to the spoken (and "seen") word, as the immediacy and persuasive power of television has edged out print media (such as newspapers) as the primary source of public information.

Among the ancients, there were almost as many ways to dissect a speech as there were ancient commentators who theorized about speechmaking. As in most areas of classical endeavor, like art and verse literature, the ancients were very much interested in *form*, that is, in mastering and propagating a tried-and-true structure. By Cicero's time, the structure of an ancient forensic speech had crystallized into the following scheme, which audiences would more or less expect:

I. *exordium,* an introduction designed to put the audience in a receptive mood for the main body of the speech;

II. *narrātiō,* a statement of the facts of the case;

III. *dīvīsiō,* an outline of the orator's treatment of the disputed points;

IV. *cōnfirmātiō,* the orator's side of the story;

V. *refūtātiō,* a refutation of the opposition's views;

VI. *perōrātiō,* a conclusion.

Undercutting this respect for the theory of speechmaking and this attention to the received structure of the model speech was the need to depart from form in order to meet the practical demands of the case. Of this there is no better example than the *prō Caeliō,* which may be divided as follows:

I. *exordium,* chs. 1–2;

II. *praemūnītiō,* chs. 3–50, including a feigned foray into a narrātiō at ch. 30;

III. *cōnfirmātiō* and *refūtātiō,* chs. 51–69, including snippets of narrātiō in the first few chapters;

IV. *perōrātiō,* chs. 70–80.

CICERO
Pro Caelio

(I,1) Si quis, iudices, forte nunc adsit ignarus legum iudiciorum consuetudinisque nostrae, miretur profecto quae sit tanta atrocitas huiusce causae, quod diebus festis ludisque publicis, omnibus forensibus negotiis intermissis, unum hoc iudicium exerceatur, nec dubitet quin tanti facinoris reus arguatur ut eo neglecto civitas stare non possit. Idem cum audiat esse legem quae de seditiosis consceleratisque civibus qui armati senatum obsederint, magistratibus vim attulerint, rem publicam oppugnarint cotidie quaeri iubeat: legem non improbet, crimen quod versetur in iudicio requirat; cum audiat nullum facinus, nullam audaciam, nullam vim in iudicium vocari, sed adulescentem inlustri ingenio, industria, gratia accusari ab eius filio quem ipse in iudicium et vocet et vocarit, oppugnari autem opibus meretriciis: Atratini ipsius pietatem non reprehendat, libidinem muliebrem comprimendam putet, vos laboriosos existimet quibus otiosis ne in communi quidem otio liceat esse. (2) Etenim si attendere diligenter atque existimare vere de omni hac causa volueritis, sic constituetis, iudices, nec descensurum quemquam ad hanc accusationem fuisse cui utrum vellet liceret nec, cum descendisset, quicquam habiturum spei fuisse, nisi alicuius intolerabili libidine et nimis acerbo odio niteretur. Sed ego Atratino, humanissimo atque optimo adulescenti, meo necessario, ignosco, qui habet excusationem vel pietatis vel necessitatis vel aetatis. Si voluit accusare, pietati tribuo, si iussus est, necessitati, si speravit aliquid, pueritiae. Ceteris non modo nihil ignoscendum sed etiam acriter est resistendum.

(II,3) Ac mihi quidem videtur, iudices, hic introitus defensionis adulescentiae M. Caeli maxime convenire, ut ad ea quae accusatores deformandi huius causa et detrahendae spoliandaeque dignitatis gratia dixerunt primum respondeam.

Obiectus est pater varie, quod aut parum splendidus ipse aut
35   parum pie tractatus a filio diceretur. De dignitate M. Caelius
notis ac maioribus natu etiam sine mea oratione tacitus facile ipse
respondet; quibus autem propter senectutem, quod iam diu
minus in foro nobiscumque versatur, non aeque est cognitus, hi
sic habeant, quaecumque in equite Romano dignitas esse possit,
40   quae certe potest esse maxima, eam semper in M. Caelio habitam
esse summam hodieque haberi non solum a suis sed etiam ab
omnibus quibus potuerit aliqua de causa esse notus. (4) Equitis
autem Romani esse filium criminis loco poni ab accusatoribus
neque his iudicantibus oportuit neque defendentibus nobis.
45   Nam quod de pietate dixistis, est ista quidem nostra existimatio
sed iudicium certe parentis. Quid nos opinemur audietis ex
iuratis; quid parentes sentiant lacrimae matris incredibilisque
maeror, squalor patris et haec praesens maestitia quam cernitis
luctusque declarat. (5) Nam quod est obiectum municipibus esse
50   adulescentem non probatum suis, nemini umquam praesenti
Praetuttiani maiores honores habuerunt, iudices, quam absenti
M. Caelio; quem et absentem in amplissimum ordinem
cooptarunt et ea non petenti detulerunt quae multis petentibus
denegarunt. Idemque nunc lectissimos viros et nostri ordinis et
55   equites Romanos cum legatione ad hoc iudicium et cum
gravissima atque ornatissima laudatione miserunt. Videor mihi
iecisse fundamenta defensionis meae, quae firmissima sunt si
nituntur iudicio suorum. Neque enim vobis satis commendata
huius aetas esse posset, si non modo parenti, tali viro, verum
60   etiam municipio tam inlustri ac tam gravi displiceret. (III,6)
Equidem, ut ad me revertar, ab his fontibus profluxi ad
hominum famam, et meus hic forensis labor vitaeque ratio
demanavit ad existimationem hominum paulo latius
commendatione ac iudicio meorum.
65   Nam quod obiectum est de pudicitia quodque omnium

accusatorum non criminibus sed vocibus maledictisque
celebratum est, id numquam tam acerbe feret M. Caelius ut eum
paeniteat non deformem esse natum. Sunt enim ista   icta
pervolgata in omnis quorum in adulescentia forn   fuit
70 liberalis. Sed aliud est male dicere, aliud accusare. A   atio
crimen desiderat, rem ut definiat, hominem notet, arg   ento
probet, teste confirmet; maledictio autem nihil habet propositi
praeter contumeliam; quae si petulantius iactatur, convicium, si
facetius, urbanitas nominatur. (7) Quam quidem partem
75 accusationis admiratus sum et moleste tuli potissimum esse
Atratino datam. Neque enim decebat neque aetas illa postulabat
neque, id quod animum advertere poteratis, pudor patiebatur
optimi adulescentis in tali illum oratione versari. Vellem aliquis
ex vobis robustioribus hunc male dicendi locum suscepisset;
80 aliquanto liberius et fortius et magis more nostro refutaremus
istam male dicendi licentiam. Tecum, Atratine, agam lenius,
quod et pudor tuus moderatur orationi meae et meum erga te
parentemque tuum beneficium tueri debeo. (8) Illud tamen te
esse admonitum volo, primum ut qualis es talem te omnes esse
85 existiment, ut quantum a rerum turpitudine abes tantum te a
verborum libertate seiungas; deinde ut ea in alterum ne dicas
quae, cum tibi falso responsa sint, erubescas. Quis est enim cui
via ista non pateat, quis est qui huic aetati atque isti dignitati non
possit quam velit petulanter, etiam si sine ulla suspicione, at non
90 sine argumento male dicere? Sed istarum partium culpa est
eorum qui te agere voluerunt; laus pudoris tui, quod ea te invitum
dicere videbamus, ingeni, quod ornate politeque dixisti.
(IV,9) Verum ad istam omnem orationem brevis est defensio.
Nam quoad aetas M. Caeli dare potuit isti suspicioni locum, fuit
95 primum ipsius pudore, deinde etiam patris diligentia
disciplinaque munita. Qui ut huic togam virilem dedit—nihil
dicam hoc loco de me; tantum sit quantum vos existimatis—hoc
dicam, hunc a patre continuo ad me esse deductum. Nemo hunc

M. Caelium in illo aetatis flore vidit nisi aut cum patre aut
100   mecum aut in M. Crassi castissima domo cum artibus
honestissimis erudiretur.

(10) Nam quod Catilinae familiaritas obiecta Caelio est, longe
ista suspicione abhorrere debet. Hoc enim adulescente scitis
ulatum mecum petisse Catilinam. Ad quem si accessit aut si
105   a me discessit umquam—quamquam multi boni adulescentes illi
homini nequam atque improbo studuerunt—tum existimetur
Caelius Catilinae nimium familiaris fuisse. "At enim postea
scimus et vidimus esse hunc in illius etiam amicis." Quis negat?
Sed ego illud tempus aetatis quod ipsum sua sponte infirmum,
110   aliorum autem libidine infestum est, id hoc loco defendo. Fuit
adsiduus mecum praetore me; non noverat Catilinam; Africam
tum praetor ille obtinebat. Secutus est tum annus, causam de
pecuniis repetundis Catilina dixit. Mecum erat hic; illi ne
advocatus quidem venit umquam. Deinceps fuit annus quo ego
115   consulatum petivi; petebat Catilina mecum. Numquam ad illum
accessit, a me numquam recessit. (V,11) Tot igitur annos versatus
in foro sine suspicione, sine infamia, studuit Catilinae iterum
petenti. Quem ergo ad finem putas custodiendam illam aetatem
fuisse? Nobis quidem olim annus erat unus ad cohibendum
120   bracchium toga constitutus, et ut exercitatione ludoque
campestri tunicati uteremur, eademque erat, si statim merere
stipendia coeperamus, castrensis ratio ac militaris. Qua in aetate
nisi qui se ipse sua gravitate et castimonia et cum disciplina
domestica tum etiam naturali quodam bono defenderet, quoquo
125   modo a suis custoditus esset, tamen infamiam veram effugere
non poterat. Sed qui prima illa initia aetatis integra atque
inviolata praestitisset, de eius fama ac pudicitia, cum iam sese
conroboravisset ac vir inter viros esset, nemo loquebatur. (12) At
studuit Catilinae, cum iam aliquot annos esset in foro, Caelius. Et
130   multi hoc idem ex omni ordine atque ex omni aetate fecerunt.
Habuit enim ille, sicuti meminisse vos arbitror, permulta

maximarum non expressa signa sed adumbrata virtutum. Utebatur hominibus improbis multis; et quidem optimis se viris deditum esse simulabat. Erant apud illum inlecebrae libidinum

135   multae; erant etiam industriae quidam stimuli ac laboris. Flagrabant vitia libidinis apud illum; vigebant etiam studia rei militaris. Neque ego umquam fuisse tale monstrum in terris illum puto, tam ex contrariis diversisque atque inter se pugnantibus naturae studiis cupiditatibusque conflatum. (VI,13)

140   Quis clarioribus viris quodam tempore iucundior, quis turpioribus coniunctior? quis civis meliorum partium aliquando, quis taetrior hostis huic civitati? quis in voluptatibus inquinatior, quis in laboribus patientior? quis in rapacitate avarior, quis in largitione effusior? Illa vero, iudices, in illo homine admirabilia

145   fuerunt, comprehendere multos amicitia, tueri obsequio, cum omnibus communicare quod habebat, servire temporibus suorum omnium pecunia, gratia, labore corporis, scelere etiam, si opus esset, et audacia, versare suam naturam et regere ad tempus atque huc et illuc torquere ac flectere, cum tristibus severe, cum

150   remissis iucunde, cum senibus graviter, cum iuventute comiter, cum facinerosis audaciter, cum libidinosis luxuriose vivere. (14) Hac ille tam varia multiplicique natura cum omnis omnibus ex terris homines improbos audacisque conlegerat, tum etiam multos fortis viros et bonos specie quadam virtutis adsimulatae

155   tenebat. Neque umquam ex illo delendi huius imperi tam consceleratus impetus exstitisset, nisi tot vitiorum tanta immanitas quibusdam facultatis et patientiae radicibus niteretur. Qua re ista condicio, iudices, respuatur, nec Catilinae familiaritatis crimen haereat. Est enim commune cum multis et

160   cum quibusdam bonis. Me ipsum, me, inquam, quondam paene ille decepit, cum et civis mihi bonus et optimi cuiusque cupidus et firmus amicus ac fidelis videretur; cuius ego facinora oculis prius quam opinione, manibus ante quam suspicione deprendi. Cuius in magnis catervis amicorum si fuit etiam Caelius, magis

165   est ut ipse moleste ferat errasse se, sicuti non numquam in eodem
homine me quoque erroris mei paenitet, quam ut istius amicitiae
crimen reformidet.

(VII,15) Itaque a maledictis impudicitiae ad coniurationis
invidiam oratio est vestra delapsa. Posuistis enim, atque id

170   tamen titubanter et strictim, coniurationis hunc propter
amicitiam Catilinae participem fuisse; in quo non modo crimen
non haerebat sed vix diserti adulescentis cohaerebat oratio. Qui
enim tantus furor in Caelio, quod tantum aut in moribus
naturaque volnus aut in re atque fortuna? ubi denique est in ista

175   suspicione Caeli nomen auditum? Nimium multa de re minime
dubia loquor; hoc tamen dico. Non modo si socius coniurationis,
sed nisi inimicissimus istius sceleris fuisset, numquam
coniurationis accusatione adulescentiam suam potissimum
commendare voluisset. (16) Quod haud scio an de ambitu et de

180   criminibus istis sodalium ac sequestrium, quoniam huc incidi,
similiter respondendum putem. Numquam enim tam Caelius
amens fuisset ut, si sese isto infinito ambitu commaculasset,
ambitus alterum accusaret, neque eius facti in altero suspicionem
quaereret cuius ipse sibi perpetuam licentiam optaret, nec, si sibi

185   semel periculum ambitus subeundum putaret, ipse alterum
iterum ambitus crimine arcesseret. Quod quamquam nec
sapienter et me invito facit, tamen est eius modi cupiditas ut
magis insectari alterius innocentiam quam de se timide cogitare
videatur.

190   (17) Nam quod aes alienum obiectum est, sumptus
reprehensi, tabulae flagitatae, videte quam pauca respondeam.
Tabulas qui in patris potestate est nullas conficit. Versuram
numquam omnino fecit ullam. Sumptus unius generis obiectus
est, habitationis; triginta milibus dixistis habitare. Nunc demum

195   intellego P. Clodi insulam esse venalem, cuius hic in aediculis
habitat decem, ut opinor, milibus. Vos autem dum illi placere
voltis, ad tempus eius mendacium vestrum accommodavistis.

(18) Reprehendistis a patre quod semigrarit. Quod quidem in hac aetate minime reprendendum est. Qui cum ex publica causa iam esset mihi quidem molestam, sibi tamen gloriosam

200 victoriam consecutus et per aetatem magistratus petere posset, non modo permittente patre sed etiam suadente ab eo semigravit et, cum domus patris a foro longe abesset, quo facilius et nostras domus obire et ipse a suis coli posset, conduxit in Palatio non magno domum. (VIII) Quo loco possum dicere id quod vir

205 clarissimus, M. Crassus, cum de adventu regis Ptolemaei quereretur, paulo ante dixit:

Utinam ne in nemore Pelio—

Ac longius mihi quidem contexere hoc carmen liceret:

Nam numquam era errans

210

hanc molestiam nobis exhiberet

Medea animo aegro, amore saevo saucia.

Sic enim, iudices, reperietis quod, cum ad id loci venero, ostendam, hanc Palatinam Medeam migrationemque hanc

215 adulescenti causam sive malorum omnium sive potius sermonum fuisse.

(19) Quam ob rem illa quae ex accusatorum oratione praemuniri iam et fingi intellegebam, fretus vestra prudentia, iudices, non pertimesco. Aiebant enim fore testem senatorem

220 qui se pontificiis comitiis pulsatum a Caelio diceret. A quo quaeram, si prodierit, primum cur statim nihil egerit, deinde, si id queri quam agere maluerit, cur productus a vobis potius quam ipse per se, cur tanto post potius quam continuo queri maluerit.

Si mihi ad haec acute arguteque responderit, tum quaeram
225   denique ex quo iste fonte senator emanet. nam si ipse orietur et
nascetur ex sese, fortasse, ut soleo, commovebor; sin autem est
rivolus arcessitus et ductus ab ipso capite accusationis vestrae,
laetabor, cum tanta gratia tantisque opibus accusatio vestra
nitatur, unum senatorem esse solum qui vobis gratificari vellet
230   inventum.

DE TESTE FVFIO.

(20) Nec tamen illud genus alterum nocturnorum testium
perhorresco. Est enim dictum ab illis fore qui dicerent uxores
suas a cena redeuntis attrectatas esse a Caelio. Graves erunt
235   homines qui hoc iurati dicere audebunt, cum sit eis confitendum
numquam se ne congressu quidem et constituto coepisse de
tantis iniuriis experiri. (IX) Sed totum genus oppugnationis
huius, iudices, et iam prospicitis animis et, cum inferetur,
propulsare debebitis. Non enim ab isdem accusatur M. Caelius a
240   quibus oppugnatur; palam in eum tela iaciuntur, clam
subministrantur. (21) Neque ego id dico ut invidiosum sit in eos
quibus gloriosum etiam hoc esse debet. Funguntur officio,
defendunt suos, faciunt quod viri fortissimi solent; laesi dolent,
irati efferuntur, pugnant lacessiti. Sed vestrae sapientiae tamen
245   est, iudices, non, si causa iusta est viris fortibus oppugnandi M.
Caelium, ideo vobis quoque causam putare esse iustam alieno
dolori potius quam vestrae fidei consulendi. Nam quae sit
multitudo in foro, quae genera, quae studia, quae varietas
hominum videtis. Ex hac copia quam multos esse arbitramini
250   qui hominibus potentibus, gratiosis, disertis, cum aliquid eos
velle arbitrentur, ultro se offerre soleant, operam navare, testimonium polliceri? (22) Hoc ex genere si qui se in hoc iudicium forte
proiecerint, excluditote eorum cupiditatem, iudices, sapientia
vestra, ut eodem tempore et huius saluti et religioni vestrae et
255   contra periculosas hominum potentias condicioni omnium
civium providisse videamini. Equidem vos abducam a testibus

neque huius iudici veritatem quae mutari nullo modo potest in voluntate testium conlocari sinam quae facillime fingi, nullo negotio flecti ac detorqueri potest. Argumentis agemus, signis

260 luce omni clarioribus crimina refellemus; res cum re, causa cum causa, ratio cum ratione pugnabit.

(X,23) Itaque illam partem causae facile patior graviter et ornate a M. Crasso peroratam de seditionibus Neapolitanis, de Alexandrinorum pulsatione Puteolana, de bonis Pallae. Vellem

265 dictum esset ab eodem etiam de Dione. De quo ipso tamen quid est quod exspectetis? quod is qui fecit aut non timet aut etiam fatetur; est enim rex; qui autem dictus est adiutor fuisse et conscius, P. Asicius, iudicio est liberatus. Quod igitur est eius modi crimen ut qui commisit non neget, qui negavit absolutus

270 sit, id hic pertimescat qui non modo a facti verum etiam a conscientiae suspicione afuit? Et, si Asicio causa plus profuit quam nocuit invidia, huic oberit maledictum tuum qui istius facti non modo suspicione sed ne infamia quidem est aspersus? (24) At praevaricatione est Asicius liberatus. Perfacile est isti loco

275 respondere, mihi praesertim a quo illa causa defensa est. Sed Caelius optimam causam Asici esse arbitratur; cuicuimodi autem sit, a sua putat esse seiunctam. Neque solum Caelius sed etiam adulescentes humanissimi et doctissimi, rectissimis studiis atque optimis artibus praediti, Titus Gaiusque Coponii qui ex omnibus

280 maxime Dionis mortem doluerunt, qui cum doctrinae studio atque humanitatis tum etiam hospitio Dionis tenebantur. Habitabat apud Titum, ut audistis, Dio, erat ei cognitus Alexandriae. Quid aut hic aut summo splendore praeditus frater eius de M. Caelio existimet ex ipsis, si producti erunt, audietis.

285 (25) Ergo haec removeantur, ut aliquando, in quibus causa nititur, ad ea veniamus.

(XI) Animadverti enim, iudices, audiri a vobis meum familiarem, L. Herennium, perattente. In quo etsi magna ex parte ingenio eius et dicendi genere quodam tenebamini, tamen

290 non numquam verebar ne illa subtiliter ad criminandum inducta
oratio ad animos vestros sensim ac leniter accederet. Dixit enim
multa de luxurie, multa de libidine, multa de vitiis iuventutis,
multa de moribus et, qui in reliqua vita mitis esset et in hac
suavitate humanitatis qua prope iam delectantur omnes versari

295 periucunde soleret, fuit in hac causa pertristis quidam patruus,
censor, magister; obiurgavit M. Caelium, sicut neminem
umquam parens; multa de incontinentia intemperantiaque
disseruit. Quid quaeritis, iudices? ignoscebam vobis attente
audientibus, propterea quod egomet tam triste illud, tam

300 asperum genus orationis horrebam. (26) Ac prima pars fuit illa
quae me minus movebat, fuisse meo necessario Bestiae Caelium
familiarem, cenasse apud eum, ventitasse domum, studuisse
praeturae. Non me haec movent quae perspicue falsa sunt;
etenim eos una cenasse dixit qui aut absunt aut quibus necesse

305 est idem dicere. Neque vero illud me commovet quod sibi in
Lupercis sodalem esse Caelium dixit. Fera quaedam sodalitas et
plane pastoricia atque agrestis germanorum Lupercorum, quorum coitio illa silvestris ante est instituta quam humanitas atque
leges, si quidem non modo nomina deferunt inter se sodales sed

310 etiam commemorant sodalitatem in accusando, ut ne quis id
forte nesciat timere videantur!

(27) Sed haec omitto; ad illa quae me magis moverunt respondeo.

Deliciarum obiurgatio fuit longa, etiam lenior, plusque
disputationis habuit quam atrocitatis, quo etiam audita est

315 attentius. Nam P. Clodius, amicus meus, cum se gravissime
vehementissimeque iactaret et omnia inflammatus ageret
tristissimis verbis, voce maxima, tametsi probabam eius
eloquentiam, tamen non pertimescebam; aliquot enim in causis
eum videram frustra litigantem. Tibi autem, Balbe, respondeo

320 primum precario, si licet, si fas est defendi a me eum qui nullum
convivium renuerit, qui in hortis fuerit, qui unguenta sumpserit,
qui Baias viderit. (XII,28) Equidem multos et vidi in hac civitate

et audivi, non modo qui primoribus labris gustassent genus hoc
vitae et extremis, ut dicitur, digitis attigissent sed qui totam
325 adulescentiam voluptatibus dedidissent, emersisse aliquando et
se ad bonam frugem, ut dicitur, recepisse gravisque homines
atque inlustris fuisse. Datur enim concessu omnium huic aliqui
ludus aetati, et ipsa natura profundit adulescentiae cupiditates.
Quae si ita erumpunt ut nullius vitam labefactent, nullius
330 domum evertant, faciles et tolerabiles haberi solent. (29) Sed tu
mihi videbare ex communi infamia iuventutis aliquam invidiam
Caelio velle conflare. Itaque omne illud silentium quod est
orationi tributum tuae fuit ob eam causam quod uno reo
proposito de multorum vitiis cogitabamus. Facile est accusare
335 luxuriem. Dies iam me deficiat, si quae dici in eam sententiam
possunt coner expromere; de corruptelis, de adulteriis, de
protervitate, de sumptibus immensa oratio est. Vt tibi reum
neminem sed vitia ista proponas, res tamen ipsa et copiose et
graviter accusari potest. Sed vestrae sapientiae, iudices, est non
340 abduci ab reo nec, quos aculeos habeat severitas gravitasque
vestra, cum eos accusator erexerit in rem, in vitia, in mores, in
tempora, emittere in hominem et in reum, cum is non suo
crimine sed multorum vitio sit in quoddam odium iniustum
vocatus. (30) Itaque ego severitati tuae ita ut oportet respondere
345 non audeo. Erat enim meum deprecari vacationem
adulescentiae veniamque petere. Non, inquam, audeo; perfugiis
nihil utor aetatis, concessa omnibus iura dimitto; tantum peto ut,
si qua est invidia communis hoc tempore aeris alieni,
petulantiae, libidinum iuventutis, quam video esse magnam,
350 tamen ne huic aliena peccata, ne aetatis ac temporum vitia
noceant. Atque ego idem qui haec postulo quin criminibus quae
in hunc proprie conferuntur diligentissime respondeam non
recuso.

(XIII) Sunt autem duo crimina, auri et veneni; in quibus una
355 atque eadem persona versatur. Aurum sumptum a Clodia,

venenum quaesitum quod Clodiae daretur, ut dicitur. Omnia sunt alia non crimina sed maledicta, iurgi petulantis magis quam publicae quaestionis. 'Adulter, impudicus, sequester' convicium est, non accusatio. Nullum est enim fundamentum horum

360   criminum, nullae sedes; voces sunt contumeliosae temere ab irato accusatore nullo auctore emissae. (31) Horum duorum criminum video auctorem, video fontem, video certum nomen et caput. Auro opus fuit; sumpsit a Clodia, sumpsit sine teste, habuit quamdiu voluit. Maximum video signum cuiusdam

365   egregiae familiaritatis. Necare eandem voluit; quaesivit venenum, sollicitavit servos, potionem paravit, locum constituit, clam attulit. Magnum rursus odium video cum crudelissimo discidio exstitisse. Res est omnis in hac causa nobis, iudices, cum Clodia, muliere non solum nobili verum etiam nota; de qua ego

370   nihil dicam nisi depellendi criminis causa. (32) Sed intellegis pro tua praestanti prudentia, Cn. Domiti, cum hac sola rem esse nobis. Quae si se aurum M. Caelio commodasse non dicit, si venenum ab hoc sibi paratum esse non arguit, petulanter facimus, si matrem familias secus quam matronarum sanctitas

375   postulat nominamus. Sin ista muliere remota nec crimen ullum nec opes ad oppugnandum M. Caelium illis relinquuntur, quid est aliud quod nos patroni facere debeamus, nisi ut eos qui insectantur repellamus? Quod quidem facerem vehementius, nisi intercederent mihi inimicitiae cum istius mulieris viro—

380   fratrem volui dicere; semper hic erro. Nunc agam modice nec longius progrediar quam me mea fides et causa ipsa coget: nec enim muliebris umquam inimicitias mihi gerendas putavi, praesertim cum ea quam omnes semper amicam omnium potius quam cuiusquam inimicam putaverunt.

385   (XIV,33) Sed tamen ex ipsa quaeram prius utrum me secum severe et graviter et prisce agere malit, an remisse et leniter et urbane. Si illo austero more ac modo, aliquis mihi ab inferis excitandus est ex barbatis illis, non hac barbula qua ista

delectatur sed illa horrida quam in statuis antiquis atque
390   imaginibus videmus, qui obiurget mulierem et qui pro me
loquatur ne mihi ista forte suscenseat. Exsistat igitur ex hac ipsa
familia aliquis ac potissimum Caecus ille; minimum enim
dolorem capiet qui istam non videbit. Qui profecto, si exstiterit,
sic aget ac sic loquetur: 'Mulier, quid tibi cum Caelio, quid cum
395   homine adulescentulo, quid cum alieno? Cur aut tam familiaris
fuisti ut aurum commodares, aut tam inimica ut venenum
timeres? Non patrem tuum videras, non patruum, non avum,
non proavum, non *abavum, non* atavum audieras consules
fuisse; (34) non denique modo te Q. Metelli matrimonium
400   tenuisse sciebas, clarissimi ac fortissimi viri patriaeque
amantissimi, qui simul ac pedem limini extulerat, omnis prope
civis virtute, gloria, dignitate superabat? Cum ex amplissimo
genere in familiam clarissimam nupsisses, cur tibi Caelius tam
coniunctus fuit? Cognatus, adfinis, viri tui familiaris? Nihil
405   eorum. Quid igitur fuit nisi quaedam temeritas ac libido? Nonne
te, si nostrae imagines viriles non commovebant, ne progenies
quidem mea, Q. illa Claudia, aemulam domesticae laudis in
gloria muliebri esse admonebat, non virgo illa Vestalis Claudia
quae patrem complexa triumphantem ab inimico tribuno plebei
410   de curru detrahi passa non est? Cur te fraterna vitia potius quam
bona paterna et avita et usque a nobis cum in viris tum etiam in
feminis repetita moverunt? Ideone ego pacem Pyrrhi diremi ut
tu amorum turpissimorum cotidie foedera ferires, ideo aquam
adduxi ut ea tu inceste uterere, ideo viam munivi ut eam tu
415   alienis viris comitata celebrares?'

(XV,35) Sed quid ego, iudices, ita gravem personam induxi ut
verear ne se idem Appius repente convertat et Caelium incipiat
accusare illa sua gravitate censoria? Sed videro hoc posterius
atque ita, iudices, ut vel severissimis disceptatoribus M. Caeli
420   vitam me probaturum esse confidam. Tu vero, mulier—iam
enim ipse tecum nulla persona introducta loquor—si ea quae

facis, quae dicis, quae insimulas, quae moliris, quae arguis,
probare cogitas, rationem tantae familiaritatis, tantae
consuetudinis, tantae coniunctionis reddas atque exponas
425   necesse est. Accusatores quidem libidines, amores, adulteria,
Baias, actas, convivia, comissationes, cantus, symphonias,
navigia iactant, idemque significant nihil se te invita dicere.
Quae tu quoniam mente nescio qua effrenata atque praecipiti in
forum deferri iudiciumque voluisti, aut diluas oportet ac falsa
430   esse doceas aut nihil neque crimini tuo neque testimonio
credendum esse fateare.

(36) Sin autem urbanius me agere mavis, sic agam tecum.
Removebo illum senem durum ac paene agrestem; ex his igitur
sumam aliquem ac potissimum minimum fratrem qui est in isto
435   genere urbanissimus; qui te amat plurimum, qui propter nescio
quam, credo, timiditatem et nocturnos quosdam inanis metus
tecum semper pusio cum maiore sorore cubitabat. Eum putato
tecum loqui:

Quid tumultuaris, soror? Quid insanis?
Quid clamorem exorsa verbis parvam rem magnam facis?
440

Vicinum adulescentulum aspexisti; candor huius te et proceritas,
voltus oculique pepulerunt; saepius videre voluisti; fuisti non
numquam in isdem hortis; vis nobilis mulier illum filium
familias patre parco ac tenaci habere tuis copiis devinctum. Non
potes; calcitrat, respuit, repellit, non putat tua dona esse tanti.
445   Confer te alio. Habes hortos ad Tiberim ac diligenter eos eo loco
parasti quo omnis iuventus natandi causa venit; hinc licet
condiciones cotidie legas; cur huic qui te spernit molesta es?'

(XVI,37) Redeo nunc ad te, Caeli, vicissim ac mihi
auctoritatem patriam severitatemque suscipio. Sed dubito quem
450   patrem potissimum sumam, Caecilianumne aliquem
vehementem atque durum:

Nunc enim demum mi animus ardet, nunc meum cor cumulatur ira

455   aut illum:

O infelix, o sceleste!

Ferrei sunt isti patres:

Egone quid dicam, quid velim? Quae tu omnia
Tuis foedis factis facis ut nequiquam velim,

460   vix ferendi. Diceret talis pater: 'Cur te in istam vicinitatem meretriciam contulisti? cur inlecebris cognitis non refugisti?'

Cur alienam ullam mulierem nosti? Dide ac dissice;
Per me *tibi* licet. Si egebis, tibi dolebit, *non mihi.*
Mihi sat est qui aetatis quod relicuom est oblectem meae.

465   (38) Huic tristi ac derecto seni responderet Caelius se nulla cupiditate inductum de via decessisse. Quid signi? Nulli sumptus, nulla iactura, nulla versura. At fuit fama. Quotus quisque istam effugere potest, praesertim in tam maledica civitate? Vicinum eius mulieris miraris male audisse cuius frater
470   germanus sermones iniquorum effugere non potuit? Leni vero et clementi patre cuius modi ille est:

Fores ecfregit, restituentur; discidit
Vestem, resarcietur,

Caeli causa est expeditissima. Quid enim esset in quo se non
475   facile defenderet? Nihil iam in istam mulierem dico; sed, si esset aliqua dissimilis istius quae se omnibus pervolgaret, quae

haberet palam decretum semper aliquem, cuius in hortos, domum, Baias, iure suo libidines omnium commearent, quae etiam aleret adulescentis et parsimoniam patrum suis sumptibus

480   sustineret; si vidua libere, proterva petulanter, dives effuse, libidinosa meretricio more viveret, adulterum ego putarem si quis hanc paulo liberius salutasset?

(XVII,39) Dicet aliquis: 'Haec igitur est tua disciplina? Sic tu instituis adulescentis? Ob hanc causam tibi hunc puerum parens

485   commendavit et tradidit, ut in amore atque in voluptatibus adulescentiam suam conlocaret, et ut hanc tu vitam atque haec studia defenderes?' Ego, si quis, iudices, hoc robore animi atque hac indole virtutis ac continentiae fuit ut respueret omnis voluptates omnemque vitae suae cursum in labore corporis

490   atque in animi contentione conficeret, quem non quies, non remissio, non aequalium studia, non ludi, non convivium delectaret, nihil in vita expetendum putaret nisi quod esset cum laude et cum dignitate coniunctum, hunc mea sententia divinis quibusdam bonis instructum atque ornatum puto. Ex hoc genere

495   illos fuisse arbitror Camillos, Fabricios, Curios, omnisque eos qui haec ex minimis tanta fecerunt. (40) Verum haec genera virtutum non solum in moribus nostris sed vix iam in libris reperiuntur. Chartae quoque quae illam pristinam severitatem continebant obsoleverunt; neque solum apud nos qui hanc sectam

500   rationemque vitae re magis quam verbis secuti sumus sed etiam apud Graecos, doctissimos homines, quibus, cum facere non possent, loqui tamen et scribere honeste et magnifice licebat, alia quaedam mutatis Graeciae temporibus praecepta exstiterunt. (41) Itaque alii voluptatis causa omnia sapientes facere dixerunt,

505   neque ab hac orationis turpitudine eruditi homines refugerunt; alii cum voluptate dignitatem coniungendam putaverunt, ut res maxime inter se repugnantis dicendi facultate coniungerent; illud unum derectum iter ad laudem cum labore qui probaverunt, prope soli iam in scholis sunt relicti. Multa enim

510   nobis blandimenta natura ipsa genuit quibus sopita virtus
       coniveret interdum; multas vias adulescentiae lubricas ostendit
       quibus illa insistere aut ingredi sine casu aliquo ac prolapsione
       vix posset; multarum rerum iucundissimarum varietatem dedit
       qua non modo haec aetas sed etiam iam conroborata caperetur.
515   (42) Quam ob rem si quem forte inveneritis qui aspernetur oculis
       pulchritudinem rerum, non odore ullo, non tactu, non sapore
       capiatur, excludat auribus omnem suavitatem, huic homini ego
       fortasse et pauci deos propitios, plerique autem iratos putabunt.
       (XVIII) Ergo haec deserta via et inculta atque interclusa iam
520   frondibus et virgultis relinquatur. Detur aliqui ludus aetati; sit
       adulescentia liberior; non omnia voluptatibus denegentur; non
       semper superet vera illa et derecta ratio; vincat aliquando
       cupiditas voluptasque rationem, dum modo illa in hoc genere
       praescriptio moderatioque teneatur. Parcat iuventus pudicitiae
525   suae, ne spoliet alienam, ne effundat patrimonium, ne faenore
       trucidetur, ne incurrat in alterius domum atque familiam, ne
       probrum castis, labem integris, infamiam bonis inferat, ne quem
       vi terreat, ne intersit insidiis, scelere careat. Postremo cum
       paruerit voluptatibus, dederit aliquid temporis ad ludum aetatis
530   atque ad inanis hasce adulescentiae cupiditates, revocet se
       aliquando ad curam rei domesticae, rei forensis reique publicae,
       ut ea quae ratione antea non despexerat satietate abiecisse et
       experiendo contempsisse videatur.
            (43) Ac multi quidem et nostra et patrum maiorumque
535   memoria, iudices, summi homines et clarissimi cives fuerunt
       quorum, cum adulescentiae cupiditates defervissent, eximiae
       virtutes firmata iam aetate exstiterunt. Ex quibus neminem mihi
       libet nominare; vosmet vobiscum recordamini. Nolo enim
       cuiusquam fortis atque inlustris viri ne minimum quidem erra-
540   tum cum maxima laude coniungere. Quod si facere vellem,
       multi a me summi atque ornatissimi viri praedicarentur quorum
       partim nimia libertas in adulescentia, partim profusa luxuries,

magnitudo aeris alieni, sumptus, libidines nominarentur, quae
multis postea virtutibus obtecta adulescentiae qui vellet
545   excusatione defenderet. (XIX,44) At vero in M. Caelio—dicam
enim iam confidentius de studiis eius honestis, quoniam audeo
quaedam fretus vestra sapientia libere confiteri—nulla luxuries
reperietur, nulli sumptus, nullum aes alienum, nulla
conviviorum ac lustrorum libido. Quod quidem vitium ventris
550   et gurgitis non modo non minuit aetas hominibus sed etiam
auget. Amores autem et deliciae quae vocantur, quae firmiore
animo praeditis diutius molestae non solent esse—mature enim
et celeriter deflorescunt—numquam hunc occupatum
impeditumve tenuerunt. (45) Audistis cum pro se diceret,
555   audistis, antea cum accusaret—defendendi haec causa, non
gloriandi loquor—genus orationis, facultatem, copiam
sententiarum atque verborum, quae vestra prudentia est,
perspexistis. Atque in eo non solum ingenium elucere eius
videbatis, quod saepe, etiam si industria non alitur, valet tamen
560   ipsum suis viribus, sed inerat, nisi me propter benivolentiam
forte fallebat, ratio et bonis artibus instituta et cura et vigiliis
elaborata. Atqui scitote, iudices, eas cupiditates quae obiciuntur
Caelio atque haec studia de quibus disputo non facile in eodem
homine esse posse. Fieri enim non potest ut animus libidini
565   deditus, amore, desiderio, cupiditate, saepe nimia copia, inopia
etiam non numquam impeditus hoc quicquid est quod nos
facimus in dicendo, quoquo modo facimus, non modo agendo
verum etiam cogitando possit sustinere. (46) An vos aliam
causam esse ullam putatis cur in tantis praemiis eloquentiae,
570   tanta voluptate dicendi, tanta laude, tanta gratia, tanta honore,
tam sint pauci semperque fuerint qui in hoc labore versentur?
Obterendae sunt omnes voluptates, relinquenda studia
delectationis, ludus, iocus, convivium, sermo paene est
familiarium deserendus. Qua re in hoc genere labor offendit
575   homines a studioque deterret, non quo aut ingenia deficiant aut

doctrina puerilis. (47) An hic, si sese isti vitae dedidisset, consularem hominem admodum adulescens in iudicium vocavisset? hic, si laborem fugeret, si obstrictus voluptatibus teneretur, hac in acie cotidie versaretur, appeteret inimicitias, in

580   iudicium vocaret, subiret periculum capitis, ipse inspectante populo Romano tot iam mensis aut de salute aut de gloria dimicaret? (XX) Nihilne igitur illa vicinitas redolet, nihilne hominum fama, nihil Baiae denique ipsae loquuntur? Illae vero non loquuntur solum verum etiam personant, huc unius mulieris

585   libidinem esse prolapsam ut ea non modo solitudinem ac tenebras atque haec flagitiorum integumenta non quaerat sed in turpissimis rebus frequentissima celebritate et clarissima luce laetetur.

(48) Verum si quis est qui etiam meretriciis amoribus inter-

590   dictum iuventuti putet, est ille quidem valde severus—negare non possum—sed abhorret non modo ab huius saeculi licentia verum etiam a maiorum consuetudine atque concessis. Quando enim hoc non factitatum est, quando reprehensum, quando non permissum, quando denique fuit ut quod licet non liceret? Hic

595   ego ipsam rem definiam, mulierem nullam nominabo; tantum in medio relinquam. (49) Si quae non nupta mulier domum suam patefecerit omnium cupiditati palamque sese in meretricia vita conlocarit, virorum alienissimorum conviviis uti instituerit, si hoc in urbe, si in hortis, si in Baiarum illa celebritate faciat, si

600   denique ita sese gerat non incessu solum sed ornatu atque comitatu, non flagrantia oculorum, non libertate sermonum, sed etiam complexu, osculatione, actis, navigatione, conviviis, ut non solum meretrix sed etiam proterva meretrix procaxque videatur: cum hac si qui adulescens forte fuerit, utrum hic tibi,

605   L. Herenni, adulter an amator, expugnare pudicitiam an explere libidinem voluisse videatur? (50) Obliviscor iam iniurias tuas, Clodia, depono memoriam doloris mei; quae abs te crudeliter in meos me absente facta sunt neglego; ne sint haec in te dicta quae

dixi. Sed ex te ipsa requiro, quoniam et crimen accusatores abs te
610   et testem eius criminis te ipsam dicunt se habere. Si quae mulier
sit eius modi qualem ego paulo ante descripsi, tui dissimilis, vita
institutoque meretricio, cum hac aliquid adulescentem hominem
habuisse rationis num tibi perturpe aut perflagitiosum esse
videatur? Ea si tu non es, sicut ego malo, quid est quod obiciant
615   Caelio? Sin eam te volunt esse, quid est cur nos crimen hoc, si tu
contemnis, pertimescamus? Qua re nobis da viam rationemque
defensionis. Aut enim pudor tuus defendet nihil a M. Caelio
petulantius esse factum, aut impudentia et huic et ceteris
magnam ad se defendendum facultatem dabit.

620   (XXI,51) Sed quoniam emersisse iam e vadis et scopulos
praetervecta videtur esse oratio mea, perfacilis mihi reliquus
cursus ostenditur. Duo sunt enim crimina una in muliere
summorum facinorum, auri quod sumptum a Clodia dicitur, et
veneni quod eiusdem Clodiae necandae causa parasse Caelium
625   criminantur. Aurum sumpsit, ut dicitis, quod L. Luccei servis
daret, per quos Alexandrinus Dio qui tum apud Lucceium
habitabat necaretur. Magnum crimen vel in legatis insidiandis
vel in servis ad hospitem domini necandum sollicitandis, plenum sceleris consilium, plenum audaciae! (52) Quo quidem in
630   crimine primum illud requiro, dixeritne Clodiae quam ob rem
aurum sumeret, an non dixerit. Si non dixit, cur dedit? Si dixit,
eodem se conscientiae scelere devinxit. Tune aurum ex armario
tuo promere ausa es, tune Venerem illam tuam spoliare
ornamentis, spoliatricem ceterorum, cum scires quantum ad
635   facinus aurum hoc quaereretur, ad necem legati, ad L. Luccei,
sanctissimi hominis atque integerrimi, labem sceleris
sempiternam? Huic facinori tanto tua mens liberalis conscia, tua
domus popularis ministra, tua denique hospitalis illa Venus
adiutrix esse non debuit. (53) Vidit hoc Balbus; celatam esse
640   Clodiam dixit, atque ita Caelium ad illam attulisse, se ad
ornatum ludorum aurum quaerere. Si tam familiaris erat Clodiae

quam tu esse vis cum de libidine eius tam multa dicis, dixit profecto quo vellet aurum; si tam familiaris non erat, non dedit. Ita si verum tibi Caelius dixit, o immoderata mulier, sciens tu
645 aurum ad facinus dedisti; si non est ausus dicere, non dedisti.

(XXII) Quid ego nunc argumentis huic crimini, quae sunt innumerabilia, resistam? Possum dicere mores M. Caeli longissime a tanti sceleris atrocitate esse disiunctos; minime esse credendum homini tam ingenioso tamque prudenti non venisse
650 in mentem rem tanti sceleris ignotis alienisque servis non esse credendam. Possum etiam alia et ceterorum patronorum et mea consuetudine ab accusatore perquirere, ubi sit congressus cum servis Luccei Caelius, qui ei fuerit aditus; si per se, qua temeritate! si per alium, per quem? Possum omnis latebras
655 suspicionum peragrare dicendo; non causa, non locus, non facultas, non conscius, non perficiendi, non occultandi malefici spes, non ratio ulla, non vestigium maximi facinoris reperietur. (54) Sed haec quae sunt oratoris propria, quae mihi non propter ingenium meum sed propter hanc exercitationem usumque
660 dicendi fructum aliquem ferre potuissent, cum a me ipso elaborata proferri viderentur, brevitatis causa relinquo omnia. Habeo enim, iudices, quem vos socium vestrae religionis iurisque iurandi facile esse patiamini, L. Lucceium, sanctissimum hominem et gravissimum testem, qui tantum
665 facinus in famam atque in fortunas suas neque non audisset inlatum a M. Caelio neque neglexisset neque tulisset. An ille vir illa humanitate praeditus, illis studiis, illis artibus atque doctrina illius ipsius periculum quem propter haec ipsa studia diligebat, neglegere potuisset et, quod facinus in alienum hominem
670 intentum severe acciperet, id omisisset curare in hospitem? quod per ignotos actum si comperisset doleret, id a suis servis temptatum esse neglegeret? quod in agris locisve publicis factum reprehenderet, id in urbe ac domi suae coeptum esse leniter fer-
ret? quod in alicuius agrestis periculo non praetermitteret, id

675   homo eruditus in insidiis doctissimi hominis dissimulandum
putaret? (55) Sed cur diutius vos, iudices, teneo? Ipsius iurati reli-
gionem auctoritatemque percipite atque omnia diligenter
testimoni verba cognoscite. Recita. L. LVCCEI TESTIMONIVM.
Quid exspectatis amplius? an aliquam vocem putatis ipsam pro
680   se causam et veritatem posse mittere? Haec est innocentiae
defensio, haec ipsius causae oratio, haec una vox veritatis. In
crimine ipso nulla suspicio est, in re nihil est argumenti, in
negotio quod actum esse dicitur nullum vestigium sermonis,
loci, temporis; nemo testis, nemo conscius nominatur, totum cri-
685   men profertur ex inimica, ex infami, ex crudeli, ex facinerosa, ex
libidinosa domo. Domus autem illa quae temptata esse scelere
isto nefario dicitur plena est integritatis, dignitatis, offici,
religionis; ex qua domo recitatur vobis iure iurando devincta
auctoritas, ut res minime dubitanda in contentione ponatur,
690   utrum temeraria, procax, irata mulier finxisse crimen, an gravis
sapiens moderatusque vir religiose testimonium dixisse
videatur.

(XXIII,56) Reliquum est igitur crimen de veneno; cuius ego
nec principium invenire neque evolvere exitum possum. Quae
695   fuit enim causa quam ob rem isti mulieri venenum dare vellet
Caelius? Ne aurum redderet? Num petivit? Ne crimen
haereret? Num quis obiecit? num quis denique fecisset
mentionem, si hic nullius nomen detulisset? Quin etiam
L. Herennium dicere audistis verbo se molestum non futurum
700   fuisse Caelio, nisi iterum eadem de re suo familiari absoluto
nomen hic detulisset. Credibile est igitur tantum facinus nullam
ob causam esse commissum? et vos non videtis fingi sceleris
maximi crimen ut alterius sceleris suscipiendi fuisse causa
videatur? (57) Cui denique commisit, quo adiutore usus est, quo
705   socio, quo conscio, cui tantum facinus, cui se, cui salutem suam
credidit? Servisne mulieris? Sic enim est obiectum. Et erat tam
demens hic cui vos ingenium certe tribuitis, etiam si cetera

inimica oratione detrahitis, ut omnis suas fortunas alienis servis
committeret? At quibus servis?—refert enim magno opere id
710   ipsum—eisne quos intellegebat non communi condicione
servitutis uti sed licentius liberius familiariusque cum domina
vivere? Quis enim hoc non videt, iudices, aut quis ignorat, in
eius modi domo in qua mater familias meretricio more vivat, in
qua nihil geratur quod foras proferendum sit, in qua inusitatae
715   libidines, luxuries, omnia denique inaudita vitia ac flagitia
versentur, hic servos non esse servos, quibus omnia
committantur, per quos gerantur, qui versentur isdem in
voluptatibus, quibus occulta credantur, ad quos aliquantum
etiam ex cotidianis sumptibus ac luxurie redundet? Id igitur
720   Caelius non videbat? (58) Si enim tam familiaris erat mulieris
quam vos voltis, istos quoque servos familiaris dominae esse
sciebat. Sin ei tanta consuetudo quanta a vobis inducitur non
erat, quae cum servis eius potuit familiaritas esse tanta? (XXIV)
Ipsius autem veneni quae ratio fingitur? ubi quaesitum est, quem
725   ad módum paratum, quo pacto, cui, quo in loco traditum?
Habuisse aiunt domi vimque eius esse expertum in servo
quodam ad eam rem ipsam parato; cuius perceleri interitu esse
ab hoc comprobatum venenum. (59) Pro di immortales! cur
interdum in hominum sceleribus maximis aut conivetis aut
730   praesentis fraudis poenas in diem reservatis? Vidi enim, vidi et
illum hausi dolorem vel acerbissimum in vita, cum Q. Metellus
abstraheretur e sinu gremioque patriae, cumque ille vir qui se
natum huic imperio putavit tertio die post quam in curia, quam
in rostris, quam in re publica floruisset, integerrima aetate,
735   optimo habitu, maximis viribus eriperetur indignissime bonis
omnibus atque universae civitati. Quo quidem tempore ille
moriens, cum iam ceteris ex partibus oppressa mens esset, extre-
mum sensum ad memoriam rei publicae reservabat, cum me
intuens flentem significabat interruptis ac morientibus vocibus
740   quanta inpenderet procella mihi, quanta tempestas civitati et

cum parietem saepe feriens eum qui cum Q. Catulo fuerat ei communis crebro Catulum, saepe me, saepissime rem publicam nominabat, ut non tam se mori quam spoliari suo praesidio cum patriam tum etiam me doleret. (60) Quem quidem virum si nulla

745   vis repentini sceleris sustulisset, quonam modo ille furenti fratri suo consularis restitisset qui consul incipientem furere atque tonantem sua se manu interfecturum audiente senatu dixerit? Ex hac igitur domo progressa ista mulier de veneni celeritate dicere audebit? Nonne ipsam domum metuet ne quam vocem

750   eiciat, non parietes conscios, non noctem illam funestam ac luctuosam perhorrescet? Sed revertor ad crimen; etenim haec facta illius clarissimi ac fortissimi viri mentio et vocem meam fletu debilitavit et mentem dolore impedivit.

(XXV,61) Sed tamen venenum unde fuerit, quem ad modum

755   paratum sit non dicitur. Datum esse aiunt huic P. Licinio, pudenti adulescenti et bono, Caeli familiari; constitutum esse cum servis ut venirent ad balneas Senias; eodem Licinium esse venturum atque eis veneni pyxidem traditurum. Hic primum illud requiro, quid attinuerit ferri in eum locum constitutum, cur

760   illi servi non ad Caelium domum venerint. Si manebat tanta illa consuetudo Caeli, tanta familiaritas cum Clodia, quid suspicionis esset si apud Caelium mulieris servus visus esset? Sin autem iam suberat simultas, exstincta erat consuetudo, discidium exstiterat, hinc illae lacrimae nimirum et haec causa est omnium horum

765   scelerum atque criminum. (62) 'Immo' inquit 'cum servi ad dominam rem totam et maleficium Caeli detulissent, mulier ingeniosa praecepit his ut omnia Caelio pollicerentur; sed ut venenum, cum a Licinio traderetur, manifesto comprehendi posset, constitui locum iussit balneas Senias, ut eo mitteret

770   amicos qui delitiscerent, deinde repente, cum venisset Licinius venenumque traderet, prosilirent hominemque comprenderent.' (XXVI) Quae quidem omnia, iudices, perfacilem rationem habent reprendendi. Cur enim potissimum balneas publicas

constituerat? in quibus non invenio quae latebra togatis
775 hominibus esse posset. Nam si essent in vestibulo balnearum,
non laterent; sin se in intimum conicere vellent, nec satis com-
mode calceati et vestiti id facere possent et fortasse non
reciperentur, nisi forte mulier potens quadrantaria illa
permutatione familiaris facta erat balneatori. (63) Atque
780 equidem vehementer exspectabam quinam isti viri boni testes
huius manifesto deprehensi veneni dicerentur; nulli enim sunt
adhuc nominati. Sed non dubito quin sint pergraves, qui
primum sint talis feminae familiares, deinde eam provinciam
susceperint ut in balneas contruderentur, quod illa nisi a viris
785 honestissimis ac plenissimis dignitatis, quam velit sit potens,
numquam impetravisset. Sed quid ego de dignitate istorum testium loquor? virtutem eorum diligentiamque cognoscite. 'In
balneis delituerunt.' Testis egregios! 'Dein temere prosiluerunt.'
Homines temperantis! Sic enim fingitis, cum Licinius venisset,
790 pyxidem teneret in manu, conaretur tradere, nondum
tradidisset, tum repente evolasse istos praeclaros testis sine nom-
ine; Licinium autem, cum iam manum ad tradendam pyxidem
porrexisset, retraxisse atque ex illo repentino hominum impetu
se in fugam coniecisse. O magnam vim veritatis, quae contra
795 hominum ingenia, calliditatem, sollertiam contraque fictas
omnium insidias facile se per se ipsa defendat! (XXVII,64) Velut
haec tota fabella veteris et plurimarum fabularum poetriae quam
est sine argumento, quam nullum invenire exitum potest! Quid
enim? isti tot viri—nam necesse est fuisse non paucos ut et
800 comprehendi Licinius facile posset et res multorum oculis esset
testatior—cur Licinium de manibus amiserunt? Qui minus enim
Licinius comprehendi potuit cum se retraxit ne pyxidem
traderet, quam si tradidisset? Erant enim illi positi ut
comprehenderent Licinium, ut manifesto Licinius teneretur aut
805 cum retineret venenum aut cum tradidisset. Hoc fuit totum
consilium mulieris, haec istorum provincia qui rogati sunt; quos

quidem tu quam ob rem temere prosiluisse dicas atque ante tempus non reperio. Fuerant ad hoc rogati, fuerant ad hanc rem
conlocati, ut venenum, ut insidiae, facinus denique ipsum ut
810   manifesto comprenderetur. (65) Potueruntne magis tempore
prosilire quam cum Licinius venisset, cum in manu teneret
veneni pyxidem? Quae cum iam erat tradita servis, si evasissent
subito ex balneis mulieris amici Liciniumque comprehendissent,
imploraret hominum fidem atque a se illam pyxidem traditam
815   pernegaret. Quem quo modo illi reprehenderent? vidisse se
dicerent? Primum ad se revocarent maximi facinoris crimen;
deinde id se vidisse dicerent quod quo loco conlocati fuerant non
potuissent videre. Tempore igitur ipso se ostenderunt, cum
Licinius venisset, pyxidem expediret, manum porrigeret,
820   venenum traderet. Mimi ergo iam exitus, non fabulae; in quo
cum clausula non invenitur, fugit aliquis e manibus, dein scabilla
concrepant, aulaeum tollitur. (XXVIII,66) Quaero enim cur
Licinium titubantem, haesitantem, cedentem, fugere conantem
mulieraria manus ista de manibus emiserit, cur non
825   comprenderint, cur non ipsius confessione, multorum oculis,
facinoris denique voce tanti sceleris crimen expresserint. An
timebant ne tot unum, valentes imbecillum, alacres perterritum
superare non possent? Nullum argumentum in re, nulla suspicio
in causa, nullus exitus criminis reperietur. Itaque haec causa ab
830   argumentis, a coniectura, ab eis signis quibus veritas inlustrari
solet ad testis tota traducta est. Quos quidem ego, iudices, testis
non modo sine ullo timore sed etiam cum aliqua spe delectationis
exspecto. (67) Praegestit animus iam videre, primum lautos
iuvenes mulieris beatae ac nobilis familiaris, deinde fortis viros
835   ab imperatrice in insidiis atque in praesidio balnearum
conlocatos. Ex quibus requiram quem ad modum latuerint aut
ubi, alveusne ille an equus Troianus fuerit qui tot invictos viros
muliebre bellum gerentis tulerit ac texerit. Illud vero respondere
cogam, cur tot viri ac tales hunc et unum et tam imbecillum quem

840 videtis non aut stantem comprehenderint aut fugientem
consecuti sint; qui se numquam profecto, si in istum locum
processerint, explicabunt. Quam volent in conviviis faceti,
dicaces, non numquam etiam ad vinum diserti sint, alia fori vis
est, alia triclini, alia subselliorum ratio, alia lectorum; non idem

845 iudicum comissatorumque conspectus; lux denique longe alia est
solis, alia lychnorum. Quam ob rem excutiemus omnis istorum
delicias, omnis ineptias, si prodierint. Sed me audiant, navent
aliam operam, aliam ineant gratiam, in aliis se rebus ostentent,
vigeant apud istam mulierem venustate, dominentur sumptibus,

850 haereant, iaceant, deserviant; capiti vero innocentis fortunisque
parcant.

(XXIX,68) At sunt servi illi de cognatorum sententia,
nobilissimorum et clarissimorum hominum, manu missi. Tandem aliquid · invenimus quod ista mulier de suorum

855 propinquorum, fortissimorum virorum, sententia atque
auctoritate fecisse dicatur. Sed scire cupio quid habeat
argumenti ista manumissio; in qua aut crimen est Caelio quaesitum aut quaestio sublata aut multarum rerum consciis servis
cum causa praemium persolutum. 'At propinquis' inquit

860 'placuit.' Cur non placeret, cum rem tute ad eos non ab aliis tibi
adlatam sed a te ipsa compertam deferre diceres? (69) Hic etiam
miramur, si illam commenticiam pyxidem obscenissima sit
fabula consecuta? Nihil est quod in eius modi mulierem non
cadere videatur. Audita et percelebrata sermonibus res est.

865 Percipitis animis, iudices, iam dudum quid velim vel potius quid
nolim dicere. Quod etiam si est factum, certe a Caelio quidem
non est factum—quid enim attinebat?—est enim ab aliquo
adulescente fortasse non tam insulso quam inverecundo. Sin
autem est fictum, non illud quidem modestum sed tamen est non

870 infacetum mendacium; quod profecto numquam hominum
sermo atque opinio comprobasset, nisi omnia quae cum
turpitudine aliqua dicerentur in istam quadrare apte viderentur.

(70) Dicta est a me causa, iudices, et perorata. Iam intellegitis
quantum iudicium sustineatis, quanta res sit commissa vobis.
875   De vi quaeritis. Quae lex ad imperium, ad maiestatem, ad statum
patriae, ad salutem omnium pertinet, quam legem Q.
Catulus armata dissensione civium rei publicae paene extremis
temporibus tulit, quaeque lex sedata illa flamma consulatus mei
fumantis reliquias coniurationis exstinxit, hac nunc lege Caeli
880   adulescentia non ad rei publicae poenas sed ad mulieris libidines
et delicias deposcitur. (XXX,71) Atque hoc etiam loco M.
Camurti et C. Caeserni damnatio praedicatur. O stultitiam!
stultitiamne dicam an impudentiam singularem? Audetisne,
cum ab ea muliere veniatis, facere istorum hominum
885   mentionem? audetis excitare tanti flagiti memoriam, non
exstinctam illam quidem sed repressam vetustate? Quo enim illi
crimine peccatoque perierunt? Nempe quod eiusdem mulieris
dolorem et iniuriam Vettiano nefario sunt stupro persecuti. Ergo
ut audiretur Vetti nomen in causa, ut illa vetus aeraria fabula
890   referretur, idcirco Camurti et Caeserni est causa renovata? qui
quamquam lege de vi certe non tenebantur, eo maleficio tamen
erant implicati ut ex nullius legis laqueis eximendi viderentur.
(72) M. vero Caelius cur in hoc iudicium vocatur? cui neque
proprium quaestionis crimen obicitur nec vero aliquod eius
895   modi quod sit a lege seiunctum, cum vestra severitate
coniunctum. Cuius prima aetas disciplinae edita fuit eisque
artibus quibus instruimur ad hunc usum forensem, ad
capessendam rem publicam, ad honorem, gloriam, dignitatem.
Eis autem fuit amicitiis maiorum natu quorum imitari indus-
900   triam continentiamque maxime vellet, eis studiis aequalium ut
eundem quem optimi ac nobilissimi petere cursum laudis
videretur. (73) Cum autem paulum iam roboris accessisset aetati,
in Africam profectus est Q. Pompeio pro consule contubernalis,
castissimo homini atque omnis offici diligentissimo; in qua
905   provincia cum res erant et possessiones paternae, tum etiam usus

quidam provincialis non sine causa a maioribus huic aetati tributus. Decessit illinc Pompei iudicio probatissimus, ut ipsius testimonio cognoscetis. Voluit vetere instituto et eorum adulescentium exemplo qui post in civitate summi viri et
910 clarissimi cives exstiterunt industriam suam a populo Romano ex aliqua inlustri accusatione cognosci. (XXXI,74) Vellem alio potius eum cupiditas gloriae detulisset; sed abiit huius tempus querelae. Accusavit C. Antonium, conlegam meum, cui misero praeclari in rem publicam benefici memoria nihil profuit, nocuit
915 opinio malefici cogitati. Postea nemini umquam concessit aequalium plus ut in foro, plus ut in negotiis versaretur causisque amicorum, plus ut valeret inter suos gratia. Quae nisi vigilantes homines, nisi sobrii, nisi industrii consequi non possunt, omnia labore et diligentia est consecutus. (75) In hoc
920 flexu quasi aetatis—nihil enim occultabo fretus humanitate ac sapientia vestra—fama adulescentis paululum haesit ad metas notitia nova eius mulieris et infelici vicinitate et insolentia voluptatum, quae, cum inclusae diutius et prima aetate compressae et constrictae fuerunt, subito se non numquam
925 profundunt atque eiciunt universae. Qua ex vita vel dicam quo ex sermone—nequaquam enim tantum erat quantum homines loquebantur—verum ex eo quicquid erat emersit totumque se eiecit atque extulit, tantumque abest ab illius familiaritatis infamia ut eiusdem nunc ab sese inimicitias odiumque propulset.
930 (76) Atque ut iste interpositus sermo deliciarum desidiaeque moreretur—fecit me invito me hercule et multum repugnante me, sed tamen fecit—nomen amici mei de ambitu detulit; quem absolutum insequitur, revocat; nemini nostrum obtemperat, est violentior quam vellem. Sed ego non loquor de sapientia, quae
935 non cadit in hanc aetatem; de impetu animi loquor, de cupiditate vincendi, de ardore mentis ad gloriam; quae studia in his iam aetatibus nostris contractiora esse debent, in adulescentia vero tamquam in herbis significant quae virtutis maturitas et quantae

940 fruges industriae sint futurae. Etenim semper magno ingenio adulescentes refrenandi potius a gloria quam incitandi fuerunt; amputanda plura sunt illi aetati, si quidem efflorescit ingeni laudibus, quam inserenda. (77) Qua re, si cui nimium effervisse videtur huius vel in suscipiendis vel in gerendis inimicitiis vis, ferocitas, pertinacia, si quem etiam minimorum horum aliquid
945 offendit, si purpurae genus, si amicorum catervae, si splendor, si nitor, iam ista deferverint, iam aetas omnia, iam res, iam dies mitigarit.

(XXXII) Conservate igitur rei publicae, iudices, civem bonarum artium, bonarum partium, bonorum virorum.
950 Promitto hoc vobis et rei publicae spondeo, si modo nos ipsi rei publicae satis fecimus, numquam hunc a nostris rationibus seiunctum fore. Quod cum fretus nostra familiaritate promitto, tum quod durissimis se ipse legibus iam obligavit. (78) Non enim potest qui hominem consularem, cum ab eo rem publicam
955 violatam esse diceret, in iudicium vocarit ipse esse in re publica civis turbulentus; non potest qui ambitu ne absolutum quidem patiatur esse absolutum ipse impune umquam esse largitor. Habet a M. Caelio res publica, iudices, duas accusationes vel obsides periculi vel pignora voluntatis. Qua re oro obtestorque
960 vos, iudices, ut qua in civitate paucis his diebus Sex. Cloelius absolutus est, quem vos per biennium aut ministrum seditionis aut ducem vidistis, hominem sine re, sine fide, sine spe, sine sede, sine fortunis, ore, lingua, manu, vita omni inquinatum, qui aedis sacras, qui censum populi Romani, qui memoriam
965 publicam suis manibus incendit, qui Catuli monumentum adflixit, meam domum diruit, mei fratris incendit, qui in Palatio atque in urbis oculis servitia ad caedem et ad inflammandam urbem incitavit; in ea civitate ne patiamini illum absolutum muliebri gratia, M. Caelium libidini muliebri condonatum,
970 ne eadem mulier cum suo coniuge et fratre et turpissimum latronem eripuisse et honestissimum adulescentem oppressisse

videatur.

(79) Quod cum huius vobis adulescentiam proposueritis, constituitote ante oculos etiam huius miseri senectutem qui hoc
975 unico filio nititur, in huius spe requiescit, huius unius casum pertimescit; quem vos supplicem vestrae misericordiae, servum potestatis, abiectum non tam ad pedes quam ad mores sensusque vestros, vel recordatione parentum vestrorum vel liberorum iucunditate sustentate, ut in alterius dolore vel pietati vel
980 indulgentiae vestrae serviatis. Nolite, iudices, aut hunc iam natura ipsa occidentem velle maturius exstingui volnere vestro quam suo fato, aut hunc nunc primum florescentem firmata iam stirpe virtutis tamquam turbine aliquo aut subita tempestate pervertere. (80) Conservate parenti filium, parentem filio, ne aut
985 senectutem iam prope desperatam contempsisse aut adulescentiam plenam spei maximae non modo non aluisse vos verum etiam perculisse atque adflixisse videamini. Quem si nobis, si suis, si rei publicae conservatis, addictum, deditum, obstrictum vobis ac liberis vestris habebitis omniumque huius
990 nervorum ac laborum vos potissimum, iudices, fructus uberes diuturnosque capietis.

VOCABULARY
AND NOTES

1–29 (chs. 1 and 2) make up the *exordium*, or opening of the speech (**exordior**, begin), which is composed of several long periodic sentences, as was considered appropriate. A *period* or *periodic sentence* (Gk. **periodos**, a circuit) has logical and syntactical subordination to a single main idea, which usually is not completed until the very end of the sentence. Among Roman writers and orators, Cicero is especially associated with the periodic style, although, as will be noted, it is certainly not the only style he employed. The exordium begins with three complex, conditional sentences, and concludes with three brief, declarative statements.

The desire to achieve periodicity is one reason the Latin verb often occurs at the end of the sentence. The Latin writer could guarantee periodicity in this way, and the Latin system of *inflection*—word endings—allowed him the freedom to do it.

Cicero probably took about three minutes to deliver this exordium, and in that critical period he presents or hints at most of the themes that run through the entire two-and-a-half-hour speech. Cicero's ornate periodic structure opens the speech with the dignity and formality appropriate to an exordium and to a matter so grave. At the same time, he makes a series of carefully crafted insinuations, by creating doubt, pity, titillation, and suspense, to deflect attention from Caelius and the formal charges and toward Clodia. We begin with an anonymous, mystified stranger.

Austin's comments on the *prō Caeliō's* exordium (at 1.1) are well worth reading, for discussion of how this exordium conformed to ancient precepts and for references to valuable discussions about exordia in Quintilian and in Cicero's *dē ōrātōre*.

1–7.   The structure of these lines is as follows:

1 (ch. 1). **Sī,** *conj.,* if. *Sī* and its derivatives *sī...nōn,* "if...not," *nisi,* "if...not," "unless," and *sīn,* "but if," are used to introduce various kinds of *conditional sentences,* Ben. 301. A conditional sentence is composed of two clauses:

(1) a *protasis* or condition (the dependent *sī*-clause
   [from Gk. *proteinō,* propose]); and
(2) an *apodosis* or conclusion (the independent clause
   [from Gk. *apodidōmi,* grant]).

In the sentence
"If it's sunny tomorrow, we'll go to the beach,"
"If it's sunny tomorrow" is the protasis, and "we'll go to the beach" is the apodosis.

In the Lat. sentence, the protasis contains the pres. subj. *adsit* and the apodosis contains another pres. subj., *mīrētur.* A condition with pres. subj.'s in both clauses is called variously an "ideal," "future less vivid," or "should-would" condition, Ben. 303. Translate "If [he] should be present, he would wonder...."

quis: quis, quid, *indef. pron.,* anyone, anybody, anything; someone, somebody, something. These pronouns, identical in declension to the interrog. pron., are usually used after *sī, nisi, nē, num,* and a few other words in place of *aliquis, aliquid,* Ben. 91, 252.1.

iūdicēs: iūdex, iūdicis, *m.,* judge; juror [**iūs,** law + **dīcō, dīcere**]. The word is applied here to the jurors, since in this kind of case they determined the defendant's guilt or innocence, rather than the presiding magistrate, who would have been referred to by his office: *praetor, quaestor,* etc.

Iūdicēs is in the *vocative* case, the case of direct address: "gentlemen of the jury." Vocatives usually have the same endings as nominatives but in modern texts are commonly set off from the rest of the sentence by commas, as here. They usually follow one or more words in their clause, Ben. 350.3.

forte: *only nom. sg.* **fors** *and abl. sg.* **forte** *are attested,* chance, happenstance, luck. *Forte* is commonly used, without prep., in the adverbial sense "by chance, perhaps."

nunc, *adv.,* (right) now, at this juncture

adsit: adsum, adesse, adfuī, be present, be on hand, be a party to [**ad** + **sum**]

ignārus: ignārus-a-um, *adj.,* having no knowledge (of), unacquainted (with); inexperienced (in) *(w. gen.)* [**in**-privative, + **(g)nārus,** knowing; *privative* (hereafter "priv.") means the *in*- negates the root meaning, from *prīvō,* deprive] lēgum: lex, lēgis, *f.,* law; *pl.,* legal system, law. Case? See *ignārus* at 1n.

2. iūdiciōrum: iūdicium, iūdicī, *n.,* trial; court of law; judgment
consuētūdinis: cōnsuētūdō, cōnsuētūdinis, *f.,* custom, habit; practices, conventions, procedures [cōnsuēscō, accustom, habituate]; here "way of life"
-que, *encl. conj.,* and; -*que* is to *et* as *'n* is to *and.*
lēgum, iūdiciōrum, cōnsuētūdinisque nostrae: an example of *tricolon,* or tripartite construction [Gk. treis, three + kōlon, part]. If the second part is longer than the first and the third longer than the second, as here, it is called *tricōlon crēscēns* [crēscō, grow].
These words are also an example of *asyndeton,* or lack of connectives [Gk. a-priv. + syn, together + deō, bind], Ben. 346.
nostrae: noster, nostra, nostrum, *poss. adj.,* our
mīrētur: mīror (1), marvel or wonder at; be astonished or bewildered by; admire, revere
profectō, *adv.,* indeed, assuredly, truly [prō + factum, thing done, fact; cf. colloq. Engl. "for sure"]. Austin, noting the word's common use as a first pers. asseverative, submits "in my opinion" (at 1.2) or "I am quite sure that..." (at 53.22).

3. quae: quī, quae, quod, *interrog. adj.,* which, what, what kind of
sit: sum, esse, fuī, futūrus, be, exist. *Sit* is pres. subj. in indir. question, Ben. 300.1.
tanta: tantus-a-um, *adj.,* such a, so great a, so much, of such magnitude
atrōcitās: atrōcitās, atrōcitātis, *f.,* dreadfulness; cruelty, savagery; outrage, wicked crime [atrox, terrible; āter, black]. In addition to these general meanings, *atrōcitās* was the technical term for what the law today calls "aggravated assault," and in a forensic context would have had a legal ring (Austin at 1.3).
huiusce: hic, haec, hoc, *dem. adj. & pron.,* this. The older forms with the complete enclitic -*ce* are emphatic, Ben. 87n1; *huiusce causae* may be rendered "...of this case before us..."
causae: causa, causae, *f.,* case, trial; reason, motive
quod: quī, quae, quod, *rel. adj.,* which. *Quod* = *propter quod,* "on account of which," "in that," "because" (Austin on 1.3). After *tanta,* we might expect a correlative *quantus* clause or a result clause beginning with *ut,* but with the *quod* clause Cicero focuses on the reason for his imaginary visitor's enquiry rather than on the result.
diēbus: diēs, diēī, *m./f.,* day. *Diēbus* is abl. of time at which, Ben. 230.
festīs: festus-a-um, *adj.,* of or pert. to a holiday, festive, festal [fēriae, holy day, holiday]

4.   **lūdīs: lūdus, lūdī,** *m.,* play, game, sport; *pl.,* public games. *Diēbus festīs lūdīsque pūblicīs* refers to the *Lūdī Megalēnsēs,* or Games in Honor of the Great Mother [Gk. **Megalē,** the Great One]. These games were held in worship of Cybele, originally a Phrygian goddess identified by the Romans variously as Rhea, Ops, and Magna Mater. Begun at Rome in 204 B.C. and originally a one-day celebration held on April 4, in Cicero's day the festivities were held on April 10 as well, and would have included races and theatrical performances. The trial had begun on April 3, 56 B.C., but had not been *intermissa* because the *lex dē vī,* "law concerning political violence," under which Caelius was being prosecuted, did not admit such delays. Cicero was, as usual, the last orator for the defense, and spoke on April 4.

pūblicīs: pūblicus-a-um, *adj.,* of or pert. to the people, public, state, as opposed to *prīvātus* [**populus,** the people]; in this section, Cicero is trying to score points with the jury: "You're working when you should be on holiday!"

omnibus: omnis-is-e, *adj.,* all, the whole (of); every

forēnsibus: forēnsis-is-e, *adj.,* of or pert. to the operation or business of the market or forum, esp. legal business [**forum,** center of business and government at Rome]

negōtiīs: negōtium, negōtī, *n.,* business [**nec + ōtium,** leisure]

intermissīs: intermittō, intermittere, intermīsī, intermissum, separate; discontinue, interrupt; allow to elapse [**inter + mittō**]. The entire phrase *omnibus forēnsibus negōtiīs intermissīs* is an abl. abs., Ben. 227.

5.   **ūnum: ūnus-a-um,** *card. num. adj.,* one, single, lone, alone

exerceātur: exerceō, exercēre, exercuī, exercitum, practice, train, keep at work; *(of a process or activity)* exercise, perform; *(of a court)* be in session [**ex-,** thoroughly + **arceō,** control]. *Exerceātur* is subj. in a causal clause within an indir. question, Ben 314.1.

Causal clauses w. *quod* ordinarily employ the indic., Ben. 286.1. The direct form of the whole question would be *quae tanta atrōcitās est hūiusce causae, quod...ūnum hoc iūdicium exercētur...?* When this is subordinated to *mīrētur, est* becomes *sit* and *exercētur* becomes *exerceātur,* Ben. 324.1.

nec *or* **neque,** *conj.,* nor, and...not.

dubitet: dubitō (1), doubt, be uncertain; hesitate, vacillate, waver. Mood? Ben. 303.

quīn, *conj., following negative verbs of doubt, hesitation or surprise,* that, but that, that...not *(+ subj.)* [**quī + ne**]

6.   **facinoris: facinus, facinoris,** *n.*, deed, action, event; crime, misdeed, villainy **[faciō]**; *facinoris* is a gen. of the charge after a verb of accusing, Ben. 208.
reus: reus, reī, *m.*, party in a lawsuit; the accused, defendant
arguātur: arguō, arguere, arguī, argūtum, shed light on, show; assert, declare; accuse, (formally) charge
ut, *conj. introducing various kinds of clauses,* that
eō: is, ea, id, *weak dem. adj. & pron.,* this, that, the; he, she, it, they
neglectō: neglegō, neglegere, neglexī, neglectum, be indifferent to, disregard, fail to attend to; overlook **[nec + legō]**. *Eō neglectō* is an abl. abs. (Ben. 227) with a circumstantial and conditional sense: "... if this [matter] were neglected..."
cīvitās: cīvitās, cīvitātis, *f.,* state, commonwealth, community **[cīvis]**
stāre: stō, stāre, stetī, statum, stand; endure, persist, survive; complementary inf. after *possit,* Ben. 328.
nōn, *adv.,* not

7.   **possit: possum, posse, potuī,** be able, can **[potis,** able + **sum]**; subj. in a result clause introduced by *ut* at 6, Ben. 284. The jurors and bystanders would think of Sulla, Sertorius, Catiline, and others who had challenged the legitimate government over the preceding three decades.

7–18. The structure of these lines is as follows:

īdem cum audiat

esse lēgem quae dē { sēditiōsīs / cōnscelerātīsque } cīvibus quī { armātī senātum obsēderint, / magistrātibus vim attulerint, cotīdiē quaerī iubeat, / rem publicam oppugnārint }

lēgem nōn improbet,
crimen quod versētur in iūdiciō requīrat;

cum audiat { nullum facinus, / nullam audāciam, in iūdicium vocārī, / nullam vim }

sed adulēscentem inlustrī { ingeniō / industriā / grātiā } accūsārī ab eius filiō quem ipse in iūdicium { et vocet / et vocārit, }

oppugnārī autem opibus meretrīciīs:

illīus pietātem nōn reprehendat,
libīdinem muliēbrem comprimendam putet,

vōs labōriōsōs existimet, quibus ōtiōsīs nē in commūnī quidem ōtiō liceat esse.

īdem: īdem, eadem, idem, *identifying demon. pron. & adj.,* same, very same
cum, *conj.,* when; as, whereas, since, because; although. *Cum* followed
by the indic. means "when"; *cum* plus the subj. may take any of
these meanings, according to context, Ben. 286.2, 288–290, 309.3.
audiat: audiō (4), hear. *Audiat* is a subj., dependent on *cum.*
esse lēgem: "that there is a law," an example of an acc. and inf. constr.
after a verb of the head (knowing, saying, thinking, etc.), Ben. 314.1.
quae: quī, quae, quod, *rel. pron.,* who, what, which; *quae* is subject of
iubeat in 10; for the constr. (*quae iubeat quaerī dē cīvibus quī...,* "[the
law] which prescribes that there be an investigation into citizens
who..."), see *quaerī* at 10n.
dē, *prep. w. abl.,* down from; concerning, about, in the matter of
sēditiōsīs: sēditiōsus-a-um, *adj.,* quarrelsome, turbulent; subversive,
factious [**sēditiō,** riot, uprising]

8.   **cōnscelerātīs: cōnscelerō** (1), defile with crime, pollute; *hence part.*
cōnscelerātus *as adj.,* debased, degenerate; wicked, criminal [**cum-**
intensive + **scelus,** crime]
cīvibus: cīvis, cīvis, *m./f.,* citizen
armātī: armō (1), arm or supply with weapons
senātum: senātus, senātūs, *m.,* Senate [**senex,** old man]. Here *senātum* is
used as a proxy for "the legitimate government," "the state."
obsēderint: obsideō, obsidēre, obsēdī, obsessum, blockade, besiege,
assault [**ob** + **sedeō**]. *Obsēderint, attulerint,* and *oppugnārint* are subj.'s
in a rel. clause within indir. statement (Ben. 314.1): cf. also *exerceātur*
at 5. They are in the perfect tense, denoting time prior to the main
verb *audiat* in primary sequence.

Primary sequence means the main verb of the sentence is in the
present or future tense. Only a present or perfect subjunctive can
depend on such a verb. Thus:
Rogat cūr illud faciās,
She is asking why you are doing that.
Rogat cūr illud fēcerīs,
She is asking why you did that.

Secondary or *historical sequence* means the main verb of the sentence
is in a past tense. Only an imperfect or pluperfect subjunctive can
depend on such a verb. Thus:
Rogābat cūr illud facerēs,
She asked why you were doing that.

> **Rogābat cūr illud fēcissēs,**
> *She asked why you had done that.* Ben. 267.

Figure of speech formed by *obsēderint, attulerint,* and *oppugnārint?* See *lēgum,* etc. at 1.

9. **magistrātibus: magistrātus, magistrātūs,** *m.,* magistracy, office; magistrate [**magister**]
    vim: vīs, vīs, *f.,* force, power, violence; *pl.* **vīrēs, vīrium,** strength. This word declines as follows:

	sg.	pl.
nom.	**vīs,** force	**vīrēs,** strength
gen.	**vīs**	**vīrium**
dat.	**vī**	**vīribus**
acc.	**vim**	**vīrēs** *or* **vīrīs**
abl.	**vī**	**vīribus**

attulerint: adferō, adferre, attulī, adlātum, bring to, carry to; **vim adferre** (+ *dat.*), offer violence against

rem: rēs, reī, *f.,* thing. *Rēs* should rarely, if ever, be translated "thing." It can usually be given an Engl. translation specific to its context or to a modifying adj. Thus, *rēs publica,* "republic," "state," "commonwealth"; *rēs mīlitāris,* "military affairs"; *rēs novae,* "revolution."

oppugnārint: oppugnō (1), attack, assault [**ob** + **pugnō**]. *Oppugnārint* = *oppugnāverint,* as often by *syncope* [Gk., a cutting away]. Note the military language: an *obsidiō* is a formal siege of a city and an *oppugnātiō* a frontal assault on a town or other fortified position.

10. **cotīdiē,** *adv.,* daily, every day [**quot,** as many as + **diēs,** day]
    quaerī: quaerō, quaerere, quaesīvī *or* **quaesiī, quaesītum,** look for, search for; inquire into, investigate; acquire, obtain; used here impersonally and in the context of a judicial inquiry, as often: cf. Lat. *quaestiō* and Engl. "inquest."
    iubeat: iubeō, iubēre, iussī, iussum, bid, command, order; here = "enjoin," "prescribe"; subj. in a rel. clause within indir. statement, Ben. 314.1.
    improbet: improbō (1), disapprove, condemn, reject [**in**-priv. + **probō,** approve]; *improbet* and *requīrat* in 10–11 are subj. because Cicero is still talking about a supposition.
    crīmen: crīmen, crīminis, *n.,* accusation, charge, indictment; ground for a charge; do not translate as "crime," which is a later extension of the meaning, first found in Livy (Austin at 1.10).

11. **versētur: versō** (1), turn again and again; *(pass.)* be engaged in, take part in, be employed in; be busy with. Mood and reason? *Versō* is a *frequentative* of *vertō,* turn. Freq. verbs signify repeated action; they are first conjugation verbs which can be formed from the perf. pass. part. of the verb whose action is looked on as repeated; e.g., *pellō,* strike, perf. pass. part. *pulsus,* has the freq. *pulsō, pulsāre,* strike repeatedly, beat.

     in, *prep. w. acc. or abl.,* in, on; into, onto; against

     requīrat: requīrō, requīrere, requīsīvī *or* **requīsiī, requīsītum,** ask for, look for, demand [**re-,** back; again + **quaerō**]. Note the *adversative asyndeton* (Ben. 341.4a; 346.b): "...he would not disapprove of the law, [but] he would ask for the charge..." For asyndeton, see *lēgum,* etc. above at 1.

     nullum: nullus-a-um, *adj.,* no, not a

12. **audāciam: audācia, audāciae,** *f.,* boldness, courage; impudence, outrageousness; an example of impudence or recklessness, "intemperate action" (Austin at 1.11) [**audax**]

     nullum facinus, nullam audāciam, nullam vim: figure of speech? See *lēgum,* etc. above at 1.

     vocārī: vocō (1), call, summon; call to court, sue; **in iūdicium vocāre,** to bring to trial. Form and reason? Ben. 314.1

     sed, *conj.,* but

13. **adulēscentem: adulēscēns, adulēscentis,** *adj.,* young, youthful; *m./f., as subst.,* youth, young man [**adolēscō,** grow up, mature]. The word has a much wider meaning than its English derivative, being used of individuals as old as thirty or even more. Caelius was twenty-seven at the time of the trial.

     inlustrī: inlustris-is-e, *adj.,* full of light, bright; clear, evident; distinguished, eminent [**in-**intensive + **lustrō,** spread light around]

     ingeniō: ingenium, ingenī, *n.,* nature, natural disposition or quality; ability, genius; ingenuity, skill [**in** + **gignō,** give birth, beget]; *ingeniō et al.* are abl.'s of quality, Ben. 224.

     industriā: industria, industriae, *f.,* diligence, hard work, constant application, assiduity [**indu,** archaic for **in,** + **struō,** build; i.e., a person who has *industria* is "active within."]

     grātiā: grātia, grātiae, *f.,* loveliness, charm; influence, prestige; kindness, gratitude. A five-minute look-up of this word in a good lexicon is well worth the effort: *grātia* has a wide range of meanings that embraces many important Roman ideas.

accūsārī: accūsō (1), censure, fault; accuse, charge; prosecute [ad + cau-sa]. Form and reason? Ben. 314.1.
ab, *prep. w. abl.,* by

14.   fīliō: fīlius, fīlī, *m.,* son, i.e., seventeen-year-old L. Sempronius Atratinus, son of L. Calpurnius Bestia *(eius),* see 301n.; *fīliō* is an abl. of agency with a pass. verb, Ben. 216.
quem ipse: be sure you understand the antecedent of *quem* and who is referred to by *ipse.*
ipse: ipse, ipsa, ipsum, *intensive pron. & adj.,* -self (here Caelius)
vocā(ve)rit: technical name for this "shortening"? Ben. 7.4. Mood of *vo-cet, vocārit?* Ben. 314.1.

15.   oppugnārī: a subtly stronger image than *vocet/vocārit.* Caelius merely sues *(vocet/vocārit)* L. Calpurnius Bestia, but is himself under siege *(oppugnārī).* Note how the word recalls the previous context in which it was used, at 9: there the imaginary stranger might have ex-pected the state itself to be under attack; here he learns that Caelius actually is. Form and reason of *oppugnārī?* Ben. 314.1.
autem, *conj., (adversative)* however, but, on the other hand; *(adding a new item)* moreover, in addition, and what's more
opibus: ops, opis, *f.,* ability, power, strength; *pl.,* resources, wealth; abl. of means, Ben. 218.
meretrīciīs: meretrīcius-a-um, *adj.,* of or pert. to a prostitute [meretrix, courtesan, prostitute, whore]; the reference, which everyone would have recognized with delight, is to Clodia, not explicitly mentioned until line 355 (ch. 30), one-third of the way through the speech; this word does not recur until 461. Note Cicero's insinuation that the trial was purchased with funds *(opēs)* provided by a person *(mer-etrix)* who is herself for sale *(mereō,* earn money). The testimony of a *meretrix* was not admissible in court.
ipsīus: L. Semprōnius Atratinus, son of L. Calpurnius Bestia, whom Caelius had just prosecuted for *ambitus* ("a going around," i.e., elec-toral bribery) on February 11, 56 B.C. *(vocārit)* and was preparing to prosecute afresh *(et vocet).* Cicero had successfully defended Bestia (and so opposed Caelius!) in his first trial. When Caelius sued Bestia a second time, Bestia's son Atratinus proceeded against Caelius on a charge of *vis,* in the hope that he could destroy Caelius before Bestia's trial came up.
Note the pronominal gen. in *-īus;* compare *huiusce* at 3.

16. **pietātem: pietās, pietātis,** *f.,* dutifulness [**pius,** loyal]. *Pietās* is so difficult to translate that it is almost best left in the Latin: it is the personal trait which in a given circumstance makes a person perform his/her duty. The translation will depend on context: "fidelity," "piety," "respect," "patriotism," "family devotion," "loyalty," "proper conduct"; here of the devotion, respect, and loyalty between parent and child. *Pietās* and *pius* are also good words to look up in a lexicon.

    reprehendat: repre(he)ndō, repre(he)ndere, repre(hē)nsī, repre(hē) nsum, grasp to hold back, check, restrain; blame, rebuke, find fault with [**re-** + **prehendō,** seize]

    nōn reprehendat, [sed]...putet, [et]...existimet: figure of speech? See *requīrat,* etc. at 11. Mood and reason? See *improbet* at 10.

    libīdinem: libīdō, libīdinis, *f.,* whim, caprice, fancy; will, desire; sexual desire, lust

    muliebrem: muliebris-is-e, *adj.,* of or pertaining to a woman, womanly [**mulier,** woman]

17. **comprimendam: comprimō, comprimere, compressī, compressum,** compress; control, hold back, restrain [**cum-**intensive + **premō,** press]. *Comprimendam (esse)* is a gerundive used in a "pass. periphrastic" construction indicating obligation or necessity: "...that womanly passion must be suppressed..." *Esse* is often deleted when used with a gerundive or perf. pass. part. in indir. statement.

    putet: putō (1), believe, think; reckon, suppose

    vōs, *pron.,* you

    labōriōsōs: labōriōsus-a-um, *adj.,* full of work, laborious, toilsome; diligent, industrious; harassed, hard-pressed [**labor**]; here = "too much labored," "overworked." Austin notes that this word underscores the discrepancy between what the jurors deserve and what they are getting, like *diēbus festīs* at 3.

    existimet: existimō (1), esteem, value; consider, deem, (ad)judge properly [**ex-,** thoroughly + **aestimō,** value]

    quibus: dat. w. *liceat;* antecedent?

18. **ōtiōsis: ōtiōsus-a-um,** *adj.,* at leisure, having spare time [**ōtium**]

    nē...quidem, *adv. emphasizing the words it surrounds,* not even

    commūnī: commūnis-is-e, *adj.,* common, general, public

    ōtiō: ōtium, ōtī, *n.,* leisure, rest, spare time; here = "holiday."

    liceat: licet, licēre, licuit *or* **licitum est,** it is permitted, it is allowed; one may (+ *dat.*). Mood? Ben. 314.1.

    esse: take after *liceat.*

18–24. The structure of these lines is as follows:

Etenim sī { attendere dīligenter / atque / existimāre } vērē dē omnī hāc causā volueritis,

sīc cōnstituētis, iūdicēs,
nec dēscēnsūrum quemquam ad hanc accūsātiōnem fuisse cui utrum vellet liceret
nec, cum dēscendisset, quicquam habitūrum speī fuisse,

nisi { alicuius intolerābilī libīdine / et / nimis acerbō ōdiō } nīterētur.

(ch. 2). **etenim,** *adv.,* (for) indeed, in fact, for the fact is that
sī: here introduces a second kind of condition, called an open condition (Ben. 302), having an indic. in both clauses. This version has a
fut. perf. indic. in the protasis and a fut. indic. in the apodosis, and
would be literally rendered "If you will have been willing (normal
Engl. idiom: "if you are willing")..., you will establish...." Account
for the Latin tense uses (sometimes called "future more vivid"), and
note the relative imprecision of corresponding English idiom.

Compare the following conditional sentences:
Sī hoc facis, errās.
If you are doing this, you are making a mistake.
Sī hoc faciēs, errābis.
If you will do (will be doing) this, you will make
a mistake.
Sī hoc fēceris, errābis.
If you will have done this, you will make a mistake.

Sī hoc faciās, errēs.
If you should do this, you would make a mistake.
The first three sentences are open conditions: the second and
third are fut. more vivid open conditions. In English these are often expressed by "If you *do* this, you will make a mistake." What
kind of condition is the fourth sentence? See *sī* at 1.
A third kind of condition is the unreal, or contrary-to-fact,
condition (Ben. 304):

> **Sī hoc facerēs, errārēs.**
> *If you were doing this* (but you are not), *you would*
> *be making a mistake* (but you are not).
> **Sī hoc fēcissēs, errāvissēs.**
> *If you had done this* (but you did not), *you would*
> *have made a mistake* (but you did not).
> The first sentence of this pair is a present contrary-to-fact con-
> dition, containing imperfect subjunctives in both clauses. The sec-
> ond sentence is a past contrary-to-fact condition, containing plu-
> perfect subjunctives in both clauses. For an ex. of a contrary-to-fact
> condition from this speech, see 58–60.

19. **attendere: attendō, attendere, attendī, attentum,** attend to, pay atten-
     tion to [**ad** + **tendō,** stretch]
     dīligenter: dīligēns, dīligentis, *adj.,* attentive, careful, assiduous
     [**dīligō**]. Third-declension adjectives whose bases end in *-nt-* form
     their corresponding adverbs in *-nter.*
     atque or **ac,** *conj.,* and. *Atque* is a somewhat stronger connective than *et*
     or *-que:* "...and *also...*"
     vērē: vērus-a-um, *adj.,* true, real; honest, upright. *Vērus* has three ad-
     verbs: *vērē,* truly, really; properly, rightly; *vērō,* in fact, surely; *vērum,*
     but, nevertheless

20. **volueritis: volō, velle, voluī,** wish, want; be willing
     sīc, *adv.,* thus, so, in this way
     cōnstituētis: cōnstituō, cōnstituere, cōnstituī, cōnstitūtum, make
     stand, set up, place; decide, conclude, "establish." [**cum**-intensive
     + **statuō,** set] This placement of *cōnstituētis* at the beginning of its
     clause in a fut. more vivid condition is regular. *Sīc cōnstituētis* sets
     up an acc. + inf. construction: "You will conclude in this way, that...."
     dēscēnsūrum...fuisse: dēscendō, dēscendere, dēscendī, dēscēnsum,
     climb down; lower or demean oneself, stoop, sink to a low level [**dē,**
     down + **scandō,** climb]. The word has a dual meaning here: the com-
     mon expression *dēscendere in forum,* or sometimes just *dēscendere,* "to
     go down to the forum to do business, be involved in a case," is con-
     flated with *dēscendere ad hanc accūsātiōnem,* "to sink to the level of
     this accusation."
     The grammatical architecture of this sentence is difficult. A
     mixed contrary-to-fact condition (for contrary-to-fact conditions see
     18n. or 58n.) is buried within an indirect statement construction af-
     ter *cōnstituētis.* Without *cōnstituētis* we would have *nec dēscendisset*

quisquam...nec...habuisset..., *nisi...nīterētur,* "no one would have sunk so low...nor... would have had...*,* unless he were relying...." When subordinated to *cōnstituētis,* the pluperf. subj.'s become fut. part.'s + *fuisse.*

21. **quemquam: quisquam, quaequam, quicquam** *or* **quidquam,** *indef. pron.,* anyone, someone; *(w. neg.)* no one. *Quemquam* is the subject of *dēscēnsūrum fuisse* as well as *habitūrum fuisse.*
    ad, *prep. w. acc.,* towards
    accūsātiōnem: accūsātiō, accūsātiōnis, *f.,* accusation; formal charge, indictment [**accūsō**]
    cui: has *quemquam* as its antecedent and sets up a relative clause with impersonal main verb *licēret,* the subject of which is the phrase *utrum vellet,* "whatever he wanted" *(vellet* is subjunctive by attraction). Case of *cui?* See *quibus* at 17.
    utrum: uter, utra, utrum, *interrog. and indef. rel. pron.,* which of two, whichever of two

22. **habitūrum: habeō, habēre, habuī, habitum,** have, hold
    speī: spēs, speī, *f.,* hope; partitive gen. after *quicquam,* "anything of hope" = "any hope," Ben. 201.2.

23. **nisi,** *conj.,* if not, unless.
    alicuius: aliquis, aliquid, *indef. pron.,* someone, somebody, something; anyone, anybody, anything
    intolerābilī: intolerābilis-is-e, *adj.,* unbearable, unendurable [**in** - priv. + **tolerō,** endure]
    nimis, *adv.,* too, too much, unduly
    acerbō: acerbus-a-um, *adj., (of taste)* bitter; disagreeable, severe; angry, hostile [**ācer**]
    ōdiō: ōdium, ōdī, *n.,* animosity, hate, hatred [**ōdī,** hate]

24. **nīterētur: nītor, nītī, nīsus** *or* **nixus sum,** rest on, lean on, rely on, depend on (+ *abl.*). Cicero likes this use of *nitor* (five times in this speech).
    ego, *pers. pron.,* I
    Atrātīnō, *etc.:* Cicero's indulgence of the green Atratinus was designed partly to nudge the jury into a similar pardon of Caelius's youthful mistakes, and partly to anticipate any sympathy the jury might have for the drubbing the young Atratinus was about to take at Cicero's hands. No doubt Cicero also wants the jury to compare his forbearance toward Atratinus with Herennius's severe harangue against Caelius, to which Cicero refers in ch. 25.

hūmānissimō: hūmānus-a-um, *adj.*, of or pert. to humankind, civilized; considerate, kind [homo, person]
optimō: optimus-a-um, *adj.*, best, excellent [superl. of bonus, good]

25.   meō: meus-a-um, *poss. adj.*, my
necessāriō, necessārius-a-um, *adj.*, essential, requisite; unavoidable, inevitable; intimate, closely related, connected; *here m. subst.*, friend [necesse, necessary]; adulēscentī, necessāriō: in apposition with *Atrātīnō.*
ignoscō: ignoscō, ignoscere, ignōvī, ignōtum, overlook, forgive, pardon *(+ dat.)* [in-priv. + (g)noscō, learn]

26.   excūsātiōnem: excūsātiō, excūsātiōnis, *f.*, excuse, defense, justification [excūsō]. "Indulgence" will work nicely here.
vel, *conj.*, or; vel...vel, either...or
necessitās: necessitās, necessitātis, *f.*, inevitability; requirement, obligation; relationship, kinship
aetātis: aetās, aetātis, *f.*, age; youth
sī voluit: mood and reason? Ben. 302.

27.   pietātī: repeated from 16 (also *piē* below at 35 of Caelius): a favorite word, and a theme in the speech.
tribuō: tribuō, tribuere, tribuī, tribūtum, allot, assign, ascribe *(+ dat.)*

28.   spērāvit: spērō (1), hope for, expect
pueritiae: pueritia, pueritiae, *f.*, boyhood, early adolescence; callowness, innocence; *pietātī, necessitātī, pueritiae:* figure of speech? See *lēgum* at 1. Cicero's condescension must have been infuriating to the spirited, youthful Atratinus.
cēterīs: cēterus-a-um, *adj.*, the rest, the remaining, the other

modo, *adv.*, only, just; nōn modo...sed etiam, not only...but also
nihil *or* nīl, *n. indecl.*, nothing

29.   ignoscendum [est]: gerundive employed in a pass. periphrastic construction, expressing obligation or necessity and here used impersonally; cf. *comprimendam* at 17.
etiam, *adv.*, also; even; still
ācriter: ācer, ācris, ācre, *adj.*, sharp; fierce; harsh; energetic, vigorous, relentless, intense
resistendum: resistō, resistere, restitī, stand still, stop, resist, oppose

30. Here begins the *praemūnītiō* [**prae,** before + **mūniō,** build up], or treatment of the issues raised and insinuations suggested by the prosecutors,
which continues through line 619 (ch. 50). Normally the *exordium* would
have been followed by a *narrātiō* [**narrō,** tell] or summary of the facts of the
case, but with his client perhaps guilty of at least some of the charges, Cicero
keeps postponing this. Instead, Cicero embarks on this extended *praemūnītiō*
in order to clear up the corrosive accusations made against Caelius in the
speeches of the prosecutors.

30–64 (chs. 3–6): a *locus dē dignitāte:* the prosecutors had evidently insinuated
that Caelius had been disrespectful to his father and was held in low repute
by his fellow townsmen.

> (ch. 3). **ac: = atque,** "and so."
>
> **quidem,** *adv.,* indeed, surely; at any rate
>
> **vidētur: videor, vidērī, vīsus sum** seem; seem a good thing, seem best
> [pass. of **videō**]
>
> **hic:** "this," = "the following."
>
> **introitus: introitus, introitūs,** *m.,* an entrance; beginning, introduction
> [**intrō,** within + **eō**]

31. **dēfēnsiōnis: dēfēnsiō, dēfēnsiōnis,** *f.,* a defense; a defense speech
> **adulēscentiae: adulēscentia, adulēscentiae,** *f.,* time of youth, young
> manhood; youthfulness, youthful "errantry"
>
> **M. Caelī:** M. Caelius Rūfus, the defendant
>
> **maximē: maximus-a-um,** *adj.,* greatest, largest [superl. of **magnus,**
> great, large]; *adv.* **maximē,** most, very much, to the greatest extent
>
> **convenīre: conveniō, convenīre, convēnī, conventum,** come together,
> assemble; be fitting, be suitable, be in agreement with (+ *dat.*). Form
> and reason? Ben. 328.
>
> **ut:** governs *respondeam* in 33 and here introduces a noun or substantive
> clause in apposition with and explaining *hic introitus* in 30.

32. **accūsātōrēs: accūsātor, accūsātōris,** *m.,* accuser, i.e., the single pros-
> ecutor in a state offense, but used generally here in the plural for
> Atratinus, L. Herennius Balbus, and P. Clodius (the latter two are
> really *subscrīptōrēs*).
>
> **dēformandī: dēformō** (1), shape, model; put out of shape, disfigure;
> disgrace, dishonor [**dē-,** expressing reversal of a process + **formō,**
> shape]
>
> **causā,** *prep. w. gen.,* for the sake of, in order to

dēformandī huius causā: the preposition *causā* (actually a fossilized abl.) takes a preceding gen., often accompanied by a gerund or gerundive to express purpose: "for the sake of this man's being defamed"; but it is better to translate actively with the noun or pronoun as object: "to defame this man." Distinguish carefully the gerundive used in a pass. periphrastic construction at 17 and 29.

dētrahendae: dētrahō, dētrahere, dētraxī, dētractum, drag down; disparage, slander, degrade

33. **spoliandae: spoliō** (1), strip, despoil; besmirch, defame, drag through the mud [**spolium,** flayed hide]

dignitātis: dignitās, dignitātis, *f.*, fitness, suitability, worthiness; distinction, personal standing, stature; rank, status [**dignus,** worthy]

grātiā: here used as a prep., "for the sake of"; parallel to and virtually identical in meaning and constr. to *causā*.

dīxērunt: dīcō, dīcere, dīxī, dictum, say, speak

prīmum, *adv.,* first; the n. acc. sg. of many common adjectives is often used adverbially, alongside or instead of the usual adverbial endings *-ē* and *-iter.*

respondeam: respondeō, respondēre, respondī, respōnsum, answer, reply; address, satisfy [**spondeō,** promise, pledge]. Mood and reason? See *ut* at 31.

34. **obiectus est: obiciō, obicere, obiēcī, obiectum,** throw in the way; put before; *(in a conversation)* bring up, cite, throw in one's teeth (+ *dat.*) [**ob** + **iaciō**]; so also at 65, 102, and 190.

pater: pater, patris, *m.,* father

variē: varius-a-um, *adj.,* different, manifold, sundry; **variē,** *adv.,* in various ways

quod, *conj.,* because

aut, *conj.,* or; **aut...aut,** either...or

parum, *adv.,* too little, insufficiently, not enough

splendidus: splendidus-a-um, *adj.,* bright, shimmering; brilliant, distinguished; magnificent, showy [**splendeō,** shine]. Another tough word to translate, having overtones of both "distinguished" and "showy." The word is an unofficial epithet of the *equitēs* or equestrian order to which Caelius's family belonged.

Cicero has probably taken up a prosecutorial statement that Caelius was too *splendidus* and turned it into a statement that Caelius's father was not *splendidus* enough, in different senses of the word.

Haury thinks that as a young *eques* Caelius had gone too far in prosecuting a noble like Antonius, a prerogative which in his view would be reserved for young *nōbilēs*; that Caelius was not, strictly speaking, a Roman would also have been offensive. If this is accurate, then just as here Cicero is trying to make the *equitēs* think ill of (supposed?) prosecutorial attacks on the equestrians, so the prosecution had had to curry favor with the senators by asserting that Caelius's prosecutions showed that he was too big for his britches. Probably Cicero has tried, perhaps successfully, to turn a prosecutorial harangue about Caelius's youth, inexperience, and extravagant living into an attack on the equestrians. Cicero frequently fathers ideas on the prosecution in this speech.

35.   **piē: pius-a-um,** *adj.,* dutiful, practicing all the proper observances; conscientious, devoted, upright, virtuous
    tractātus: tractō (1), haul; conduct; control [freq. of **trahō,** drag]
    dīcerētur: causal clauses normally employ the indic., but Cicero here employs the subj. to show that the reason given is not his own. The use of the subj. *exerceātur* at 5, also after *quod,* has a similar logic: the reason given is felt to be the imaginary speaker's, not Cicero's.
    M. Caelius: this is Marcus Caelius the Elder.

35–42.   The structure of this period is as follows:

Dē dignitāte M. Caelius
nōtīs ac maiōribus nātū etiam sine meā ōrātiōne tacitus facile ipse respondet;
quibus autem propter senectūtem,
    quod iam diū minus in forō nōbīscumque versātur, nōn aequē est cognitus,

hī sīc habeant, quaecumque in equite Rōmānō dignitās esse possit,
    quae certē potest esse maxima,
    eam semper in M. Caeliō habitam esse summam hodiēque habērī
    nōn sōlum ā suīs
    sed etiam ab omnibus quibus potuerit aliquā dē causā esse nōtus.

36.   **nōtīs: noscō, noscere, nōvī, nōtum,** learn; *(perf.)* know; *hence part.* **nōtus-a-um** *as adj.,* known; well-known; here "those who know [him]" (a quasi-pass. meaning)
    maiōribus: maior, maius, *adj.,* larger, greater [compar. of **magnus,** great, large]; *m. pl. subst.* **maiōres,** older men, elders
    nātū: (g)nāscor, (g)nāscī, (g)nātus sum, be born, arise; *nātū* is a supine in *-ū* functioning as an abl. of respect or specification, "by birth," "in respect to birth"; however, it is best omitted in translation.
    sine, *prep. w. abl.,* without
    ōrātiōne: ōrātiō, ōrātiōnis, *f.,* conversation, discussion; statements, discourse; treatise, speech [**ōrō,** beseech]

tacitus: taceō, tacēre, tacuī, tacitum, be silent; fall or become silent; pass over in silence or without comment; *hence part.* **tacitus-a-um** *as adj.,* silent
facile: facilis-is-e, *adj.,* easy [**faciō,** make]; **facile,** *n. acc. sg. used as adv.,* easily; on the n. acc. sg. used adverbially, see *prīmum* at 33n.
ipse: what word does this intensive adjective modify?

37. **quibus:** dat. with *cognitus* in 38; antecedent is *hī* in 38.
     propter, *prep. w. acc.,* on account of, because of
     senectūtem: senectūs, senectūtis, *f.,* old age [**senex,** old man]
     iam, *adv.,* now, already; **iam diū,** for a long time now, long since now
     diū, *adv.,* for a long time

38. **minus: minor, minus,** *adj.,* smaller, less [compar. of **parvus,** small]; **minus,** *adv.,* less; recall that the compar. adv. is regularly the n. acc. sg. of the corresponding compar. adj.
     forō: forum, forī, *n.,* marketplace, business district, public square, piazza
     cum, *prep. w. abl.,* with. When used with a pers. pron., and often with rel. pron.'s, *cum* becomes an enclitic, like *-ne* or *-que:* e.g., *mēcum, sēcum, quibuscum.* Thus *nōbīscumque* = "and with us."
     versātur: indic. after *quod,* as usual.
     aequē: aequus-a-um, *adj.,* equal; fair, just; favorable; advantageous; *adv.* **aequē,** in like manner, equally; likewise, similarly
     cognitus: cognoscō, cognoscere, cognōvī, cognitum, learn; *(perf.)* know
     hī...habeant: "let these people consider," a volitive subj., expressing a wish; note also *habitam esse* and *habērī* below (40–41), in a different sense.

39. **quaecumque: quīcumque, quaecumque, quodcumque,** *indef. rel. adj.,* whichever
     equite: eques, equitis, *m.,* horseman; equestrian, a Roman class. The *equitēs* ranked just below the *senātōrēs* in the Roman social and political system. Since senators, who had traditionally derived their livelihoods from the land, were barred from taking public contracts or engaging in overseas business ventures—being "in trade" was considered a "dirty" affair —the *equitēs* reaped the fruits of Roman expansion during the one hundred and fifty years of overseas conquest from the close of the Second Punic War in 201 B.C. through Cicero's day.
     Rōmānō: Rōmānus-a-um, *adj.,* Roman
     possit: subj. in a subordinate clause in indir. statement.

40. **certē: certus-a-um,** *adj.,* certain, sure
potest: as noted at *iubeat* at 10 and *exerceātur* at 5, rel. and other normally indic. clauses are put into the subj. when the main clause on which they depend is put into indir. speech. Why not here? (Hint: does Cicero agree with the view expressed?)
semper, *adv.,* always, ever

41. **summam: summus-a-um,** *adj.,* highest, topmost; distinguished, excellent
hodiē, *adv.,* today
sōlum: sōlus-a-um, *adj.,* lone, alone; *hence adv.* **sōlum,** only; **nōn sōlum...:** take as correlative with *sed etiam;* cf. *nōn modo* at 28.
suīs: suus-a-um, *reflex. adj.,* his/her/its/their/one's own; *here subst.* **suī, suōrum,** one's own (friends, family, acquaintances, retainers, etc.)

42. **quibus:** case and reason? See *quibus* at 37.
potuerit: mood and reason? Ben. 314.1.
aliquā: aliquī, aliquae, aliquod, *indef. adj.,* any, some; take w. *dē causā.*
(ch. 4) **equitis...fīlium:** inf. phrase used as subject of the impersonal verb *oportuit* in 44. Cicero is pulling out all the stops!

43. **locō: locus, locī,** *n.,* place, position; *(in a proceeding)* "point."
pōnī: pōnō, pōnere, posuī, positum, place, put; take as complementary inf. after *oportuit.*

44. **neque...neque:** neither...nor
hīs: deictic (Cicero would have gestured toward the jury box; *deictic* is derived from Gk. *deiknumi,* "point out").
iūdicantibus: iūdicō (1), judge, decide, try a case
oportuit: oportet, oportēre, oportuit, it is fitting, it is proper, it is right (+ *dat.*)
dēfendentibus: dēfendō, dēfendere, dēfendī, dēfēnsum, defend, protect, answer a charge; *dēfendentibus nōbīs* refers particularly to Cicero, generally to the other defense attorneys, and more remotely to the equestrian class as a whole.

45. **nam,** *conj.,* for; **nam quod:** "as for the fact that..."; Cicero uses this formula frequently in the first parts of the speech to deal with the several minor but potentially damaging insinuations of the prosecution.
existimātiō: existimātiō, existimātiōnis, *f.,* opinion, judgment; reputation, honor, character [**existimō**]

46. **parentis: parēns, parentis,** *m./f.,* parent, father, mother [old part. of
     pariō, give birth; bring forth]. "This is a matter between son and
     father," Cicero says, "and for the latter's judgment, not ours."
     quid: quis, quid, *interrog. pron.,* who, what
     opīnēmur: opīnor (1), think, suppose, conjecture, believe, reckon; imag-
     ine, conceive. Mood and reason? See *sit* at 3.

47. **iūrātīs: iūrō** (1), swear an oath; *hence subst.* **iūrātus, -ī,** *m.,* he who has
     been sworn: juror (often = *iūdicēs*)
     quid parentēs sentiant: direct object of *dēclārat* in 49. Mood and reason
     of *sentiant*? Ben. 300.
     sentiant: sentiō, sentīre, sēnsī, sēnsum, think, feel, perceive
     lacrimae: lacrima, lacrimae, *f.,* tear; *usu. in pl.,* shedding of tears, weeping
     mātris: māter, mātris, *f.,* mother
     incrēdibilis: incrēdibilis-is-e, *adj.,* not to be believed, incredible; ex-
     traordinary [**in**-priv. + **crēdō**]

48. **maeror: maeror, maerōris,** *m.,* mourning, grief, sadness, sorrow
     [**maereō,** mourn]
     squālor: squālor, squālōris, *m.,* dirtiness, filthiness; neglected condi-
     tion [**squāleō,** be covered with roughness, as with dirt]. A dishev-
     eled or unkempt condition was an outward sign of mourning.
     praesēns: praesum, praeesse, praefuī, be in charge of *(+ dat.); hence part.*
     praesēns, praesentis *as adj.,* present, at hand; effective, powerful,
     moving
     maestitia: maestitia, maestitiae, *f.,* sadness, dejection, gloominess
     [**maestus,** sad, fr. **maereō**]
     cernitis: cernō, cernere, crēvī, crētum, see, discern; comprehend,
     understand

49. **luctus: luctus, luctūs,** *m.,* grief, sorrow; expression of mourning, lamen-
     tation [**lūgeō,** mourn]
     dēclārat: dēclārō (1), make clear, demonstrate, prove [**clārus**]; note the
     sg. verb with a compound subject: the different signs of grief are
     part of a common state of lamentation. This appeal by Cicero to
     the parents' wretched condition will be turned into a full-blown
     miserātiō in ch. 79.
     (ch. 5). **mūnicipibus: mūniceps, mūnicipis,** *m./f.,* citizen or townsman
     of a *mūnicipium,* a free or "municipal" town, possessing Roman citi-
     zenship but governed by its own laws and magistrates. These are
     the residents of *Interamnia Praetuttiōrum* in Picenum, about eighty
     miles northeast of Rome, Caelius's "fellow citizens."

50.   **probātum: probō** (1), prove, show; approve
      nēminī: nom. **nēmō,** dat. **nēminī,** acc. **nēminem,** *m./f.,* no one [**nē** +
         homō]
      umquam, *adv.,* ever

51.   **Praetuttiānī:** see 49n.
      honōrēs: honor, honōris, *m.,* esteem, honor, respect; political office, po-
         sition; reward, acknowledgment
      habuērunt: "conferred"
      quam, *adv. used w. comparatives,* than
      absentī: absum, abesse, āfuī, āfutūrus, be away (from); be different
         (from); *hence part.* **absēns, absentis** *as adj.,* absent

52.   **quem:** a so-called "connecting relative" (Ben. 251.6): translate as though
         = *et eum.*
      et: = *etiam,* as often.
      amplissimum: amplus-a-um, *adj.,* large, spacious; magnificent, splen-
         did; distinguished, eminent; usually an epithet of a Roman senator,
         here of a *decuriō.*
      ordinem: ordō, ordinis, *f.,* order, arrangement; class, rank; Caelius had
         probably been chosen a *decuriō,* or member of the local senate.

53.   **cooptā(vē)runt: cooptō** (1), choose, elect
      petentī: petō, petere, petīvī *or* **petiī, petītum,** demand, require; desire,
         request, seek
      dētulērunt: dēferō, dēferre, dētulī, dēlātum, confer
      multīs: multus-a-um, *adj.,* much; *pl.,* many

54.   **dēnegā(vē)runt: dēnegō** (1), say no, deny, refuse, reject
      īdem: m. nom. pl., referring to the *Praetuttiānī*
      lectissimōs: legō, legere, lēgī, lectum, collect, gather; choose, select;
         read; *hence part.* **lectus-a-um** *as adj.,* choice, excellent
      virōs: vir, virī, *m.,* man; husband; courageous man
      nostrī ordinis: identify the reference.

55.   **lēgātiōne: lēgātiō, lēgātiōnis,** *f.,* deputation, embassy [**lēgō, lēgāre,**
         send, appoint]; Austin (at 5.5) notes that the usual number in such a
         lēgātiō was at least ten.

56.   **gravissimā: gravis-is-e,** *adj.,* heavy; weighty, serious; eminent, venerable

ornātissimā: ornō (1), equip, prepare; adorn, decorate; honor, extol; *hence part.* **ornātus-a-um** *as adj.,* distinguished, eminent; eloquent; when used as adjectives, participles may have comparatives and superlatives like ordinary adjectives.

laudātiōne: laudātiō, laudātiōnis, *f.,* praise, commendation; character testimonial [**laudō, laus**]

mīsērunt: mittō, mittere, mīsī, missum, send

videor mihi: "I think that...(I have done something)"

57.   **iēcisse: iaciō, iacere, iēcī, iactum,** throw, hurl; establish, found

fundāmenta: fundāmentum, fundāmentī, *n.,* foundation of a building, basis; support, absolute requirement [**fundus,** farm, ground]

firmissima: firmus-a-um, *adj.,* strong, solid, steady; constant, faithful

sī: identify the kind of condition, Ben. 302.

58.   **suōrum:** see *suīs* at 41n.

neque...posset, sī...displicēret: pres. contrary-to-fact condition, see 18n., Ben. 304.

enim, *conj.,* certainly, indeed; *(explaining what preceded)* for

satis *or* **sat,** *adj.,* enough, sufficient; *adv.,* enough, sufficiently

commendāta: commendō (1), entrust to someone's care or protection; recommend [**cum + mandō,** entrust]

59.   **huius aetās:** awkward to render into reasonable Engl.: try "this young man"; but what is the case of *huius*?

tālī: tālis-is-e, *adj.,* such a, such a remarkable, such an excellent

vērum: see *vērē* at 19n.

60.   **mūnicipiō: mūnicipium, mūnicipī,** *n.,* a town, usually in Italy, with Roman citizenship but governed by its own laws; see the description at 49n.

tam, *adv.,* so, so much, as

displicēret: displiceō, displicere, displicuī, displease, be displeasing to (+ *dat.*) [**dis-,** indicating separation + **placeō,** please]

61 (ch. 6).   **equidem,** *adv., usually w. first pers.,* indeed, truly; for my part, "my experience has been that..." These personal remarks are a way that Cicero builds equity for his client, by attaching him to himself (see also 119).

ut: here introduces a purpose clause, Ben. 282.

revertar: revertor, revertī, reversus sum, turn back, return; turn to a new point

fontibus: fōns, fontis, *m.*, fountain, natural spring; origin, source
prōfluxī: prōfluō, prōfluere, prōfluxī, flow forth; be derived, spring, emanate from [prō + fluō, flow]
ad hominum fāmam: a common arrangement for a prepositional phrase with a gen.

62. hominum: homō, hominis, *m./f.*, man, human being, person; *pl.*, people generally
     fāmam: fāma, fāmae, *f.*, report, saying, "talk"; public opinion, reputation; good name, renown. A complex word, whose meanings range from rumor to news story, and from a report on good deeds to notoriety for wickedness.
     labor: labor, labōris, *m.*, effort, work, toil; hardship, suffering
     vītae: vīta, vītae, *f.*, life; course of a life and accomplishments, career
     ratiō: ratiō, ratiōnis, *f.*, calculation, accounting; method, plan; judgment, reason

63. dēmānāvit: dēmānō (1), flow down, spread out [dē + mānō, flow]. Note sg. verb w. pl. subject again, as w. *dēclārat* in 49.
     paulō, *adv., often used w. comparatives,* a little, by a little, somewhat [paulus, small, trifling]; really a fossilized abl. of degree of difference, Ben. 223.
     lātius: lātus-a-um, *adj.,* broad, wide; extensive, far-ranging, widespread; here *-ius* indicates a compar. adv.

64. commendātiōne: commendātiō, commendātiōnis, *f.*, an entrusting or committal; commendation, praise, recommendation; approval, esteem, excellence. Explain cases of *commendātiōne* and *iūdiciō* (hint: not abl. of comparison), Ben. 218.
     meōrum: "of my (own) people," "of my friends"; cf. *suōrum* at 58, with which it is balanced.

65–101 (chs 6–9): the first half of the *locus dē pudīcitiā* ("treatment of morals"): Cicero rebuts charges that Caelius had been a passive homosexual. Ancient ideas about what constitutes healthy, normal, or acceptable sexuality were often quite different from our own sensibilities. For good notes, see Treggiari, p. 106, n. 132.

65. pudīcitia: pudīcitia, pudīcitiae, *f.*, sexual purity, chastity, virtue; reputation [pudet, it shames]
     quodque: not a form of *quīque,* as might be expected: here = *et quod.* The two *quod* clauses explain the *id* that follows them.

66. **vōcibus: vōx, vōcis,** *f.,* voice; word, saying; opinion, pronouncement, utterance
     maledictīs: maledīcō, maledīcere, maledīxī, maledictum, speak ill of, abuse, slander; *hence subst.* **maledictum, -i,** insult, taunt; *pl.,* vituperation, invective. Latin is fond of using a "concrete" noun, often in the pl., where English prefers an abstract noun. Case of *crīminibus, vōcibus, maledictīs?* Ben. 218.

67. **celebrātum: celebrō** (1), crowd, fill up a place; celebrate, honor; make known, proclaim [**celeber,** crowded; famous]
     numquam, *adv.,* never, at no time; not in any circumstances [**nē + umquam**]
     acerbē: acerbus-a-um, *adj.,* bitter, sour; disagreeable, severe [**ācer**]; **acerbē ferre,** be indignant at; take badly. Part of speech of *acerbē?*
     feret: ferō, ferre, tulī, lātum, bear, carry
     ut: here introduces a result clause set up by *tam,* Ben. 284.

68. **paeniteat: paenitet, paenitēre, paenituit,** it causes regret (to), it wearies, it grieves, it displeases; the person to whom the regret is caused is in the acc., here *eum.*
     dēformem: dēformis-is-e, *adj.,* misshapen, ugly, without good looks; base, disgraceful [**dē-**priv. + **forma**]
     (g)nascor, (g)nascī, (g)nātus sum, be born, arise *(+ abl.)*
     nōn dēformem esse nātum: entire inf. clause stands as subject to *paeniteat:* compare 42–44.

69. **pervolgāta = pervulgāta: pervulgō** (1), make public, make known; prostitute oneself; *hence part.* **pervulgātus-a-um** *as adj.,* customary, usual; well-known, familiar
     in: "against"
     omnīs: = *omnēs; -īs* is an alternative acc. m./f. pl. form for i-stem nouns and adj's.
     forma: forma, formae, *f.,* shape, appearance; beauty; stature, "features"
     speciēs: speciēs, speciēī, *f.,* sight, look, appearance; beautiful appearance [**speciō,** look at]
     fuit: singular even with a compound subject because *forma et speciēs* is taken as one thought.

70. **līberālis: līberālis-is-e,** *adj.,* of or pert. to a free man; gentlemanly, honorable; handsome

aliud: **alius, alia, aliud,** *adj. & pron.,* other, another; **alius...alius,** one... another

male, *adv.,* badly, wrongly

71.   **crīmen:** see 10n.

     dēsīderat: dēsīderō (1), long for, wish for; miss, lack, want [**sīdus,** star]

     rem ut dēfīniat: = *ut rem dēfīniat.* Why does Cicero put *rem* first?

     dēfīniat: dēfīniō (4), limit, mark off; delimit, restrict; explain, interpret [**fīniō,** finish, fr. **fīnis,** end]

     notet: notō (1), mark, signify, denote

     argūmentō: argūmentum, argūmentī, *n.,* evidence, proof; subject, theme [**arguō,** shed light, prove]

72.   **teste: testis, testis,** *m./f.,* witness

     cōnfirmet: cōnfirmō (1), strengthen; corroborate, prove

     maledictiō: maledictiō, maledictiōnis, *f.,* reviling abuse; slander

     prōpositī: prōpōnō, prōpōnere, prōposuī, prōpositum, put forward, tell; *hence subst.* **prōpositum, -ī,** plan, objective, "the point." Case and reason of *prōpositī*? Ben. 201.2.

73.   **praeter,** *prep. w. acc.,* besides, except, aside from

     contumēliam: contumēlia, contumēliae, *f.,* outrage, rough treatment; insulting language, affront [**contumax,** obstinate]

     quae: the antecedent is *maledictiō* in the previous sentence.

     sī: introduces another open condition, this time with present indicatives in both the protasis and apodosis, and translated straightforwardly into English.

     petulantius: petulāns, petulantis, *adj.,* aggressive, impudent, out of control; wild, malicious; (sexually) wanton, immodest

     iactātur: iactō (1), throw, hurl; toss, toss about, buffet [freq. of **iaciō,** hurl]

     convīcium: convīcium, convīcī, *n.,* loud cry, shout, clamor; abuse, insult [**cum** + **vox**]

     convīcium (nōminātur): Latin regularly ellipses the first, English the second repeated element.

74.   **facētius: facētus-a-um,** *adj.,* witty, charming

     urbānitās: urbānitās, urbānitātis, *f.,* refinement, sophistication; wit, charm [**urbs,** city]

     nōminātur: nōminō (1), name, call, refer to

     (ch. 7) **quam:** = *et eam,* connecting relative, Ben. 251.6

     partem: pars, partis, *f.,* part, portion, section

75. **admīrātus: admīror, admīrārī, admīrātus sum,** wonder at, marvel at;
be surprised **[mīror]**
molestē: molestus-a-um, *adj.,* distressing, vexing; troublesome, annoy-
ing, irksome **[mōlēs,** bulk, burden; but note the quantity of the *-o*];
molestē ferre, take badly, be disturbed; cf. *acerbē feret* in 67.
potissimum: potis-is-e, *adj.,* able, possible; *hence adv.* **potissimum,**
chiefly, for the most part, above all; see *prīmum* at 33n.
esse...datam (partem): acc. and inf. after *molestē tulī,* Ben. 184.

76. **datam: dō, dare, dedī, datum,** give, grant, assign
decēbat: decet, decēre, decuit, it is becoming; it is proper, it is appropriate, it is fitting
aetās illa: Atratinus was seventeen or eighteen at the time, and so not
yet *rōbustus.*
postulābat: postulō (1), ask for, demand; require, expect; accuse,
prosecute

77. **id...poterātis:** parenthetical
animum: animus, animī, *m.,* mind, soul, spirit, rational thought.
Contrast with *anima,* "breath," "life force": all creatures have *anima,*
only humans have *animus.*
advertere: advertō, advertere, advertī, adversum, turn or direct toward; guide, steer
pudor: pudor, pudōris, *m.,* regard for shame; modesty, seemliness;
dishonor, humiliation; Cicero has craftily slipped from Caelius's
pudīcitia ("sexual propriety") to Atratinus's *pudor* ("sense of right
and wrong").
patiēbātur: patior, patī, passus sum, experience, suffer, endure; allow,
permit
pudor patiēbātur...in tālī illum ōrātiōne versārī: "his decency suffered
his being engaged in such a speech"; *illum* is object of *patiēbātur* and
subject of *versārī.*

78. **vellem...suscēpisset:** "I would have wished [that] someone else had
undertaken..." Hopeless wishes for the present usually employ the
potential impf. subj. *(vellem),* a use of the impf. that is analogous to
its use in pres. unreal conditions (see 58n.).

79. **rōbustiōribus: rōbustus-a-um,** *adj.,* made of oak, oaken; solid, strong;
mature, grown-up, "experienced in the ways of the world" **[rōbur,**
oak tree; strength]

suscēpisset: suscipiō, suscipere, suscēpī, susceptum, take upon one-self, begin, undertake; plupf. subj. referring to an action one now wishes *had* taken place in the past.

80. **aliquantō: aliquantus-a-um,** *adj.,* of some size, moderate, not small; *hence subst.,* a good deal. Case? Ben. 223.
   līberius: līber, lībera, līberum, *adj., (in var. senses)* free; open, frank, out-spoken. Part of speech? See *lātius* at 63.
   fortius: fortis-is-e, *adj.,* strong, hardy, resolute; energetic, vigorous, forceful; brave, audacious
   magis, *adv.,* more [comp. of **multum,** much]
   mōre: mōs, mōris, *m.,* custom, habit, manner, mode
   nostrō: Cicero sometimes uses "our," "we," and "us" when speaking of himself: this usage in Latin is, however, not as affected as it would be in English. Translate "my," "I," etc.
   refūtārēmus: refūtō (1), push back, check, repel; disprove, refute; poten-tial subjunctive: "We would have refuted..."; compare *vellem* at 78.

81. **licentiam: licentia, licentiae,** *f.,* freedom to do what one wants, liberty; opportunity, privilege; dissoluteness, excess, licentiousness [**licet,** it is allowed]
   tēcum: = *cum tē,* as usual.
   Atrātīne: voc.
   agam: agō, agere, ēgī, actum, guide, lead; drive, impel; do. The form could be pres. subj. or fut. indic.: how does context help you decide which?
   lēnius: lēnis-is-e, *adj.,* mild, gentle, moderate

82. **tuus-a-um,** *poss. adj.,* your *(sg.)*
   moderātur: moderor, moderārī, moderātus sum, keep within limits, regulate, restrain, direct *(+ dat.)* [**modus,** limit]
   meum...beneficium: object of "tuērī;" encloses a prepositional phrase.
   ergā, *prep. w. acc.,* towards, for, to *(+ obj. of person's feelings)*; with respect to

83. **beneficium: beneficium, beneficī,** *n.,* a favor, good deed
   tuērī: tueor, tuērī, tūtus *or* **tuitus sum,** regard, look at; look after, care for, guard, protect. Form and reason? Ben. 328.
   dēbeō: dēbeō, dēbēre, dēbuī, dēbitum, owe, ought [**dē + habeō**]

83–87. The structure of this period is as follows:

Illud tamen	tē	esse admonitum volō,
prīmum	ut	quālis es
		tālem tē omnēs esse existiment,
	ut	quantum ā rērum turpitūdine abes
		tantum tē ā verbōrum lībertāte sēiungās;
deinde	ut	ea in alterum nē dīcās quae, cum tibi falsō respōnsa sint, ērubēscās.

(ch. 8) **illud:** internal acc. with *esse admonitum:* "I want you to be warned *about that....*"

tamen, *adv.,* nevertheless, nonetheless; here = "all the same," "in spite of the awful things you've said"

84. **[esse] admonitum: admoneō, admonēre, admonuī, admonitum,** remind; caution, warn; advise, urge. Constr.? Ben. 184. Translate *[esse] admonitum* as if *admonērī* (the perf. is used to indicate completed action, without reference to time).

ut: this first *ut* introduces a purpose clause (Ben. 282) that explains why he is giving the forthcoming advice.

ut quālis...tālem, ut quantum...tantum: carefully translate these double pairs of correlatives. The second *ut,* at 85, introduces an indir. command (Ben. 295) dependent on *admonitum esse* and in apposition to *illud.*

85. **turpitūdine: turpitūdō, turpitūdinis,** *f.,* ugliness; shamelessness; disgrace, infamy, notoriety [**turpis,** base]

86. **verbōrum: verbum, verbī,** *n.,* word

lībertāte: lībertās, lībertātis, *f.,* freedom; licence, abandon; frankness, outspokenness, candor

sēiungās: sēiungō, sēiungere, sēiūnxī, sēiūnctum, separate, sever, disjoin; exclude, isolate [**sē,** apart, aside + **iungō,** join]. Mood and reason? See *ut quālis* at 84.

deinde, *adv.,* afterwards, next, secondly, then

ut...nē: virtually equivalent to *nē* (also at 347–351) in a negative indir. command; but see Austin at 8.11.

in: "against."

alterum: alter, altera, alterum, *adj.,* one or the other of two; another

87. **falsō: fallō, fallere, fefellī, falsum,** deceive, trick; be concealed; *hence part.* **falsus-a-um** *as adj.,* false; *hence adv.* **falsō,** erroneously, mistakenly

respōnsa sint: mood? See *cum* at 7.
ērubēscās: ērubēscō, ērubēscere, ērubuī, grow red or blush at *(w. shame)*, feel ashamed [**ruber,** red]

88.　**via: via, viae,** *f.,* road, path, way
　　pateat: pateō, patēre, patuī, lie exposed, be open; be visible, be evident; extend in space, stretch, spread out; subj. in a rel. clause of characteristic
　　aetātī, dignitātī: dependent on *male dīcere* in 90.

89.　**quam:** the antecedent is *dignitātī.*
　　petulanter: part of speech? See *dīligenter* at 19.
　　etiam sī: "even if," "although"
　　ulla: ullus-a-um, *adj.,* any
　　suspiciōne: suspiciō, suspiciōnis, *f.,* suspicion, mistrust
　　at, *conj.,* but, however

90.　**partium:** "role"; the pl. is regular in this sense (Austin at 8.15).
　　culpa: culpa, culpae, *f.,* blame, fault; wrongdoing

91.　**agere:** "to egg on"
　　laus: laus, laudis, *f.,* praise, commendation; renown, reputation; action or deed that wins fame or glory; excellence, praiseworthiness
　　invītum: invītus-a-um, *adj.,* unwilling, not wishing, reluctant

92.　**ingenī:** parallel with *pudōris:* translate ...*[laus] ingenī [tuī]*...; note also the parallel *quod* clauses.
　　polītē: poliō (4), smooth, make smooth, polish; bring to a refined state; *hence part.* **polītus-a-um** *as adj.,* polished, refined, accomplished

93 (ch. 9). **vērum,** *adv.,* but, nevertheless; see 19n.
　　brevis: brevis-is-e, *adj.,* short, brief

94.　**quoad,** *interrog. and rel. adv.,* how far, as far as, until
　　fuit: take with *mūnīta* in 96, an example of a "double perfect," virtually equivalent to *est mūnīta.*

95.　**etiam,** *adv.,* also, even, still
　　dīligentiā: dīligentia, dīligentiae, *f.,* hard work, diligence

96.　**disciplīnā: disciplīna, disciplīnae,** *f.,* instruction, teaching; knowledge, discipline; system, method. Case and reason of *dīligentiā disciplīnāque?* Ben. 218.

mūnīta: mūniō (4), build a wall, fortify; secure, defend, protect [**moenia,** defensive works]

quī ut: = *et is ut* = *et ut is,* Ben. 251.6.

togam: toga, togae, *f.,* toga [rel. to **tegō,** cover]

virīlem: virīlis-is-e, *adj.,* of or pert. to a man, manly; adult; courageous [**vir,** man]; **toga virīlis:** the adult toga assumed by an adolescent boy at about sixteen years of age.

ut...dedit: *ut* + indic. is to be translated "as" or "when."

— nihil dīcam...: a good example of *anacoluthon,* or a sudden change of grammatical construction in mid-sentence, Ben. 374.6.

97. hōc locō: abl. of place where, Ben. 228.

98. continuō: continuus-a-um, *adj.,* uninterrupted, lasting; *hence adv.* **continuō,** immediately, forthwith; continuously

dēductum: dēdūcō, dēdūcere, dēduxī, dēductum, bring down, lead down

99. flōre: flōs, flōris, *m.,* flower; here figurative w. *aetātis,* "bloom of youth," "flower of youth"

100. Crassī: M. Licinius Crassus, said to be the wealthiest man at Rome at this time, as ambitious and cunning as others of his day, yet noted for his moderate lifestyle.

castissimā: castus-a-um, *adj.,* (morally) pure, temperate; chaste, pious, holy

domō: domus, domūs, *f.,* house, home; *domus* has forms from both the second and fourth declensions. As we will see, the speech is full of references to "good" and "bad" houses.

artibus: ars, artis, *f.,* skill, way, art

101. honestissimīs: honestus-a-um, *adj.,* honored, respected, in good repute; honorable, proper, virtuous

ērudīrētur: ērudiō (4) educate, instruct, teach, train [**ex** + **rudis,** unrefined]

102–167 (chs. 10–14). Cicero rebuts the prosecution's allegations that the youthful Caelius had been (politically and perhaps sexually) involved with Catiline, the unscrupulous, and in the end revolutionary, politician. There must have been some truth to the charges, and Cicero is at his most careful and skillful in this passage. Its staccato style (see 110n.) is in marked contrast with the first half of the *locus dē pudīcitiā* (chs. 6–9).

102 (ch. 10). **nam quod:** "as for the fact that...," see 45n.
Catilīnae: Catilīna, Catilīnae, *m.,* L. Sergius Catilina, a demagogic aristocrat, commonly known in English as Catiline, who unsuccessfully
attempted to overthrow the legitimate government of Rome during
Cicero's consulship in 63 B.C. For more information on his career, see
intro., secs. 14–15, as well as the bibliography.
familiāritās: familiāritās, familiāritātis, *f.,* close friendship, relationship, intimacy [**familiāris,** a friend, acquaintance, from **familia,**
household]
obiecta Caeliō est: for this common use of *obicere* + dat., see 34n.
longē: longus-a-um, *adj.,* long; *adv.* **longē,** far from. Note the strong first
position.

103.   **istā: iste, ista, istud,** *pronoun and pronominal adj.,* that of yours; that, this.
Iste often has a contemptuous ring (Ben. 246.4); hence *istā suspiciōne*
= "suspicion of the kind you mention" (Austin at 10.2).
abhorrēre: abhorreō, abhorrēre, abhorruī, shudder at, shrink back
from; be inconsistent with, deviate or differ from; be free from
[Caelius] dēbet.
scītis: sciō, scīre, scīvī, scītum, know, be aware

104.   **cōnsulātum: cōnsulātus, cōnsulātūs,** *m.,* consulship, chief executive
magistracy of the Roman Republic. Two *cōnsulēs* ("consuls") were
elected each year; they held great powers during their terms of office. See also intro., sec. 13. The event Cicero describes was in the
summer of 64 B.C.
cōnsulātum...petīsse Catilīnam: fully explain this construction, Ben. 314.
ad quem: = *et ad eum,* connecting rel., Ben. 251.6.
sī: with perf. indic.'s in the protasis, introduces an open condition.
However, an independent (here hortatory) subj. or an imperative
can replace a pres. indic. in the apodosis of an open condition,
Ben. 302.4. The apodosis has the jussive subj. *existimētur:* "if he ap-
proached that man..., then let him be thought...." Compare:
> **Sī hoc fēcit,   hoc luit.**
> *If he did this,   he is paying for it.*
> **Sī hoc fēcit,   hoc luat!**
> *If he did this,   let him pay for it.*
The second sentence is still an open condition, but a jussive subj.
now stands in the apodosis. An imperative is also possible:
> **Sī hoc fēcistī,   hoc lue!**
> *If you did this,   pay for it!*
accessit: accēdō, accēdere, accessī, accessum, approach, come near to

105. **discessit: discēdō, discēdere, discessī, discessum,** depart from, leave; deviate from
quamquam, *conj.,* although
bonī: has a political ring ("good conservatives," "the better element," "supporters of senatorial prerogatives"); so similarly the compar. *melior* and superl. *optimus.* Thus Catiline once seemed to Cicero a *cīvis meliōrum partium* (141), a *cīvis mihi bonus et optimī cuiusque cupidus et firmus amīcus ac fidēlis* (161); *multōs fortīs virōs et bonōs* (154) fell for him, and many *bonīs* (160) were fooled, for Catiline only pretended to be dedicated to the *optimīs...virīs* (134). But Catiline turned out to be *improbus* (106), cultivated *hominibus improbīs multīs* (133), and gathered together *hominēs improbōs audācīsque* (153).

Cicero's whole portrait of Caelius is designed to show that his sober life is such that he could not possibly have cavorted with such a man. Note *Quī...tantus furor [est] in Caeliō?* (172), where *furor* refers to the political disturbances so common in Rome at the end of the Republic (cf. the personified *Furor impius* [of civil strife], Verg., *Aen.* I.294); P. Clodius Pulcher is *furentī* at 745 (*populārēs* are often *furentēs* for Cicero). In contrast, Caelius's vigilance and valiance at prosecuting powerful people who have harmed the Republic show that he is no *cīvis turbulentus* (957); he has followed an *optimī ac nōbilissimī ... cursum* (902) and is *probātissimus* (908; contrast *improbus* above); and in the peroration Cicero will personally guarantee Caelius's continued status as a *cīvem bonārum artium, bonārum partium, bonōrum virōrum* (950), working hard for the *rēs pūblica* (repeated 3 times). It is no accident that the *furor*-laden image of Sextus Cloelius (960–970) follows immediately thereafter.

These "political catchwords" (so Syme, pp. 149–161, a very useful discussion) are frequently combined with mention of specific political figures. Thus the death of Metellus Celer, a staunch optimate politician, snatched him away from *bonīs omnibus atque ūniversae cīvitātī* (735–736); juxtaposed is his *furentī fratrī* ("brother-in-law," i.e., P. Clodius Pulcher) at 745: "Only the good die young!" This Us vs. Them view that Cicero often holds should be contrasted with the demands of *amīcitia.*

These features of the speech as well as more general references to the political problems of the period (e.g., 876–893) and frequent invocations of the good old days all underscore the deeper political implications of this private case, and Cicero's keen awareness of them even as he throws up a smoke screen.

Cicero's remarks here are somewhere between a rhetorical flourish and an outright lie: his description of Catiline's following at *in Catilīnam*, II.8–10 (delivered at the time of the attempted coup) is quite different.

illī: ille, illa, illud, *pron. and pronominal adj.,* that; he, she, it; that famous

106. **nēquam,** *indecl. adj.,* worthless, good-for-nothing, bad [**nē** + **aequus**]
improbō: improbus-a-um, *adj.,* base, immoral; unprincipled, disloyal; impudent, outrageous [**in**-priv. + **probus,** upright, honest]
studuērunt: studeō, studēre, studuī (+ *dat.*), be zealous about, strive after; be a partisan of, support, favor
tum, *adv.,* at that time, then; consequently, then
existimētur: see 104n.

107. **Caelius Catilinae:** note the *juxtaposition* [**iūxtā,** near + **pōnō,** place].
Catilīnae: case and reason? Ben. 192.1.
nimium: nimius-a-um, *adj.,* very great, very much; too great, excessive; immoderate, extravagant; *hence adv.* **nimium,** too much, unduly [**nimis,** too much]
familiāris: familiāris-is-e, *adj.,* of or pert. to a household or family, familial; intimate, friendly (+ *dat.*); *hence subst.* **familiāris, -is,** *m./f.,* friend. *Familia* includes all the members of a Roman household, and therefore has a wider sense than its English derivative "family." In addition to family members, one's *familiārēs* included household servants and friends. (Hence the collection of Cicero's letters now referred to as *epistulae ad familiārēs* were addressed to family members as well as to close political associates.)
At enim...: an objection Cicero imagines the prosecution will have to his assertion that Caelius's early support of Catiline should not prejudice him. Translate: "'Well,' you say, 'but later we....'" or "'But,' someone may say, 'later we....'" (like *aliquis dīcat*). This figure of speech is called *occupātiō,* or anticipated objection.
posteā, *adv.,* afterwards, later, subsequently

108. **vīdimus: videō, vidēre, vīdī, vīsum,** see
hunc: Caelius
illīus: Catiline
amīcīs: amīcus-a-um, *adj.,* amicable, friendly; politically supportive; *hence subst.* **amīcus, -i,** *m.,* friend; political adherent. *Amīcus* here implies a far wider nexus of political connections than *familiāris.* For Caelius's support of Catiline, see intro., sec. 28.

negat: negō (1), say that...not, say no, deny. Note Cicero's use of a rhetorical question (Ben. 162.3) to express mock impatience: "Really, now, does anybody deny this?"

109. **tempus: tempus, temporis,** *n.,* time; occasion; opportunity; **illud tempus aetātis:** "his youth"
       suā: refers to *illud tempus aetātis,* not to the subject of the main clause.
       sponte, *f., abl. (other cases very rarely),* willingly, of one's own accord; automatically, by itself. *Suā sponte* is answered by *aliōrum libīdine.*
       īnfirmum: īnfirmus-a-um, *adj.,* weak, feeble; unstable, vulnerable

110. **īnfestum: īnfestus-a-um,** *adj.,* aggressive, hostile; dangerous, harmful; unsafe, imperiled, threatened. Note how alliteration (repetition of the same consonant sound [Ben. 375.3]) and assonance (repetition of the same vowel sound) emphasize the parallel word order of this sentence:

       quod ipSUM SUā Sponte   INFirMUM,
          aliōrUM   auteM libīdine   INFESTUM EST....

       id: refers back to *illud tempus aetātis.* This "redundant use" (Austin at 10.10) helps the main sentence (*ego illud tempus aetātis...dēfendō*) regroup after the intervening *quod*-clause.
       Fuit [Caelius], etc.: Note the rapid, staccato style of this entire section, characterized by brief, uncomplicated sentences, asyndeton (Ben. 346), linking verbs, and simple vocabulary, all contributing to the conversational effect. Note also the repeated use of *hic* and *ille* to refer to Caelius and Catiline, respectively, and the repetition of certain vocabulary words (noted *ad locc.*). This coordination of simple phrases or clauses without conjunctions is *parataxis* [Gk. **para,** beside + **tassō,** arrange]. It is particularly effective when contrasted with the style of the section immediately preceding, chs. 6–9.

111. **adsiduus: adsiduus-a-um,** *adj.,* continuous, uninterrupted [**adsideō,** from **ad** + **sedeō**]
       praetōre: praetor, praetōris, *m.,* praetor, presiding judge of a court. For almost a century and a half after the founding of the Republic, *praetor* was the title of the two chief executives of the Roman Republic, later called *cōnsulēs;* note the derivation of the word, from *praeeō,* "go ahead," "command," which illustrates its military origins. In 366 B.C. was created the office of *praetor urbānus,* "city praetor," to handle justice in Rome. Thereafter, the office evolved with the spread of

Rome's power outside Italy. In 242, at the end of the First Punic War, came the *praetor peregrīnus,* "praetor with jurisdiction over foreign cases," to handle cases involving non-Romans. With the decision in 227 B.C. to administer newly acquired Sicily and Sardinia as tribute-paying *prōvinciae,* two new *praetōrēs* were created, and two more to govern Spain in 197 B.C. In 82 B.C., Sulla raised the number of praetors to eight, but made them presidents of the ever more busy *quaestiōnēs perpetuae* ("standing courts").

At the start of his term, it was customary for the new praetor to issue an *ēdictum,* a statement of official policy for the coming year. In theory *ēdicta* merely explained how the praetor intended to carry out the *iūs cīvīle* ("civil law"), but in practice they went a good deal farther, and gradually a body of law developed called the *iūs praetōrium* ("praetorian law"), alongside the *iūs cīvīle.* The praetorian edicts, then, were of great importance in the development of Roman law. (With the rise of imperial administration under Augustus and his successors, the praetorship, like most Republican offices, declined in prestige and importance. Around A.D. 130 the Emperor Hadrian codified the praetorian edict into an *ēdictum perpetuum* from which the praetors could not deviate.)

praetōre mē: constr.? Ben. 227.1. This was 66 B.C., when Caelius was sixteen.
Africam: Africa, Africae, *f.,* Africa; the praetorian province of Africa. Geographically, *Africa* meant to the Romans the northern coastal lands; farther south spanned the Sahara Desert, which was inhospitable and impassable everywhere except in the east, in the Nile river valley (Egypt, governed by the Ptolemies of Alexandria, and independent of Rome until 30 B.C.). To the west, *Africa* ended at the Straits of Gibraltar (beyond which was open sea). Politically, *Africa* was organized as a Roman province in 146 B.C., encompassing land once controlled by Carthage (modern-day Tunisia and Libya).

112. **praetor:** "as a praetor," in apposition to *ille,* = *Catilīna.*
       obtinet: obtineō, obtinēre, obtinuī, obtentum, hold, possess; administer, govern *(a province)*
       secūtus est: sequor, sequī, secūtus sum, follow; **secūtus est tum annus:** 65 B.C.
       annus: annus, annī, *m.,* year
       causam...dīxit: *causam dīcere* = "to plead a case," here in his own defense.

113. **pecūniīs: pecūnia, pecūniae,** *f.,* possessions, property, wealth; money, cash. *Pecūnia* is derived from *pecū,* "flock," "herd," since livestock was a principal store of value in the agrarian society of early Rome.

repetundīs: repetō, repetere, repetīvī *or* **repetiī, repetītum,** strike or attack again; seek or claim again; bring or take back. Armed with *imperium* and the immunities that inhered in the office, a provincial governor's power was virtually unchecked during his term. Once out of office, he could be prosecuted by the provincials for *rēs* or *pecūniae repetundae* (restitution to a province of money or property illegally extorted by its governor). See also intro., sec. 10.

-(i)undum and *-(i)undus-a-um* are the original forms of third and fourth conj. gerunds and gerundives; the forms in *-(i)endum* and *-(i) endus-a-um* arose in classical Latin, probably by analogy with the *-e-* in the pres. part. forms *-(i)ēns, -(i)entis* (see Palmer, p. 281).

hic: Caelius

114. **advocātus: advocātus, advocātī,** *m.,* "one called in" to help, legal supporter, assistant [**advocō**]. The *advocātus* was "a supporter present in court to give help in legal matters" (Austin at 10.14). Roughly speaking, *advocātī* were to the defense what *subscrīptōrēs* were to the prosecution: "junior counsel." Cicero pleads: "Caelius didn't even help Catiline in court, let alone in his revolutionary plans!"

venit: veniō, venīre, vēnī, ventum, come

umquam: strong last position

deinceps, *adv.,* in succession, successively, in turn; after that, then; **deinceps...petīvī:** 64 B.C.

quō: case and reason? Ben. 230.

116. **recessit: recēdō, recēdere, recessī, recessum,** draw back, recede; leave, withdraw

(ch. 11) **tot,** *adv.,* so many, such a number of

annōs: case and reason? Ben. 181.

117. **īnfāmiā: īnfāmia, īnfāmiae,** *f.,* bad repute, infamy; discredit, disgrace, dishonor

iterum, *adv.,* again, a second time; this was the summer of 63 B.C.

118. **ergō,** *adv.,* consequently, then, therefore; *(with rhetorical question)* "Well, then,...?"

fīnem: fīnis, fīnis, *m.,* boundary, end, limit; *pl.,* territory, land. **Quem... ad fīnem:** "For how long?"

custōdiendam: custōdiō (4), keep safe, protect

119. **Nōbīs quidem...:** a difficult sentence to render into idiomatic English. *Et* connects the two purpose constructions *ad cohibendum bracchium togā* and *ut exercitātiōne lūdōque campestrī tunicātī ūterēmur.* The

sentence seems to be sarcastic: in effect, "whereas the *tīrōcinium forī* is supposed to be only one year, as it was when I was young, the logical result we are forced to conclude from the prosecution's line of argument is that they believe Caelius's probationary period should have gone on nearly forever indeed!" Cicero's logic in this section is hardly coherent, and deliberately so.

nōbīs: Why does Cicero make these personal comments at crucial moments? For another ex. of Cicero's use of this strategy, see 61n.

ōlim, *adv.,* once, formerly, at that time, someday; *ōlim* is derived from *olle,* the Old Latin form of *ille* (which developed by analogy with the other pronouns *ipse, is,* and *iste*).

annus...ūnus: i.e., the *tīrōcinium forī* (see intro., sec. 2).

cohibendum: cohibeō, cohibēre, cohibuī, cohibitum, hold together, contain; confine, restrain; check, hinder [**cum-** + **habeō**]

erat: take with *cōnstitūtus.*

120. **bracchium: bracchium, bracchī,** *n.,* forearm; arm

togā: case and reason? Ben. 218; **ad cohibendum bracchium togā:** in other words, as Austin says at 11.20, "extravagant gesture was forbidden." In his *contrōversiae,* "Debates," L. Annaeus Seneca the Elder (c. 55 B.C. – 37/41 A.D.) writes: *apud patrēs nostrōs, quī forēnsia stīpendia auspicābantur, nefās putābātur bracchium extrā togam exserere,* "Among our predecessors, who inaugurated the forensic exercises, it was considered positively dreadful for someone to remove his arm from his cloak" (v.6).

exercitātiōne: exercitātiō, exercitātiōnis, *f.,* exercise, physical training; practice, experience [**exercitō,** freq. from **exerceō**]

121. **campestri: campestris-is-e,** *adj.,* of or pert. to a field or level plain, or to the *Campus Martius,* "Field of Mars." Both army exercises and meetings of the *comitia centuriāta* (a public assembly organized according to military "hundreds") were held in the Campus Martius.

tunicātī: tunicātus-a-um, *adj.,* clothed in a tunic, wearing (only) a tunic

ūterēmur: ūtor, ūtī, ūsus sum, use, make use of, employ *(+ abl.)*

eademque erat: take with *castrēnsis ratiō ac mīlitāris* below, after the intervening condition.

si...coeperāmus: some individuals apparently skipped the *tīrōcinium forī.* Kind of condition? Ben. 302.3.

statim, *adv.,* immediately, at once, without delay

merēre: mereō, merēre, meruī, meritum, earn; win, gain; deserve, merit

122. **stīpendia: stīpendium, stīpendī,** *n.,* soldier's pay; tax, contribution [**stips,** a small payment + **pendeō**]; **stīpendia merēre:** draw pay as a soldier; serve (as a soldier). The long *-ī-* in *stīpendium* results from contraction from **stipipendium.*
     coeperāmus: coepī, coepisse, coeptus sum, begin. This "defective" verb is conjugated only in the perf.
     castrēnsis: castrēnsis-is-e, *adj.,* of or pert. to a military encampment or military service [**castra,** camp]
     mīlitāris: mīlitāris-is-e, *adj.,* of or pert. to the army, military

123. **sē ipse:** good Latin, but omit *ipse* in translation.
     gravitāte: gravitās, gravitātis, *f.,* heaviness, weight; seriousness, importance; authority, dignity
     castimōniā: castimōnia, castimōniae, *f.,* purity, morality, "clean living" (Austin at 11.23) [**castus,** moral, proper, upright]
     cum...tum: "both...and"

124. **domesticā: domesticus-a-um,** *adj.,* of or pert. to a house, family, or home, domestic; private, personal, one's own
     nātūrālī: nātūrālīs-is-e, *adj.,* natural, inborn, innate
     quōdam: quīdam, quaedam, quiddam *or* **quoddam,** *indef. pron. & adj.,* a certain (one); a particular (one)
     bonō: "goodness," "good behavior"
     quōquō: quisquis, quaeque, quodquod *or* **quidquid (quicquid),** *indef. pron. & pronominal adj.,* whoever, whatever; each (one), every (one), all

125. **modō: modus, modī,** *m.,* measure, (correct) quantity; limit, end; moderation, restraint; manner, way; **quōquō modō:** "however much" (Austin at 11.26)
     custōdītus esset: custōdiō: keep safe, protect, preserve; subj. by attraction to *dēfenderet* (Ben. 324.1)
     suīs: "his own friends": see *suīs* at 41n.
     vēram: "backed by truth," "justifiable" (Austin at 11.26).
     effugere: effugiō, effugere, effūgī, flee, slip away, escape; keep away from, avoid

126. **poterat:** according to the rule given above at 18n. for unreal conditions, we might expect *posset.* However, the apodosis of these conditions is usually indic. if the apodosis expresses ability, obligation, or necessity (verbs like *posse, dēbēre,* etc.), Ben. 304.3.
     quī: "he who"
     initia: initium, initī, *n.,* beginning, start; *pl.,* initial phase, early period

integra: integer, integra, integrum, *adj.*, untouched, untried; intact, un-damaged, whole; moral, upright [rel. to *tag-, root of tangō]

127. inviolāta: inviolātus-a-um, *adj.*, undamaged, unharmed; unsullied, morally pure, unstained
praestitisset: praestō, praestāre, praestitī, prastātum, stand out, be superior; present or show oneself to be (+ *nom.*); produce, provide
fāma: picks up *īnfāmiam* at 125.
sēsē: alternate form of *sē*

128. conrōborāvisset: conrōborō (1), strengthen, reinforce, fortify; *hence* sē conrōborāre, grow up, mature [con- + rōborō, strengthen, from rōbur, oak, hard wood]
inter, *prep. w. acc.*, between, among, amid
loquēbātur: loquor, loquī, locūtus sum, speak; (+ *dē*) to speak evil of (Löfstedt, as quoted in Austin at 11.29)
at: "Yes, I grant that..." (Austin at 12.29)

129. (ch. 12) studuit: take *Caelius* as subject.
aliquot, *indecl. adj.*, a number of, some, several
annōs: annus, annī, *m.*, year

130. hoc idem: "the very same thing," i.e., his support of Catiline
ordine (equestrī).
fēcērunt: faciō, facere, fēcī, factum, do, make

131. sīcutī *and* sīcut, *adv. and conj.*, just as, in the same manner as (+ *correl.*); just as [for instance], as indeed [is the case];
meminisse: meminī, meminisse, recall, remember; pay heed to; another so-called defective verb (see *coeperāmus* above at 122n.)
arbitror (1), think, reckon, suppose
permulta: permultus-a-um, *adj.*, very many. Adj. and verb compounds in *per-* could be coined at will: they are lively and colloq. (not unlike Engl. "really" + adj.), and extremely common in this speech: see *perfacile* at 274, *perattentē* at 288, *periūcundē* and *pertristis* at 295, *perturpe* and *perflāgitiōsum* at 613, *percelerī* at 727, and *percelebrāta* at 864.

132. maximārum: take with *virtūtum.*
expressa: exprimō, exprimere, expressī, expressum, press or squeeze out; copy, depict; stamp out a design *(on a coin)*; relate, describe; this verb is commonly used in sculpture and numismatics.

signa: signum, signī, *n.,* sign, mark; indication
adumbrāta: adumbrō (1), cast a shadow on, shade; outline, silhouette, sketch out; *hence part.* **adumbrātus-a-um** *as adj.,* unfinished, sketchy; pretended, counterfeit, false. *Adumbrāta* is further metaphorical language, this time from drawing and painting; Catiline's *signa maximārum virtūtum* were "shadowy" and "shady," i.e., only hazily visible, and misleading anyway.
virtūtum: virtūs, virtūtis, *f.,* manliness, courage; excellence, "character"; goodness, virtue. *Virtūs* is a word well worth looking up in a good lexicon in order to see its range of meanings.

133.   **ūtēbātur: ūtor, ūtī, ūsus sum,** use, employ *(+ abl.)*
improbīs: improbus-a-um, *adj.,* wicked; incorrect, improper, unprincipled; greedy, unfair; a political term (see 105n.).
et quidem: concessive as well as adversative: "Yes, but..." (Austin at 12.5, with references)

134.   **dēditum esse: dēdō, dēdere, dēdidī, dēditum,** give up, surrender; dedicate or devote oneself to
simulābat: simulō (1), pretend, feign, simulate [**similis**]; picks up *nōn expressa* and *adumbrāta* in 132 above; cf. also 154.
apud, *prep. w. acc.,* at; among
inlecebrae: inlecebra, inlecebrae, *f.,* allurement, enticement; attraction, charm; inducement (to) [**inliciō,** entice]
libīdinum: "of debauchery"

135.   **stimulī: stimulus, stimulī,** *m.,* cattle prod, goad; spur or goad to fury, passion, action; mental torment, unrest

136.   **flagrābant: flagrō** (1), burn, blaze; be ardent or excited
vitia: vitium, vitī, *n.,* defect, fault, shortcoming; moral failing, vice
vigēbant: vigeō, vigēre, viguī, be vigorous, flourish, thrive

137.   **mōnstrum: mōnstrum, mōnstrī,** *n.,* evil omen, portent; monstrous and wicked person [**moneō**]
terrīs: terra, terrae, *f.,* land

138.   **tam,** *adv.,* so
contrāriīs: contrārius-a-um, *adj.,* opposite, opposed; hostile, injurious; antithetical, incompatible, different
dīversīs: dīvertō, dīvertere, dīvertī, dīversum, turn aside; *hence part.* **dīversus-a-um** *as adj.,* different, opposite

139. **pugnantibus: pugnō** (1), contend, struggle with, fight
       nātūrae: nātūra, nātūrae, *f.,* nature; birth; character, temperament, in-
       nate abilities, one's "make-up" [**(g)nāscor**]
       studiīs: studium, studī, *n.,* eagerness, zeal; affection, devotion; a pur-
       suit or activity, course of study
       cupiditātibus: cupiditās, cupiditātis, *f.,* passionate desire, longing;
       lust, immoderate desire; ambition, avarice, greed; *pl.,* acts of desire
       [**cupidus**]
       cōnflātum: cōnflō (1), blow on; cause; make by combining, weld; an-
       other metaphor, this time from welding: hence perhaps "welded
       together," "mixed together."

140 (ch. 13). **quis (est)...quis (est)...**(7x): good ex. of *(ep)anaphora* (rhetorical rep-
       etition) and *ellipsis* (the deletion of words that can be understood
       from context).
       clāriōribus: clārus-a-um, *adj.,* bright, shining, clear; clear, distinct,
       plain; well-known, notorious, famous, illustrious. *Clārissimus*
       is a common honorific title for men of high rank: Cicero may be
       alluding to C. Julius Caesar and Crassus, who had once flirted
       with backing Catiline (and then backed away when he became too
       wild).
       tempore: tempus, temporis, *n.,* time; season; occasion, opportunity
       iūcundior: iūcundus-a-um, *adj.,* pleasant, agreeable, delightful; conge-
       nial (to be with); agreeable (to the senses) [**iuvō,** please]

141. **turpiōribus: turpis-is-e,** *adj.,* disgusting, repulsive; depraved, dishon-
       orable, shameful
       coniunctior: coniungō, coniungere, coniunxī, coniunctum, join to-
       gether, connect, unite; *hence part.* **coniunctus-a-um** *as adj.,* closely
       related to, intimate with
       meliōrum: melior, melius, *adj.,* better [comp. of **bonus**]
       cīvis meliōrum partium: a political phrase, see 105n.; it echoes *optimīs*
       virīs at 133, and is contrasted with *taetrior hostis* at 142.
       aliquandō, *indef. adv.,* at some time, once; at any time, ever; at times, oc-
       casionally. This is a variation (so Austin, p. 163, at 13.13) on *quōdam*
       tempore just before.
142. **taetrior: taeter, taetra, taetrum,** *adj.,* disgusting, offensive; repulsive,
       loathsome; the word suggests disease (Austin at 13.14).
       hostis: hostis, hostis, *m.,* enemy
       voluptātibus: voluptās, voluptātis, *f.,* a pleasure, delight, enjoyment;
       pl., entertainments, shows; sexual adventures [rel. to **volō**]

inquinātior: inquinō (1), make dirty, stain; contaminate, pollute; be-smirch, defame; *hence part.* inquinātus-a-um *as adj.*, dirty, polluted; corrupt(ed), guilty

143. labōribus: labor, labōris, *m.*, labor, work; hardship, suffering, distress
patientior: patior, patī, passus sum, experience, undergo; bear, endure; not prevent, permit, tolerate; *hence part.* patiens, patientis *as adj.*, enduring, hardy; easy-going, long-suffering, tolerant
rapācitāte: rapācitās, rapācitātis, *f.*, rapacity, greed [rapāx, rapācis, grasping; greedy, rapacious]; the only occurrence in extant Republican Latin of this very rare word.
avārior: avārus-a-um, *adj.*, covetous, greedy; miserly, stingy [aveō, long for, crave]

144. largītiōne: largītiō, largītiōnis, *f.*, gift-giving, generosity, largess; brib-ery, corruption [largior, bestow generously]
effūsior: effundō, effundere, effūdī, effūsum, pour out, shed; bring forth, produce abundantly; use up, spend, fritter away; *hence part.* effūsus *as adj.*, relaxed, slack; unrestrained, extravagant, lavish; here almost "generous"
admīrābilia: admīrābilis-is-e, *adj.*, remarkable, wonderful; admirable; strange, paradoxical [admīror]

145. comprehendere: comprehendō, comprehendere, comprehendī, comprehēnsum, take hold of, grasp; seize, wrest, "bag," "nab"; per-ceive, comprehend [prehendō]; the rare use of this word here means to embrace one with kindness and affection so as to put him under obligation, hence "to have many friends" (L&S, s.v.).
amīcitiā: amīcitia, amīcitiae, *f.*, friendship, friendly relations; political friendship or alliance; see 108n.
tuērī: tueor, tuērī, tuitus sum, look at, watch; keep safe, preserve, protect
obsequiō: obsequium, obsequī, *n.*, compliance, deference, obedience [obsequor, yield, obey]

146. commūnicāre: commūnicō (1), share; communicate, discuss together, consult [commūnis, common, universal]
servīre: serviō (4), serve (as a slave); be at the service of; be devoted to, gratify
temporibus: "times of need" (Austin at 13.19); dat. w. *servīre* (rather than abl. of time when).

147. pecūnia: pecūnia, pecūniae, *f.*, property, possessions; money [pecus, cattle]
corporis: corpus, corporis, *n.*, body

scelere: scelus, sceleris, *n.,* utterly evil deed, crime, villainy
etiam: modifies preceding *scelere,* as usual

148. **sī opus esset:** "if there was need," "if need be." The condition is "mixed":
the apodosis has an indicative (*fuērunt...servīre*), usual in open conditions (cf. 18n., Ben. 302), while the protasis has a subjunctive (*esset*),
usual in future less vivid and unreal conditions (cf. 1n. and 18n., 58n.,
Ben. 303, 304).

   Sī opus esset looks like a present unreal protasis, but the meaning "if
there were need (but there isn't)" is clearly inappropriate here. Rather,
a future less vivid protasis (*sī opus sit,* "if there should be need"), has
been shifted into the past (*sī opus esset,* "if there was need").
versāre: "adapt" (Austin at 13.21)
suam naturam: "his ways" (Austin at 13.21)
regere: regō, regere, rēxī, rēctum, keep straight, guide, direct; control,
manage; govern, rule
ad tempus: "to suit the occasion" (Austin at 13.21)

149. **hūc,** *adv.,* to this place; to this point, to this degree, this far
illūc, *adv.,* to that place; **hūc...illūc,** *et sim.,* to and fro, this way and that
torquēre: torqueō, torquēre, torsī, tortum, turn, twist; bend, direct
flectere: flectō, flectere, flexī, flectum, bend, curve; turn aside, deflect;
adapt, adjust
tristibus: tristis-is-e, *adj.,* depressed, sad; ill-humored, morose; austere,
severe, stern
sevērē: sevērus-a-um, *adj.,* stern, strict; serious, austere

150. **remissīs: remittō, remittere, remīsī, remissum,** send back, return;
loosen, release, relax; *hence part.* **remissus-a-um** *as adj.,* good-hu-
mored, easy-going; lenient, forbearing
senibus: senex, senis, *m.,* old man; venerable or grand old man of yesteryear; *paterfamiliās* of comedy; *hence adj.,* old, aged. *Senex* referred
to men aged 40½ on; compare *adulēscēns* at 13, *iuventūs* just below.
iuventūte: iuventūs, iuventūtis, *f.,* young men, the young (men aged
twenty to forty years) [**iuvenis,** young man]
cōmiter: cōmis-is-e, *adj.,* affable, gracious, obliging

151. **facinerōsīs: facinerōsus-a-um,** *adj.,* crime-stained, wicked [**facinus,**
(evil) deed]
audāciter: audax, audācis, *adj.,* bold, daring, spirited; rash, reckless
[**audeō,** dare]. *Audacter* is more common, but Cicero seems to use
these forms interchangeably, probably depending on rhythm.

libīdinōsīs: **libīdinōsus-a-um,** *adj.,* wanton, willful, capricious; sensual, lustful [**libīdō**]

luxuriōsē: **luxuriōsus-a-um,** *adj.,* fertile, luxuriant; excessive, extravagant [**luxuriēs/luxuria,** lush growth]

vīvere: **vīvō, vīvere, vīxī, vīctum,** live

152 (ch. 14). multiplicī: **multiplex, multiplicis,** *adj.,* having many folds or twists; manifold, numerous; complex, versatile; varied, many-sided [-**plex,** cognate with Engl. "-fold"]

153.   conlēgerat: **conligō, conligere, conlēgī, conlectum,** gather together, collect; acquire, obtain; deduce, infer

154.   bonōs: for the political ring, see 105n.

speciē: **speciēs, speciēī,** *f.,* outward appearance, "look"; seeming appearance, semblance, cloak; splendor, show

adsimulātae: **adsimulō** (1), feign, pretend, simulate; *adsimulātae* picks up *simulābat* in 134; it is also *pleonastic* after *speciē*. Pleonasm (Gk. **pleon,** rather much) refers to the stylistic use of excess or unnecessary words. It is a distinctive feature of the early period of Latin literature (for a poetic ex. consider the Medea selection at 205–216n.), and also of English literature from Anglo-Saxon times well into the modern period (the King James Bible has many examples).

We usually find pleonasm overwrought and wordy today, although there are many colloq. expressions that use it (e.g., "circle around," "that X there,"). The Roman rhetorical writer Quintilian also criticized its excesses: *est et pleonasmos vitium, cum supervacuīs verbīs ōrātiō onerātur: 'ego oculīs meīs vīdī,' satis enim 'vīdī,'* "pleonasm is also a vice, since the speech is loaded up with excess verbiage: 'I saw [it] with my own eyes'; for [it is] sufficient [to say], 'I saw [it],'" *īnstitūtiō ōrātōria* viii.3.53.

155.   tenēbat: **teneō, tenēre, tenuī, tentum,** hold, possess; conceive, comprehend, know

dēlendī: **dēleō, dēlēre, dēlēvī, dēlētum,** annihilate, destroy; end, stop

imperī: **imperium, imperī,** *n.,* the right to command, administrative authority; jurisdiction; power; a command, magistracy; sovereignty, dominion [**imperō,** order, command]

156.   impetus: **impetus, impetūs,** *m.,* thrust, attack, assault; impulse, vigor; burst of emotion, passion

exstitisset: exsistō, exsistere, exstitī, appear, arise, become; show oneself or prove oneself to be (a certain way), be
exstitisset...nīterētur: another mixed condition; see above at 148n.

157. **immānitās: immānitās, immānitātis,** *f.,* enormity, monstrous size, vastness; savagery, brutality, ferocity
facilitātis: facilitās, facilitātis, *f.,* ease; easygoing nature, obliging or accommodating attitude; many edd. (including Austin at 14.2) find Madvig's proposal, *facultātis,* "ability," attractive here.
patientiae: patientia, patientiae, *f.,* endurance; forbearance, patience [**patior**]
rādīcibus: rādīx, rādīcis, *f.,* root; *pl.,* foundations, sources

158. **quā rē:** "for which reason;" ends the digression started at 131.
condiciō: condiciō, condiciōnis, *f.,* contract, agreement; consideration, proposition, possibility, "line of argument"; situation, circumstances [**condīcō, condīcere,** arrange, settle; note the quantity of the -*ī*-]. *Ista condiciō* = *istīus reī condiciō* (Austin at 14.3), "consideration of that matter," namely, the prosecution's contention that odium should attach to Caelius because of the alleged connection with Catiline.
respuātur: respuō, respuere, respuī, spit out; refuse, reject; mood and reason (also of *haereat*)? Ben. 275.

159. **crīmen:** remember *not* to translate "crime"; see 10n.
haereat: haereō, haerēre, haesī, haesum, stick, adhere, attach, cling to

160. **cum quibusdam bonīs:** some edd. read *cum quibusdam etiam bonīs,* which gives more point to *bonīs* (contra Austin) but also an inferior closing cadence.
inquam: parenthetical and emphatic: "I say." This verb is irreg. and defective. The extant pres. forms are:

inquam, I say   ——
inquis, you say   ——
inquit, he, she, it says   **inquiunt,** they say.

A few other forms are also attested, Ben. 134.
quondam, *adv.,* once, formerly
paene, *adv.,* almost, nearly, all but

161. **dēcēpit: dēcipiō, dēcipere, dēcēpī, dēceptum,** catch, entrap; deceive, mislead; cheat, deprive. Cicero had considered defending Catiline when he was on trial for *repetundae,* "extortion," in 65 b.c.

cupidus: **cupidus-a-um,** *adj.,* having a strong desire, eager, longing; avaricious, greedy

162. amīcus: "political ally"
    fidēlis: **fidēlis-is-e,** *adj.,* faithful, constant, loyal, devoted; principled, constant; trustworthy, reliable
    oculīs: **oculus, oculī,** *m.,* eye

163. prius: **prior, prius,** *adj.,* former, previous, first; *hence adv.* **prius,** before, sooner; previously, rather
    opīniōne: **opīniō, opīniōnis,** *f.,* belief, opinion, thought; estimation, expectation; esteem, reputation
    manibus: **manus, manūs,** *f.,* hand; group of armed men, band, force; here used figuratively, to balance *oculīs.*
    ante, *adv.,* beforehand, previously; *prep. w. acc.,* before, in front of
    dēpre(he)ndī: **dēpre(he)ndō, dēpre(he)ndere, dēpre(he)ndī, dēpre(hē)nsum,** catch, seize; detect, catch red-handed; comprehend, understand

164. catervīs: **caterva, catervae,** *f.,* crowd, mass (of followers); band, company (of soldiers or esp. of irregular armed men); large number, crowd
    magis est ut: "it is more reasonable that" (Austin at 14.11)

165. molestē ferat: cf. *acerbē feret* at 67, and *molestē tulī* at 75.
    errā(vi)sse: **errō** (1), wander, roam; blunder, make a mistake
    nōn numquam: a double negative expressing a positive, as is common in Latin: "not never," = "sometimes."

166. **quoque,** *adv.,* also, likewise, too
    errōris: **error, errōris,** *m.,* error, mistake

167. reformīdet: **reformīdō** (1), shrink back in fear, dread

168–189 (chs. 15–16). Cicero concludes the Catilinarian material by supplying logical (and often less than logical) reasons why Caelius would not have been involved with the conspiracy.

168 (ch. 15). **itaque,** *adv.,* and so, consequently, therefore
    impudīcitiae: **impudīcitia, impudīcitiae,** *f.,* sexual immorality, lasciviousness, perversion; the word often refers to homosexuality and effeminacy; see *pudīcitiā* at 65n., *pudōre* at 95.

coniūrātiōnis: coniūrātiō, coniūrātiōnis, *f.*, a swearing *(of an oath)* together, alliance, league; conspiracy, plot

169. invidiam: invidia, invidiae, *f.*, ill-will, spite, indignation; jealousy, envy; odium, dislike, prejudice [invidus, hostile; jealous]; *ad coniūrātiōnis invidiam:* "to arousing prejudice in connexion with the conspiracy" (Austin at 15.14).
dēlapsa: dēlābor, dēlābī, dēlapsus sum, fall, glide or slip down; slide or slip into an inferior or less relevant subject
id: compare the similar *id* at 110.

170. titubanter, *adv.,* in an unsteady, uncertain manner, falteringly, hesitatingly [titubō, totter; stumble]. Since participles are verbal adj.'s, adv.'s can be formed from them, so *titubanter* from *titubāns, titubantis.*
strictim, *adv.,* closely, compactly; briefly, superficially [strictum, from stringō, tie together; touch lightly]

171. participem: particeps, participis, *adj.,* participating in, sharing in; *hence subst.,* a participant, partner; fellow soldier, comrade [pars + -ceps, same root as capiō, take]

172. haerēbat: echoes *haereat* at 159: what was there wished for from the jury is here asserted as fact; *crīmen haerēbat* is a common phrase in Cicero; it recurs in this speech at 697.
vix, *adv.,* not easily, with difficulty; hardly, scarcely
disertī: disserō, disserere, disseruī, dissertum, discuss; speak about, treat of; *hence part.* disertus-a-um *as adj. (note the irreg. spelling),* eloquent, well-spoken; glib, slick-talking [serō, link, join]
cohaerēbat: cohaereō, cohaerēre, cohaesī, cohaesum, stick together, cohere; be consistent; note the jingle with *haerēbat* just before.

173. furor: furor, furōris, *m.,* frenzy, madness; rage, passion, fury, anger; violent behavior; civil discord [furō, rage, rave]; for the political connotation, see 105n.
tantum: take with *volnus.*
mōribus: mōs, mōris, *m.,* custom, usage, manner, habit, tradition; *pl.,* habits, customs, character

174. volnus: volnus, volneris, *n.,* a hurt, injury, wound; blow, misfortune; character flaw, defect; "disability" (Austin at 15.20); *-vo-* is a common spelling for *-vu-*

rē: rēs, reī, *f.*, thing; matter, fact; business, affair; property, situation

fortūna: fortūna, fortūnae, *f.*, chance, luck; good luck, prosperity; condition, circumstances, lot

ubi, *adv.*, where; when

dēnique, *adv.*, finally, at length, at last, in short, to sum up

175. nimium: nimius-a-um, *adj.*, too much, excessive; extravagant; *hence n. acc. sg.* nimium *as adv.*, too much, too [nimis]

minimē: minimus-a-um, smallest, least; youngest; *hence adv.* minimē, to the least extent, by no means

176. dubia: dubius-a-um. *adj.*, uncertain, wavering; doubted, undetermined [duo]

socius: socius-a-um, *adj.*, sharing, in partnership with; *as subst.*, an accomplice, associate, partner; ally

nōn modo: supply a *nōn* from *nisi* or *numquam,* and transl. "not only if he had not been an ally of the conspiracy, but unless he had been most opposed to that crime,..."

177. inimīcissimus: inimīcus-a-um, *adj.*, unfriendly, hostile; *as subst.*, an enemy

sceleris: scelus, sceleris, *n.*, evil or heinous deed, crime, sin

178. coniūrātiōnis accūsātiōne: a reference to Caelius's successful prosecution of C. Antonius Hybrida, in March 59 B.C. Antonius was actually charged with *repetundae,* or possibly even with *māiestas* ("treason"), in connection with his corrupt maladministration of Macedonia, rather than with his wavering loyalty at the time of the Catilinarian crisis. Nevertheless, Antonius's conviction and disgrace (exile and resultant loss of *dignitās*) were a blow to Cicero, whose political fortunes were just then ebbing (he himself was just months from exile); Austin, pp. 158–159, collects the ancient evidence surrounding Antonius's trial.

We have an interesting fragment from Caelius's prosecution speech, in which he imagines Antonius so drunk and debauched that he is incapable of preparing himself for battle:

Namque ipsum offendunt tēmulentō sopōre prōflīgātum, tōtīs praecordiīs stertentem, ructuōsōs spīritūs gemināre, praeclārāsque contubernālēs ab omnibus spondīs trānsversās incubāre et reliquās circumiacere passim. Quae tamen exanimātae terrōre, hostium adventū perceptō, excitāre Antōnium

cōnābantur, nōmen inclāmābant, frustrā ā cervīcibus tollēbant, blandius
alia ad aurem invocābat, vehementius etiam nōnnulla feriēbat; quārum cum
omnium vōcem tactumque nōscitāret, proximae cuiusque collum amplexū
petēbat, neque dormīre excitātus neque vigilāre ēbrius poterat, sed sēmisomnō
sopōre inter manūs centuriōnum concubīnārumque iactābātur.

"For [the centurions] found Antonius lying overcome in a drunken sleep, snoring with his whole belly, repeatedly belching out his breath; the more eminent of his female retinue were lying all across the couches, and the rest were lying around higgledy-piggledy. They, however, scared to death with the realization that the enemy [i.e., the Catilinarians] were coming, tried to rouse Antonius: they called his name; they lifted him by the neck to no avail; one called into his ear alluringly, while another slapped him vehemently. When he finally recognized the voice and touch of each, he sought to embrace whichever girl was nearest; now awake, he could not sleep, and he could not stay awake drunk, but tossed and turned in a kind of dreamlike stupor in the hands of his centurions and harlots."

Caelius must have been a formidable adversary! Of course, despite Cicero's spin, it made perfect sense for Caelius to prosecute someone in order to deflect attention from his own similar activities; so also on the *ambitus* charge below in ch. 16.

potissimum: potis, *indecl. adj.,* having power, able, capable; *comp.* **potior, potius,** better, preferable, preferred; stronger, more effective; *superl.* **potissimus-a-um,** chief, principal, most prominent, most important, most powerful, especial; *hence adv.* **potius,** rather, more; **potissimum,** chiefly, especially, most of all, above all; "in this particular way"

179.   **commendāre: commendō** (1), entrust, commit; recommend, point out favorably, commend, "distinguish"

179–189 (ch. 16). The exact circumstances behind this section are obscure, and it is uncertain to which election, or to whose, the passage refers; possibly Catiline's candidacy in 63 B.C. is meant, but we cannot be sure. The bribery charge is tangential, technically unconnected with the prosecution under the *lēx dē vī,* but advanced in order to add fuel to the fire.

quod: adverbial, "in this connection..." (Austin at 16.25)
haud, *adv.,* hardly, scarcely, not at all, by no means

sciō: sciō (4), know
an, *conj,* or, or rather; **haud sciō an...putem,** "I am inclined to think
[that...]," "I almost know," "I almost think," "I might say," = "perhaps," "probably"; cf. also *nesciō an,* "I rather think"
ambitū: ambitus, ambitūs, *m.,* a going around, circuit, revolution; improper or illegal canvassing for office, corruption, electoral bribery
[**ambiō,** go around, canvass (for votes)]

180. **sodālium: sodālis, sodālis,** *m.,* companion, friend; fellow member of a
fraternal or religious organization, esp. a *sodālicium* (society organized for political bribery). The *sodālicia* were a serious problem in
the late Republic; in 55 B.C. they would be outlawed by the *lēx Licinia
dē sodāliciīs* (itself prefigured by a senatorial decree of February 56
B.C.) (Austin at 16.26).
sequestrium: sequester, sequestris, *m.,* a third party acting as a depositary or escrow agent; the middleman with whom a bribe promised
to a third party is deposited
quoniam, *conj.,* seeing that...now, now that; because, since; *quoniam* ordinarily takes the indicative, and is trisyllabic (*quo-ni-am*).
incidī: incidō, incidere, incidī, incāsum, fall or drop into; happen, oc-
cur; come to a certain point [**cadō,** fall]

181. **similiter: similis-is-e,** *adj.,* similar, like

182. **āmēns: āmēns, āmentis,** *adj.,* demented, insane; distracted, excited,
frantic [**ā** + **mēns**]; take with preceding *tam.*
īnfīnītō: īnfīnītus-a-um, *adj.,* indefinite, unrestricted; unlimited, vast
commaculā(vi)ssent: commaculō (1), spot, stain; defile, pollute; stain
one's reputation, smear [**maculō,** stain, from **macula,** a spot]

183. **alterum:** L. Calpurnius Bestia.
factī: factum, factī, *n.,* action, deed, fact

184. **perpetuam: perpetuus-a-um,** *adj.,* unbroken, uninterrupted; complete,
entire; lasting, permanent, perpetual
optāret: optō (1), choose, select; wish (for), desire

185. **semel,** *adv.,* once, ever
perīculum: perīculum, perīculī, *n.,* experiment, test, attempt; danger,
risk; a criminal trial, suit at law; *perīculum ambitūs subeundum* is a
standard construction for "face prosecution for bribery," which recurs as *subīret perīculum capitis* at 580.

subeundem (esse): subeō, subīre, subiī *or* subiī, subitum, go up to, approach; undergo, endure, face

186. iterum, *adv.*, again, a second time
arcesseret: arcessō, arcessere, arcessīvī *or* arcessiī, arcessītum, send for, summon; call into court, arraign, indict
quamquam, *conj. w. indic.*, though, although, however much

187. sapienter: sapiō, sapīre, sapiī *or* sapīvī, taste; have good taste, be discerning, be sensible, be wise; *hence part.* sapiēns, sapientis *as adj.*, intelligent, sensible, wise

188. īnsectārī: īnsector (1), pursue, chase; rail at, inveigh against, harry, attack [sector, sectārī, harass, *freq. of* sequor, follow]
innocentiam: innocentia, innocentiae, *f.*, innocence; honesty, integrity
timidē: timidus-a-um, *adj.*, fearful, fainthearted, cowardly
cōgitāre: cōgitō (1), think, suppose; ponder, reflect (upon), consider; intend, plan

190–216 (chs. 17–18). The prosecution had evidently staged an *argūmentum ē victū*, "a 'proof' drawn from one's way of life."

190 (ch. 17). aes: aes, aeris, *n.*, copper; bronze; coin; money
aliēnum: aliēnus-a-um, *adj.*, belonging to another, another's; alien, foreign; aes aliēnum, "another's money," i.e., a debt
nam quod...obiectum est: for *nam quod,* see 45n.; for *obiectum est,* see 34n.
sūmptus: sūmptus, sūmptūs, *m.*, expenditure, outlay, expense; lavish or extravagant expense

191. tabulae: tabula, tabulae, *f.*, board; writing tablet; *pl.*, account book
flāgitātae: flāgitō (1), ask urgently, demand, require [rel. to flāgrō, burn, be ardent]
pauca: paucī-ae-a, *adj.*, few, a few; only a few, hardly any

192. potestāte: potestās, potestātis, *f.*, ability, power; office, magistracy. The *paterfamiliās* was said to hold his entire family *in potestāte suā,* "under his authority," including all unmarried children (regardless of age), and strictly speaking he had in law almost absolute legal power over them. What is significant here is that the family's property was held entirely in his name.
cōnficit: cōnficiō, cōnficere, cōnfēcī, cōnfectum, make, complete; exhaust, weaken

versūram: versūra, versūrae, *f.,* a turning around; the borrowing of money to pay a debt, process of exchanging one creditor for another

193. omnīnō, *adv.,* entirely, wholly; by all means, to be sure
generis: genus, generis, *n.,* birth, descent, origin; kind, type, class
obiectus est: see 34n.

194. habitātiōnis: habitātiō, habitātiōnis, *f.,* residence, dwelling, habitation; rent. The meaning "rent" is attested just once in (classical) Latin, in Suetonius (over 150 years later). In extant Republican Latin the word means "residence," but it is just possible that "rent" is the meaning here in view of the context. (However, *mercēdēs habitātiōnis annuās* [Caes. *B.C.* 3.21.1], which would have been *habitātiōnem annuam* had Caesar there felt *habitātiō* to mean "rent," may tell against this.)
trīgintā, *indecl. card. num. adj.,* thirty
mīlibus: mīlle, *indecl. num. adj.,* thousand; *n. pl. noun* mīlia, mīlium, thousands; abl. of price, Ben. 225.
habitāre: habitō (1), live in a place, dwell, inhabit, live, reside
dēmum, *adv.,* at length, at last; nunc dēmum, now, now at length, at last, "yet it is only now that...," "I am at last beginning to see that..."

195. intellegō: intellegō, intellegere, intellexi, intellectum, understand, perceive, comprehend, realize
P. Clōdī: almost certainly *not* Cicero's nemesis P. Clodius Pulcher (so also at 315). (1) Clodius was *aedīlis plēbis* (plebeian aedile), and therefore will have been presiding over the *Lūdī Megalēnsēs* alluded to in the exordium (*diēbus fēstīs lūdīsque pūblicīs* at 3–4); (2) Cicero could hardly make such cursory references to Clodius's speech if this were Clodius Pulcher; and (3) Cicero could not have delivered the *prosōpopoeia* involving Clodius Pulcher (432–448) in the form given there if he had actually been in court. No doubt this P. Clodius is some lesser member of the *gēns,* or perhaps a *cliēns* (see Gruen [1995], p. 307): Prosecution by such a person would have kept Clodia out of the limelight better than if her brother had prosecuted. Of course, if this was the Clodian strategy, it failed miserably once Cicero brought Clodia in, which the prosecutors probably expected—or hoped—he would not do. See also Austin, App. VI, pp. 155–156.
īnsulam: īnsula, īnsulae, *f.,* island; apartment building
vēnālem: vēnālis-is-e, *adj.,* for sale [vēnum, sale]
aediculīs: aedicula, aediculae, *f.,* a small chapel; *pl.,* a small house or apartment [aedēs]

196.   **decem,** *indecl. card. num. adj.,* ten
       opīnor: opīnor (1), think, believe, suppose, imagine, conjecture, deem, judge; **(ut) opīnor,** *parenthetical,* as I think, as I believe, according to my opinion
       dum, *conj., (+ indic.)* while; *(+ subj.)* until
       placēre: placet, placēre, placuit *or* **placitum est,** it is pleasing, it is agreeable

197.   **voltis:** = *vultis.*
       ad tempus eius: the usage is like that at 148.
       mendācium: mendācium, mendācī, *n.,* a lie, falsehood, false statement [**mendāx,** lying, untruthful, deceitful]
       accommodāvistis: accommodō (1), adjust, adapt, conform

198 (ch. 18). Cicero returns to the theme of ch. 3.
       sēmigrārit: sēmigrō (1), go or move away [**sē,** showing separation + **migrō,** go away, depart]

199.   **hāc:** deictic (see 44n.)

200.   **glōriōsam: glōriōsus-a-um,** *adj.,* glorious, renowned, illustrious, famous; boastful, vainglorious, bragging, haughty [**glōria,** glory]

201.   **victōriam: victōria, victōriae,** *f.,* victory; *sibi glōriōsam victōriam* refers to Caelius's successful prosecution of Antonius Hybrida, for which see intro. sec. 29 and lines 576–578, 954–957 (note how skilfully Cicero handles his own awkward situation in all these passages).
       cōnsecūtus: cōnsequor, cōnsequī, cōnsecūtus sum, follow up; obtain, gain; win; overtake, pursue
       per, *prep. w. acc.,* through

202.   **permittente: permittō, permittere, permīsī, permissum,** let go, let loose; give up, surrender; allow, permit
       suādente: suādeō, suādēre, suāsī, suāsum, advise, recommend, exhort, urge, persuade

203.   **longē: longus-a-um,** *adj.,* long, lasting; remote, far-reaching
       quō facilius: purpose clauses with comparative adverbs begin w. *quō* (which is abl. of degree of difference [Ben. 223]): "by which amount it would be easier...."
       nostrās domūs: the *domus* theme again, see 100n.

204.   **obīre: obeō, obīre, obiī** *or* **obitum,** go or come to, travel to, traverse, visit; go to meet, meet, undertake, enter upon

  ā suīs: "by his friends" (cf. *suōrum* and *meōrum* at 58 and 64)

  colī: colō, colere, coluī, cultum, till, cultivate; inhabit, live in; care for, protect, cherish; worship, reverence

  condūxit: condūcō, condūcere, condūxī, conductum, draw, lead, bring or collect together; unite; hire, rent; be useful to, be profitable, serve

  Palātiō: Palātium, Palātī, *n.,* Palatine Hill

205.   **magno: magnus-a-um,** *adj.,* great, large, big; ample, eminent, powerful; **nōn magnō,** *subst.,* "for not a great price," abl. of price, Ben. 225.

205–216. The mythology and context are complex. Jason's wicked uncle Pelias had improperly seized Jason's crown in Iolcus, and in order to kill his nephew, commanded him to fetch the Golden Fleece in Colchis, a distant land near the Black Sea. Jason and his men, the Argonauts ("the crew of the ship called the *Argō*) sailed to Colchis; unfortunately, the Fleece was guarded by fierce monsters, which Jason was able to overcome only through the help of the witch Medea, the daughter of Aeetes, king of Colchis. Later, Jason, desiring to marry a Greek, tried to separate from Medea, for which she killed their children and his intended.

In his prosecution speech, Atratinus had called Caelius *pulcherrimum Iāsōnem,* "a pretty-boy Jason," thus starting a chain of insults, retorts, and references, all based on the literature surrounding the folktale witch Medea. Caelius himself retorted by labeling Atratinus *Pelias cincinnātus,* "a Pelias with curls," implicitly comparing Atratinus's prosecution of Caelius with Pelias's attempt to kill Jason; *pulcherrimus* and *cincinnātus* imply effeminacy and homosexuality (as perhaps also *pulchellus,* Cicero's derisive form of P. Clodius Pulcher's name); for Caelius's other barbs, and a complete set of fragments from his speeches (with sources), see the second edition (forthcoming).

As Cicero mentions here, Crassus had picked up the theme in his defense speech, quoting from the *Mēdēa exsul* (Medea the Exile), written by the early Roman poet Q. (Quintus) Ennius (239 B.C.–169 B.C.), the first poet known to use dactylic verse in Latin poetry (quotations in Cicero are italicized):

utinam nē in nemore Peliō secūribus
caesa accidisset abiegna ad terram trabēs,
nēve inde nāvis incohandae exordium
coepisset, quae nunc nōminātur nōmine
Argō, quia Argīvī in eā dēlectī virī
vectī petēbant pellem inaurātam arietis

Colchīs, imperiō rēgis Peliae, per dolum;
nam numquam era errāns mea domō ecferret pedem
Mēdēa, animō aegra, amōre saevō saucia.

Would that in the Pelian grove, cut by axes, the fir-wood trunk had not fallen to earth, and had not begun the starting point of initiating a ship, which is now named with the name Argo, because, carried in her, Argives, picked men, sought the gilded fleece of the ram, among the Colchians, by command of King Pelias, through trickery. For never would my mistress, meandering [mentally as well as physically; overtone of "erring," too], have set foot from home, Medea, sick in [her] mind, stricken by savage love.

Oh! that axes had not felled fir trees in a Pelian grove, and that from these no beginning had been made of that ship; it is now called "Argo," because carefully selected Argive heroes were carried by her in their quest for the golden fleece of the ram in Colchis: this by the orders of King Pelias—a trick it was! For then never would my misguided mistress have set foot outside her home—Medea, sick at heart, smitten with cruel love!

The first version is less a translation than a trot or a crib, although it does have the virtue of reproducing the deliberate pleonasm of the original (see 134n.), which seems overblown to us and is omitted in the freer translation that follows. It is worth noting that *ecferret* is a *past,* not present, contrary-to-fact apodosis (as often in "early" Latin, where classical style would require the plpf. subj. *extulisset*). For further information on this work, and on the style of Ennius in general, see Jocelyn, pp. 113–118 and 342–356.

Crassus had changed the context to refer to the ship that had transported Ptolemy Auletes, the king of Egypt, from Alexandria to Naples. Auletes ("the flute-player"), officially a "friend and ally of the Roman people," had been overthrown by his own people, in part because of high taxes made necessary by his bribery of Roman politicians. He had come to Italy to lobby the Senate and the "triumvirs" to effect his reinstatement. The Alexandrian philosopher Dio had led a delegation representing the new government to Italy; members of this delegation were roughed up in Naples, and Dio himself was killed. These events gave rise to three of the five charges against Caelius (see intro., sec. 31), some of which may have been (partly) true. For an insightful and entertaining discussion, see Wiseman (1995), pp. 54–62.

Here Cicero reverts to the "society" approach to the case (i.e., Clodia and her involvement), giving the audience a tantalizing hint of what is to come (as in ch. 1).

206.   **clārissimus: clārus-a-um,** *adj.,* bright, clear; evident, plain; well-known, illustrious, famous; *vir clārissimus* is a common honorific title (like our congressional "the distinguished gentleman from Ohio").

M. (Marcus) Crassus: on the career of this crafty politician, see intro., sec. 17, and the bibliography.

adventū: adventus, adventūs, *m.,* coming, approach, arrival

rēgis: rēx, rēgis, *m.,* king

Ptolemaeī: Ptolemaeus, Ptolemaeī, *m.,* Ptolemy, name of a royal house of Egypt; here Ptolemy Auletes, king during most of the period from 80 B.C. to 51 B.C. The Ptolemies were a Macedonian house that ruled Egypt from the death of Alexander the Great in 323 B.C. (Ptolemy I Soter was one of Alexander's generals), to the most famous member of the house, Cleopatra VII, who killed herself in 30 B.C. (her death ended the line; thereafter Egypt was administered as an imperial estate, overseen on the Emperor's behalf by an equestrian *praefectus*).

207.   **quereretur: queror, querī, questus sum,** complain or grumble about, lament

   ante, *adv.,* previously, earlier; *prep. w. acc.,* before, in front of

208.   **utinam,** *adv.,* how I wish that, if only, would that!, oh that! **[utī (= ut) + nam];** *utinam* reinforces subj. wishes; it is especially common with hopeless wishes (as here), Ben. 279.2.

   nē, *adv.,* not; *conj.,* in order that...not, lest, for fear that; *nē,* rather than *nōn,* is usual in negative wishes.

   nemore: nemus, nemoris, *n.,* a wood (adjacent to or containing pasture land), glade; sacred grove

   Pēliō: Pēlius-a-um, *adj.,* of or pert. to Pelion, a mountain in Thessaly, from which came the wood for the Argo

   Utinam nē in nemore Pēliō: see above at 205–216.

209.   **contexere: contexō, contexere, contexuī, contextum,** weave or join together; connect, link; proceed, "continue the context" (Austin at 18.1) **[con- + texō, weave]**

   carmen: carmen, carminis, *n.,* song, poem

   licēret: licet, licēre, licuit *or* **licitum est,** it is allowed or permitted, one may; here a potential subj., Ben. 280.3.

210.   **era: era, erae,** *f.,* woman, mistress, lady of the house

211.   **exhibēret: exhibeō, exhibēre, exhibuī, exhibitum,** hold out, present; reveal, show; produce, cause

212.   **Mēdēa: Mēdēa, Mēdēae,** *f.,* Medea (see 205n.)

aegrō: **aeger, aegra, aegrum,** *adj.,* sick; exhausted, weak; sick at heart, troubled; lovesick; *animō aegrō* is abl. of quality, Ben. 224.

amōre: **amor, amōris,** *m.,* desire, love; love affair; case and reason? Ben. 218.

saevō: **saevus-a-um,** *adj., (of people)* harsh, savage, ferocious; *(of things)* cruel, harsh, severe

saucia: **saucius-a-um,** *adj.,* wounded; affected, stricken, "smitten"

213.   sīc: "anticipatory of *hanc...fuisse*" (Austin at 18.5)
reperiētis: **reperiō, reperīre, repperī, reppertum,** find (out), discover; acquire, get; devise, invent [**re** + **pariō,** give birth; bring forth]
id locī: for the construction, Ben. 201.2.
vēnerō: **veniō, venīre, vēnī, ventum,** come

214.   ostendam: **ostendō, ostendere, ostendī, ostentum** *or* **ostēnsum,** show, display; exhibit, present; demonstrate, establish
hanc...fuisse: an indirect statement construction in apposition to *quod... ostendam;* translate *"quod ostendam,* namely, that *hanc migrātiōnem..."*
Palātīnam: **Palātīnus-a-um,** *adj.,* of or pert. to the Palatine Hill, which overlooked the *Forum Rōmānum* and was the wealthiest and most fashionable quarter of Rome, where Clodia lived and to which Caelius moved, probably in 59 or 58 B.C.
migrātiōnem: **migrātiō, migrātiōnis,** *f.,* a change of residence, a move

215.   sīve *or* seu, *conj.,* or
malōrum: **malus-a-um,** *adj.,* bad, evil, wicked; *hence subst.* **malum, malī,** misfortune, woe, trouble; evil-doing, wickedness, misdeed; cf. *male dīcere* at 70.
potius: "rather"

216.   sermōnum: **sermō, sermōnis,** *m.,* conversation, talk; idle talk, gossip, rumor

217–261 (chs. 19–22): Cicero impugns the witnesses.

217 (ch. 19). **ob,** *prep. w. acc.,* because of, on account of; **quam ob rem** (sometimes written as one word, *quamobrem), interrog. adv.,* for what reason, why; *rel. adv.,* for which reason, why; *causal adv.,* for which reason, wherefore, therefore
illa: n. acc. pl. dir. obj. of *pertimēscō* in 219.

218. **praemūnīrī: praemūniō** (4), fortify in front of a place; strengthen, bolster; bring evidence forward, adduce in defense

     fingī: fingō, fingere, fīnxī, fictum, create, fashion; suppose, imagine; fabricate, misrepresent

     frētus: frētus-a-um, *adj.,* relying, trusting, or depending on (+ *abl.*); **frētus vestrā prūdentiā:** Cicero likes this kind of construction when addressing juries, see also 547, 920.

     prūdentiā: prūdentia, prūdentiae, *f.,* wisdom, sagacity, good sense; practical knowledge, common sense (Austin at 19.10) [**prūdēns**, sagacious] Cicero refers frequently to the jury's *prūdentia* (also 557; of the judge Domitius at 371) and *sapientia* (244, 253, 339, 547, 921 [along w. *hūmānitās*]): "If you want to have *prūdentia* and *sapientia,* you'll agree with the defense."

219. **pertimēscō: pertimēscō, pertimēscere, pertimuī,** become very scared of or frightened from

     āiēbant: āiō, *irreg.,* say yes, affirm, assent, agree; say, assert. Only the present forms *āiō, ais, ait* and *āiunt* and a few others are attested.

     fore: = *futūrum esse.*

     senātōrem: senātor, senātōris, *m.,* senator [**senex**]

220. **pontificiīs: pontificius-a-um,** *adj.,* of or pert. to a *pontifex* or to a pontifical college. A *pontifex* was a Roman high priest; nothing certain can be said about the curious derivation (from *pōns,* bridge + *faciō*).

     comitiīs: comitium, comitī, *n.,* place of public assembly in the forum; judicial, legislative, or electoral assembly; *(pl.)* an assembly for elections, the election(s) [**con- + eō**]

     pulsātum esse: pulsō (1), push, strike; strike repeatedly, beat; urge, drive on, impel, move, agitate, disturb, disquiet; attack, assault, assail; Austin (at 19.12) notes that this is *iniūria,* not *vīs.* This charge was probably lumped together with the others.

     dīceret: subj. in a subordinate clause in indir. statement. We can "unwrap" this sentence to reveal its grammar and reconstruct what Cicero maintains the senator said:

(1) āiēbant enim fore (=futūrum esse) testem senātōrem quī sē pontificiīs comitiīs pulsātum (esse) ā Caeliō dīceret.

(2) āiunt enim fore (=futūrum esse) testem senātōrem quī sē pontificiīs comitiīs pulsātum (esse) ā Caeliō dīcat.

(3) Erit testis senātor quī sē pontificiīs comitiīs pulsātum (esse) ā Caeliō dīcet.

(4) "Ego pontificiīs comitiīs pulsātus sum ā Caeliō."

This analysis reveals how a future tense verb such as *dīcet* (third sentence) will be represented in primary sequence (second sentence) by a present subj. *dīcat,* and in secondary sequence (first, actual sentence) by an impf. subj. *dīceret* (which might not seem logical at first glance).
quō: = *et eō,* connecting rel.

221. **quaeram:** Cicero uses *requīram* similarly (to announce what he plans to ask a witness) at 836. In each passage, by revealing what is normally guarded defense strategy, Cicero hopes to underscore just how groundless the prosecution's case is.
prōdeō, prōdīre, prōdiī, prōditum, go or come forward, make an appearance, be produced (as a witness); appear
cūr, *adv.,* why
statim, *adv.,* immediately, at once [**stō**]
nihil ēgerit: "took no legal action" (Austin at 19.13)

222. **agere:** like *ēgerit* just before, but here used absolutely, = "to bring a case"
māluerit: mālō, mālle, māluī, choose rather, prefer [**mage/magis +volō**]
prōductus [sit]: prōdūcō, prōdūcere, prōdūxī, prōductum, lead or bring forward; present (evidence, witnesses) before a court

223. **tantō post:** *post* here is an adv., *tantō* an abl. of degree of difference, Ben. 223.
continuō: continuus-a-um, *adj.,* joining, connecting; connected, uninterrupted; continuous, successive; *hence adv.* **continuō,** immediately, at once; continuously, without interruption

224. **acūtē: acūtus-a-um,** *adj.,* sharp, pointed; keen, shrewd, intelligent; here "pointedly," "artfully"
argūtē: arguō, arguere, arguī, argūtum, make clear, make known, show; declare, assert; *hence part.* **argūtus-a-um** *as adj.,* bright; adroit, clever, smart
responderit: respondeō, respondēre, respondī, respōnsum, promise in return; answer, reply [**spondeō,** promise]

225. **dēnique,** *adv.,* at length, in the end, at last; finally, lastly; to sum up, in short
ēmānet: ēmānō (1), flow or trickle out, pour forth; be derived, arise, originate
oriētur: orior, orīrī, ortus sum, rise, arise; emerge or spring from, crop up from

226. **fortasse,** *adv.,* perhaps, possibly, it may be that [rel. to **forte**]
soleō: soleō, solēre, solitus sum, be accustomed to, make it a practice to, be apt to
commovēbor: commoveō, commovēre, commōvī, commōtum, shake, agitate; stir one's feelings, impress, "touch"
sīn, *conj.,* but if, if however [**sī** + **ne,** by *apocope,* Gk., "a cutting off"]

227. **rīvolus: rīvolus, rīvolī,** *m.,* small stream or brook, tributary [dim. of **rīvus,** stream]; this word was often spelled *rīvulus* (cf. *volnus* at 174n.): it is always figurative in Cicero.
arcessītus: arcessō, arcessere, arcessīvī, arcessītum, go or send for, fetch, invite; summon before a court, arraign, indict; here "drawn (from)"
ductus: dūcō, dūcere, dūxī, ductus, lead
capite: caput, capitis, *n.,* head; life; source, fountain, origin

228. **laetābor: laetor** (1), rejoice, be delighted
cum: concessive, as shown by the context, Ben. 309.3.
grātiā, opibus: abl. w. *nītātur*

229. **sōlum: sōlus-a-um,** *adj.,* alone, sole, only
grātificārī: grātificor (1), show kindness to, gratify, oblige; do a favor (+ *dat.*) [**grātia** + **faciō**]
vellet: mood and reason? Ben. 283.
esse...inventum: inveniō, invenīre, invēnī, inventum, come upon, find; procure, acquire, (manage to) get; find (out), discover

231. **DE TESTE FVFIO:** This *titulus,* or break marking an abridgement, is found in only one MS, and is rejected by Austin and most edd., since it is not clear that it is needed. If it is genuine, then Fufius is the *ūnum senātōrem* of 229.
Fūfiō: Fūfius, Fūfī, *m.,* Roman gentile name. Possibly this is Q. Fūfius Calēnus, tribune in 61, praetor in 59, consul *suffectus* in 47 (a consul chosen in a special election to complete the unexpired term of a deceased consul was called a *cōnsul suffectus*). As an *amīcus* ("political ally") of both Clodius and Caesar, he was, from at least 61 until Cicero's death, "a thorn in the side of Cicero" (Gruen [1995], p. 171), and then some.
If the *titulus* is genuine, and this identification is correct, then (1) Cicero's twitting of him in the preceding lines is disingenuous

(a man of praetorian rank is not to be dismissed so easily), though quite in line with oratorical liberties; and (2) Cicero is scoring political points—against his *inimīcus* Fufius Calenus himself, and against the triumviral power Fufius supported (especially Caesar).

232 (ch. 20). **tamen:** "in any case"; "in spite of what someone may have said" (Austin at 20.24)

nocturnōrum: nocturnus-a-um, *adj.,* of or pert. to the night, nocturnal, nighttime [**nox**]; appropriate to the speech's consistent contrast between darkness/secrecy and light/revelation.

233. **perhorrēscō: perhorrēscō, perhorrēscere, perhorruī,** shudder, tremble greatly, be very frightened of [**per-** + **horrēscō**]

est...dīcerent...: How does the run of this sentence reinforce Cicero's contention that the prosecution's case is not to be believed?

uxōrēs: uxor, uxōris, *f.,* wife

234. **cēna: cēna, cēnae,** *f.,* dinner

redeuntīs: redeō, redīre, rediī, reditum, come or go back, return; *redeuntīs:* acc. pl.

attrectātās esse: attrectō (1), touch; handle roughly, assault; the word here means to assault sexually or criminally, like *contrectāre;* also, *mala tractātiō* is a technical term for "maltreatment" (Austin at 20.26).

235. **audēbunt: audeō, audēre, ausus sum,** dare, venture [**avidus,** eager]

eīs: dat. of agent, the regular usage with the gerundive in the pass. periphrastic construction; Ben. 189.1.

sit...cōnfitendum: cōnfiteor, cōnfitērī, cōnfessus sum, admit, acknowledge; allow, concede, grant; reveal, make known [**fateor,** admit]

236. **congressū: congressus, congressūs,** *m.,* meeting, conference; interview, engagement; "private meeting" (Austin at 20.1) [**congredior,** meet]

cōnstitūtō: cōnstituō, cōnstituere, cōnstituī, cōnstitūtum, put, place, set; assent, agree upon; *hence subst.* **cōnstitūtum,** arrangement, agreement, accommodation (here for monetary compensation; see Ulpian in *dīgesta,* 13.5.1.5, 13.5.3.2)

coepisse: coepī, coepisse, coeptum, *defective,* have begun, began; this verb is normally used only in the perf. system.

237. **iniūriīs: iniūria, iniūriae,** *f.,* unlawful, injurious, or unjust conduct; injustice, injury, harm [**in**-priv. + **iūs**]; see the distinction between *injūria* and *vīs* above at 220n.

experīrī: experior, experīrī, expertus sum, put to the test, try out; experience, undergo; resort to trial, go to law; "get legal satisfaction" (Austin at 20.1)

(IX) **tōtum: tōtus-a-um,** *adj.,* whole, entire; all

oppugnātiōnis: oppugnātiō, oppugnātiōnis, *f.,* military assault, attack; an accusation. Note the recurrence of this theme, begun in *oppugnārint* at 9 and brought to its fullest development in the comic Battle of the Baths (at 754–872). Here the theme runs to *oppugnandī* in 245, through a variety of military words and phrases.

238. **iam:** "already"

prōspicitis: prōspiciō, prōspicere, prōspexī, prōspectum, look forward (at), look out (at); take care, anticipate, foresee; provide for [**prō + speciō**]

īnferētur: īnferō, īnferre, intulī, illātum, bring or carry in; march forward, advance, attack; hurl, throw

239. **prōpulsāre: prōpulsō** (1), drive away, beat off, repulse; ward off, avert [freq. of **prōpellō,** push forward]

240. **palam,** *adv.,* openly, publicly

tēla: tēlum, tēlī, *n.,* spear, javelin; weapon

clam, *adv.,* secretly, under cover

241. **subministrantur: subministrō** (1), supply, furnish; this section restates the argument of the exordium (12–17), and naturally we (and the jury) think of Clodia immediately; but we are also to think of deeper political forces at work.

(ch. 21). **invidiōsum: invidiōsus-a-um,** *adj.,* full of envy, hateful, hostile, resentful; envied, unpopular [**invidia,** envy, grudge; odium, unpopularity, from **invidus,** envious]

eōs: may refer to the *gēns Clōdia* or to the formal prosecutors. (1) A reference to Clodia *via* her family would suit the general picture of 240–241 nicely. In 245, Cicero says it is appropriate (*iūsta*) for these *virīs fortibus* to *oppugnandī,* which also supports a reference to the *Claudiī* (so too *oppugnātur* in 240), rather than *accūsandī,* the technical term that would apply to the prosecutors. (2) On the other hand, the language of 242–244 probably refers especially to Atratinus, who is protecting his father. Cicero neatly conflates the interests of the *gēns Claudia* and of Atratinus: the jurors would hardly have time to distinguish the two.

242. **glōriōsum etiam:** "even a source of pride"; *etiam* regularly emphasizes the word it follows.
　　funguntur: fungor, fungī, fūnctus sum, do, perform *(+ abl.)*
　　officiō: officium, officī, *n.,* favor; duty, obligation [root of **ops,** help + **faciō**]

243. **laesī: laedō, laedere, laesī, laesum,** harm, hurt, injure; trouble, vex; wrong, harm
　　dolent: doleō, dolēre, doluī, dolitum, suffer pain; grieve (for), lament

244. **īrātī: īrātus-a-um,** *adj.,* full of anger, enraged, furious [**īra**]
　　efferuntur: efferō, efferre, extulī, ēlātum, bring or carry out or away; announce, proclaim; *(pass., of emotions)* be carried away
　　pugnant: pugnō (1), fight
　　lacessītī: lacessō, lacessere, lacessīvī *or* **lacessiī, lacessītum,** provoke, rouse, urge on; harass, trouble, vex [**laciō,** allure]
　　sapientiae: sapientia, sapientiae, *f.,* good sense, soundness of judgment, prudence, wisdom [**sapiō,** be sensible]; gen. of quality, Ben. 203. An inf. often follows *esse* plus a gen. of quality, Ben. 203.5.

245. **iūsta: iūstus-a-um,** *adj.,* righteous, upright; just, fair; rightful, lawful [**iūs**]
　　virīs fortibus: "for resolute men"; dat. of reference.

246. **ideō,** *adv.,* for this or that reason, therefore, consequently

247. **dolōrī: dolor, dolōris,** *m.,* physical pain; mental anguish, distress, grief; anger, animosity, indignation, resentment; *aliēnō dolōrī:* "someone else's spite" (Austin at 21.12).
　　fideī: fidēs, fideī, *f.,* faith, trust, confidence; here = "bond," "oath," "duty."
　　cōnsulendī: cōnsulō, cōnsulere, cōnsuluī, cōnsultum, consider, reflect, deliberate; ask for advice, consult; have regard for, look after, give thought to *(+ dat.)*; construction? Ben. 338.1a.
　　sit: mood and reason? Ben. 300.

248. **multitūdō: multitūdō, multitūdinis,** *f.,* a great number; the common people, mob, rabble
　　quae [sint] genera, quae [sint] studia, quae [sit] varietās: ellipsis.
　　genera: "classes"
　　studia: "political allegiances," a sense of *studium* which arises from its use to mean zeal about and devotion to a person or cause (L&S, s.v., II.A; *OLD,* s.v., 5)
　　varietās: varietās, varietātis, *f.,* variety, diversity; a motley, an assortment; fickleness, unpredictability, capriciousness [**varius,** manifold]

249. cōpiā: cōpia, cōpiae, *f.*, wealth, resources; supply; ample supply, abundance; troops, forces
quam multōs: "How many...?"; rhetorical question.
arbitrāminī: arbitror (1), judge, decide; believe, reckon, think [arbiter, judge]

250. quī...soleant: constr.? Ben. 283.
potentibus: potēns, potentis, *adj.*, able, powerful; having power over, ruling over, master of; endowed with; powerful, influential
grātiōsīs: grātiōsus-a-um, *adj.*, beloved, well-regarded; popular, influential; the wide meanings of the adj. parallel those of the noun (for which see 13n.).
disertīs: "slick talkers"; cf. 172n.
aliquid: aliquis, (aliqua), aliquid, *indef. pron.*, someone, somebody, something; *aliquis* is a little more specific than *quis* (cf. 1n.); this is why the latter is used after *sī*.

251. ultrō, *adv.*, to the far side; besides, moreover, and what's more; of one's own accord, voluntarily, spontaneously [rel. to ulterior and ultimus]
offerre: offerō, offerre, obtulī, oblātum, carry or bring to, present; show, reveal; offer, volunteer, cause, occasion
soleant: mood and reason? Ben. 283.
operam: opera, operae, *f.*, effort, pains, work; services, help; care, attention
nāvāre: nāvō (1), devote oneself to; operam nāvāre, busy oneself, work hard, work energetically. This word is derived from the same root as *(g)nāvus,* diligent, energetic, industrious (cf. Vergil's description of drones as *ignāvum...pecus,* "a lazy swarm" [*Aen.* I.435]).
testimōnium: testimōnium, testimōnī, *n.*, evidence, proof; attestation, testimony [testis]

252. pollicērī: polliceor, pollicērī, pollicitus sum, promise

253 (ch. 22). prōiēcerint: prōiciō, prōicere, prōiēcī, prōiectum, throw, fling forward; throw away, reject; *(pass. or reflex.)* rush forward, plunge into; sē...prōiēcerint: "have intruded themselves" (Austin at 22.18): fut. perf. indic. in a fut. more vivid condition.

exclūditōte: exclūdō, exclūdere, exclūsī, exclūsum, keep or shut out, exclude; separate, cut off, hinder, prevent; leave out, omit [claudō, close]. The forms of the so-called fut. act. imp. are as follows:

	sg.	pl.	sing.	pl.
1st	–	–	–	–
2nd	-tō	-tōte	exclūditō, you shall keep out!	exclūditōte, you shall keep out!
3rd	-tō	-ntō	exclūditō, he shall keep out!	exclūduntō, they shall keep out!

The fut. (better labeled "second") imp., is found primarily in formulaic writing such as legal texts, maxims, and recipes, and was used instead of the pres. (better labeled "ordinary") imp. to convey solemnity or rigor.

cupiditātem: "ambition"

sapientiā vestrā: abl. of means

254. **salūtī: salūs, salūtis,** *f.,* health, soundness; safety, welfare, well-being; greeting, salutation

    religiōnī: religiō, religiōnis, *f.,* reverence for the gods; a feeling of constraint or scruple, sense of duty or responsibility, "conscience" (Gardner); like *fideī* above, the word can signify the obligation created by an oath; the word is derived probably from the root *lig-* found in *ligō, ligāre,* to tie, bind.

255. **contrā,** *adv.,* opposite, over against, on the opposite side; otherwise; *hence prep. w. acc.,* against, in opposition to

    perīculōsās: perīculōsus-a-um, *adj.,* dangerous, hazardous, perilous, full of danger

    potentiās: potentia, potentiae, *f.,* might, force, power; political power, authority, influence; *hominum potentiās* picks up *potentibus* in 250.

    condiciōnī: condiciō, condiciōnis, *f.,* contract, proposition, agreement; circumstance, state of affairs, position, plight; Gardner suggests "security."

256. **prōvīdisse: prōvideō, prōvidēre, prōvīdī, prōvīsum,** see up ahead or at a distance; foresee, expect; see to it that, provide that; care for, look after

    videāminī: "be deemed" (*OLD,* s.v., 22)

    abdūcam: abdūcō, abdūcere, abdūxī, abductum, take or lead away, remove; steer clear of, separate (oneself) from

257. **vēritātem: vēritās, vēritātis,** *f.,* truth, truthfulness, honesty; real life, reality

    mūtārī: mūtō (1), alter, change, transform, become different (often for the worse)

258. **voluntāte: voluntās, voluntātis,** *f.,* will, wish; intention, inclination; good will, favor, affection

collocārī: **conlocō** (1), put in place, set up, establish; base, ground in, make dependent on; fill up, occupy, spend
sinam: sinō, sinere, sīvī *or* **siī, situm,** leave alone, let be; allow, let, permit
quae: antecedent is *voluntāte.*
nūllō negōtiō: "with no trouble at all" (Englert)

259.   **flectī: flectō, flectere, flexī, flectum,** bend, twist, turn; change, alter, influence
dētorquērī: dētorqueō, dētorquērī, dētorsī, dētortum, turn away, deflect; distort, misrepresent, "twist"
argūmentīs: "deductions" (Austin at 54.12)
signīs: signum, signī, *n.,* sign, mark; evidence. The evidence referred to by the technical language here is not the physical or factual evidence we might expect, but rather theoretical "deductions."

260.   **lūce: lūx, lūcis,** *f.,* light; case and reason? Ben. 217.1.
refellēmus: refellō, refellere, refellī, refute, rebut, disprove [**re + fallō**]

261.   **pugnābit: pugnō** (1), fight

262–284 (chs. 23–24): The attempt on Dio's life will have been considered particularly heinous because it was a violation of the laws of hospitality and of international relations (since Dio was a *lēgātus*).

262 (ch. 23). **patior: patior, patī, passus sum,** suffer, undergo; experience; allow, permit; **facile patior:** "I am very pleased" (Austin at 23.29)

263.   **perōrātam: perōrō** (1), speak from beginning to end; explain or state thoroughly; harangue; wind up a case, conclude
sēditiōnibus: sēditiō, sēditiōnis, *f.,* "a going apart," violent political discord, rebellion, insurrection, riot
Neāpolītānīs: Neāpolītānus-a-um, *adj.,* of or pertaining to Naples, Neapolitan. Naples is a town in Campania, originally a Greek settlement [**Neāpolis,** Gk. "new city"]. The reference is unclear. Austin thinks it refers to some "local dispute," but it may be connected with Dio and the eastern situation.

264.   **Alexandrīnōrum: Alexandrīnus-a-um,** *adj.,* of or pertaining to Alexandria, a city in Egypt at the mouth of the Nile founded by Alexander the Great.
pulsātiōne: pulsātiō, pulsātiōnis, *f.,* repeated striking or hammering; assault on a person, "a roughing up"

Puteolānā: Puteolānus-a-um, *adj.,* of or pert. to Puteolī, modern Pozzuoli, a prosperous seaport town near Naples; here "at Puteoli"
bonīs: "property"
Pallae: Palla, Pallae, *m.,* Palla, an unknown individual
vellem (ut) dictum esset: *vellem* is a potential subjunctive in a present hopeless wish: "I should have wished"; *dictum esset* is a substantive clause without *ut* (as usual after *vellem*), 78n., Ben. 296.1a, Ben. 280.4.

265. **Diōne: Diō, Diōnis,** *m.,* Dio

266. **exspectētis: exspectō** (1), wait for, expect; mood? Ben. 283.2.
quod: "considering that"
timet: timeō, timēre, timuī, fear, be afraid

267. **fatētur: fateor, fatērī, fassus sum,** accept as true, concede, acknowledge, admit; profess, declare
rēx: Ptolemy Auletes
adiūtor: adiūtor, adiūtōris, *m.,* helper, abetter, supporter; agent

268. **cōnscius: cōnscius-a-um,** *adj.,* sharing knowledge, privy, aware, in the know; *hence subst.,* an accomplice, accessory, confidant (Grant)
P. Asicius: prosecuted by the lawyer-poet C. Licinius Calvus (Catullus's friend), and successfully defended by Cicero, just before this trial.
iūdiciō: we say "in court" in English, but this abl. is in origin an abl. of separation, Ben. 214.1a.
līberātus: līberō (1), set free, release; absolve, acquit
quod: anticipates *id* in 270 (*quod* cannot here be a connecting rel., since we already have the conj. *igitur*)
igitur, *conj.,* and so, therefore, then, accordingly

269. **ut [is] quī....**
commīsit: committō, committere, commīsī, commissum, combine, unite; commit, do, perpetrate
neget: negō (1), say no, say that...not; deny, refuse
absolūtus sit: absolvō, absolvere, absolvī, absolūtum, loosen; set free, detach; absolve, acquit

270. **id:** resumptive, and not wholly unlike *id* at 110: both "collect" the preceding thought(s) in preparation for the main verb to come.
pertimēscat: pertimēscō, pertimēscere, pertimuī, become very much afraid of; deliberative subj., Ben. 277.

nōn modo...vērum etiam: = *nōn modo...sed etiam.*

ā factī (suspiciōne): Shackleton Bailey would emend to *ā factō,* which better suits the sense of this passage (and is supported by *factī... suspiciōne* in 272–273 as well), since the antithesis should properly be between *factum* and *suspiciō* rather than between *factum* and *cōnscientia.*

cōnscientiae: cōnscientia, cōnscientiae, *f.,* joint knowledge, complicity; moral sense, conscience

271. **sī...invidia:** that is, Asicius had profited politically from the revelation that Ptolemy Auletes was behind Dio's murder, even if some disgrace attached to his being brought to trial.

  plūs: plūs, plūris, *n.,* more; *hence acc. sg.* **plūs** *as adv.,* more; *plūs* is a neuter noun in the singular, usually followed by a partitive gen., but an adj. in the plural.

  prōfuit: prōsum, prōdesse, prōfuī, be of use, help; be helpful, advantageous or beneficial, profit *(+ dat.)*

272. **oberit: obsum, obesse, obfuī,** be a disadvantage, do harm, hinder; hurt, injure *(+ dat.)*

  nōn modo...nē...quidem: "not only *not...,* but not even...," Ben. 343.2a. But to get good English, put the negative once with the verb *est aspersus:* "who was not besmirched...." The logic of the Latin construction is that the negative *nōn,* joined to the verb, does double duty.

273. **est aspersus: aspergō, aspergere, aspersī, aspersum,** strew, (be)sprinkle, spatter; besmirch, disgrace, sully [**ad** + **spargō**]

  (ch. 24) **At...līberātus:** an imagined prosecutorial objection. You may want to put quotation marks around this sentence, and begin your translation with "But, you will say that..."

274. **praevāricātiōne: praevāricātiō, praevāricātiōnis,** *f.,* technical term for secret and illegal collusion between prosecution and defense [**praevāricārī,** collude, from **prae** + **vāricārī,** straddle]; evidently the prosecution had expected this line of argument, and had claimed that Asicius's acquittal did not matter because of *praevāricātiō* at his trial.

  perfacile: perfacilis-is-e, *adj.,* very easy

  istī locō: dat. w. *respondēre;* cf. Gk. *topos,* meaning both "place" and "point."

275. **praesertim,** *adv.,* especially, above all, particularly

276.   **optimam:** a good example of how the Latin superlative must sometimes be translated "very...," rather than with "-est."

      cuicuimodī: "of whatever kind," for *cuiuscuiusmodī,* perhaps considered too awkward [**quisquis** + **modus**]; an asterisk in front of a form indicates an extrapolated, hypothetical, or otherwise non-occurring form.

277.   **sit:** mood?

      ā suā [causā].

      (causam Asicī) esse sēiunctam: sēiungō, sēiungere, sēiūnxī, sēiūnctum, disjoin, separate; distinguish, dissociate; *[causam] sēiūnctam* would have had a legal ring, since *coniūnctae causae* is a legal term denoting cases in which one serves as a precedent for the other; hence *sēiūncta* = "not a precedent."

278.   **doctissimī: doceō, docēre, docuī, doctum,** tell, inform; demonstrate, show; teach, instruct; *hence part.* **doctus-a-um** *as adj.,* learned, well-versed, experienced

      rēctissimīs: regō, regere, rēxī, rēctum, direct, guide; manage, control; rule, govern; *hence part.* **rēctus-a-um** *as adj.,* straight, direct; correct, right; upright, refined, virtuous

279.   **optimīs artibus:** *ars* is often used of moral qualities, almost equivalent to *virtūs* (Austin at 24.17).

      praeditī: praeditus-a-um, *adj.,* endowed or equipped with, possessing, "with the advantage of" (Austin at 24.17) (+ *abl.*). The thematic treatment of 278–279 is chiastic: *rēctissimīs studiīs* answers *doctissimī,* and *optimīs artibus* answers *hūmānissimī.*

      Titus Gāiusque Copōniī: not much is known about these two brothers, except what is mentioned here. Dio of Alexandria had stayed at Titus's house in Rome. Supply *sēiūnctam esse causam putant* as predicate.

280.   **mortem: mors, mortis,** *f.,* death

      cum: take with *tum etiam,* "both...and also."

      doctrīnae: doctrīna, doctrīnae, *f.,* teaching, instruction, training; learning, knowledge; picks up *doctissimī* above.

281.   **hūmānitātis: hūmānitās, hūmānitātis,** *f.,* culture, civilization; education, refinement; kindness, humane behavior; picks up *hūmānissimī* above.

      hospitiō: hospitium, hospitī, *n.,* hospitality; guest friendship; lodgings, guest room, inn

      tenēbantur: teneō, tenēre, tenuī, tentum, hold, possess; hold fast, restrain, keep back

282. **apud,** *prep. w. acc.,* at, near, by, with, among; before, in the presence of; at the house of (like Fr. *chez*)
erat...cognitus: cognōscō, cognōscere, cognōvī, cognitum, learn; *(perf.),* know, recognize

283. **Alexandrīae: Alexandrīa, Alexandrīae,** *f.,* Alexandria; here locative case. The locative is an old case expressing "place in which." During the classical period it was used almost exclusively with the names of towns and small islands, and with the phrases "in the country" (*rūre*) and "at home" (*domī*). For most other kinds of nouns, its function was supplanted by the ablative, Ben. 232. Its forms are as follows:

	sg.	pl.	sg.	pl.
1st decl.	*-ae*	*-īs*	*Rōmae*	*Athēnīs*
2nd decl.	*-ī*	*-īs*	*Corinthī*	*Delphīs*
3rd decl.	*-e/-ī*	*-ibus*	*Karthāgine/Karthāginī*	*Gadibus*

splendōre: splendor, splendōris, *m.,* brightness, brilliance, luster; distinction, eminence; sumptuous lifestyle, lavish living, showiness; used in a different sense at 946. *Splendor* and its derivatives (*splendidus* at 34) are especially used as unofficial epithets of the equestrian order.
frāter: frāter, frātris, *m.,* brother

284. **prōductī erunt: prōdūcō, prōdūcere, prōdūxī, prōductum,** bring forward or out; advance, promote; prolong, continue; put off, postpone

285–311 (chs. 25–26). Cicero addresses the accusations and insinuations made by L. Herennius Balbus, a *subscrīptor* and final prosecution speaker, about whom we know little else. Evidently he delivered a moralizing diatribe against youthful excess, though Cicero has good cause to exaggerate its content. Cicero's treatment of Herennius is in some ways similar to his treatment of Atratinus (e.g., *familiārem,* complimenting his style, etc.); see 25n.

285 (ch. 25). **ergō,** *adv.,* accordingly, consequently, therefore, for that reason
removeantur: removeō, removēre, remōvī, remōtum, move back or away, remove; withdraw; mood and reason? Ben. 275.
aliquandō, *adv.,* at some time, at any time, once; sometimes, occasionally; at last, finally; "at least"
in quibus: antecedent is *ea.*

286. **veniāmus: veniō, venīre, vēnī, ventum,** come; mood and reason? Ben. 282.

287.   **animadvertī: animadvertō, animadvertere, animadvertī, animadver-
sum,** turn or give the mind to, take notice of, pay attention to; notice, perceive, observe [**animus** + **advertō,** sometimes written as two
words: *animum advertō* or *animōs advertō*]

288.   **perattentē: perattentus-a-um,** *adj.,* very attentive; note the strong last
position: "very attentively indeed."
in quō: "in which connection," "on which point"
etsī, *conj.,* although, even if
magnā: magnus-a-um, *adj.,* great, large; **magnā ex parte:** "in a great/
large degree/extent"

289.   **dīcendī genere quōdam:** "a particular quality of style"; *dīcendī genus*
denotes literary or oratorical style (picked up again at 299).

290.   **nōn numquam:** Lat. likes such double negatives.
verēbar: vereor, verērī, veritus sum, revere, be in awe of; fear, dread,
be afraid. For other examples of the fearing construction, compare
timēre nē (310–311), *verear nē* (417), *metuet nē* (749), *timēbant nē* (827),
Ben. 296.2.

Clauses of fearing are actually wishes subordinated to an intro-
ductory verb of fearing, and one fears the reverse of the wish, i.e.,
that the wish will not come true. Hence, ignore the *nē* in transl. A
simple demonstration:

Nē hoc faciat!	+	**Timeō!**
May he not do this!	+	*I fear (that he will)!*

becomes:
Timeō nē hoc faciat!
I fear that he will do this!

When *ut* follows *timēre* or a similar verb of fearing, the negative
sense must be supplied:

Utinam hoc faciat!	+	**Timeō!**
May he do this!	+	*I fear (that he will* not*)!*

becomes:
Timeō ut hoc faciat!
I fear that he will not *do this!*

subtīliter: subtīlis-is-e, *adj.,* fine, thin, delicate; precise, accurate; keen, perceptive; unadorned, simple, plain [**sub + tēla,** woven material]. *Subtīlis* is commonly used to describe the "plain" style of oratory.

crīminandum: crīminor (1), accuse, bring a charge against (maliciously), slander

inducta: indūcō, indūcere, indūxī, inductum, lead or bring in *(esp. onto a stage)*; induce, persuade

291. **sēnsim,** *adv.,* slowly, gradually; carefully, gently; little by little, imperceptibly

lēniter: lēnis-is-e, *adj.,* smooth, mild, gentle, easy, calm; gentle, mild, moderate, lenient [rel. to **lentus,** pliant]

accēderet: accēdō, accēdere, accessī, accessum, go or come near to; approach with hostility, attack; happen, befall

291–296. A mapping of this sentence:

Dīxit enim	multa dē luxuriē,	
	multa dē libīdine,	
	multa dē vitiīs iuventūtis,	
	multa dē mōribus	
et, quī	in reliquā vītā	mītis esset
	et in hāc suāvitāte humānitātis quā prope iam dēlectantur omnēs versārī periūcundē solēret,	

fuit   in hāc causā pertristis quīdam $\begin{cases} \text{patruus} \\ \text{cēnsor,} \\ \text{magister;...} \end{cases}$

292. **luxuriē: luxuriēs, luxuriēī,** *f.,* lush growth of vegetation, fruitfulness; excessively rich living, dissipation [**luxus,** extravagance]

iuventūtis: iuventūs, iuventūtis, *f.,* young men, the youth; period of youth

293. **mōribus: mōs, mōris,** *m.,* way, manner, habit; custom, practice, usage; *(pl.)* virtuous habits, ethics, "character"

quī: Herennius; **quī...esset:** rel. clause of characteristic with an accessory notion of concession, Ben. 283.3b: translate "..., although he is mild..., and although he is accustomed...."; note the pres. transl. of *esset* and *solēret.*

reliquā: reliquus-a-um, *adj.,* the rest of, the remaining; **in reliquā vītā:** "otherwise."

mītis: mītis-is-e, *adj.,* succulent, sweet; mild, placid, calm; kindly, indulgent

hāc: "this that we see round us," "familiar," "usual"

294. **suāvitāte: suāvitās, suāvitātis,** *f.,* pleasantness, agreeability; attraction, attractiveness, charm [**suāvis,** pleasant, agreeable]
    prope: take as an adv. modifying *omnēs.*
    dēlectantur: dēlectō (1), delight, charm, amuse; *(pass.)* be delighted by, delight in, take pleasure in *(+ abl.)*
    versārī...in (294): here nearly = "to display" (Austin at 25.9); cf. *versārī in* above at 38 with a different meaning.

295. **periūcundē: periūcundus-a-um,** *adj.,* very welcome or agreeable
    pertristis: pertristis-is-e, *adj.,* very sad or mournful; thoroughly austere, severe, or stern
    quīdam: "shall we say?"
    patruus: patruus, patruī, *m.,* father's brother, paternal uncle (proverbially stern, critical, and censorious, especially in Roman comedy)

296. **cēnsor: cēnsor, cēnsōris,** *m.,* a censor; severe critic, moralizer [**cēnseō,** value, estimate]. The *cēnsor* was a Roman magistrate responsible for public leases and for the maintenance of good public morals; the term was then applied to a grim moralizer. Cicero describes the *cēnsor* as *magister mōrum (epistulae ad familiārēs,* 3.13.2).
    magister: magister, magistrī, *m.,* master, director; teacher, schoolmaster [**magis,** greater]; note *asyndeton* (Gk. "lack of connectives").
    obiurgāvit: obiurgō (1), scold, castigate, harangue; cf. *obiurgātiō* at 313; *iurgī* at 357, *obiurget* at 390.
    sīcut, *conj.,* as, just as, in the same way as
    sīcut nēminem umquam parēns [obiurgāvit].

297. **incontinentiā: incontinentia, incontinentiae,** *f.,* lack of self-restraint, self-indulgence, wild living [**in-** priv. + **contineō,** restrain]
    intemperantiā: intemperantia, intemperantiae, *f.,* lack of moderation, extravagance, excess; arrogance, impudence, insolence [**temperō,** practice self-restraint]

298. **disseruit:** "he lectured on," "he discoursed about"; in a context like this, the finite verb can have a "stuffy," almost professorial ring (but contrast the part. *disertī* above at 172).
    Quid quaeritis, iūdicēs?: "What more can I say?" (Englert, p. 44).
    ignōscēbam: the imperfect often denotes the start of an action *(inceptive:* "I began to excuse"), Ben. 260.3. The phrasing of the entire section

reveals Cicero's concern over the impact of Herennius's speech, which he must have sensed made a great impression on the jurors (so *audīrī ā vōbīs meum familiārem, L. Herennium, perattentē* at 288, *vōbīs attentē audientibus* here).

attentē: attendō, attendere, attendī, attentum, pay close attention, note well; *hence part.* **attentus-a-um** *as adj.,* attentive, heedful, with concentration

299. **proptereā,** *adv.,* for that reason, consequently, therefore; Cicero often writes *proptereā quod,* "because," with the same meaning as *quod,* "because."

-met, *encl. particle;* this little suffix emphasizes the pronoun to which it attaches, often with contrastive force (here the contrast is with *vōbīs* in 298).

triste: see 149n.

illud: modifies *genus;* translate the entire phrase "that very (*tam*) grim and harsh kind of oratory that Herennius employed."

300. **asperum: asper, aspera, asperum,** *adj.,* harsh, rough; severe, stern

horrēbam: horreō, horrēre, horruī, be rough or bristly; shudder, shiver, tremble at; be horrified by. Austin takes *horrēbam* in its physical meaning and so "probably ironical" (at 25.13); the passage is certainly mock-comic, and the reader should use her or his mind's eye to imagine Cicero's possible facial expressions and body language as he uttered these words.

301 (ch. 26). **movēbat: moveō, movēre, mōvī, mōtum,** set in motion, move; stir up, excite; affect, influence, "touch"; distress, trouble

fuisse...praetūrae: implied indirect statement: start with "namely, that Caelius..." after translating *quae mē minus movēbat.* Cicero seems to be quoting directly from Herennius's speech; Herennius had evidently started off (*prīma pars*) by positing a close relationship between Caelius and his father (Bestia), followed by the ambitious Caelius's perfidious betrayal in his quest for a career-making prosecution. Probably Herennius exaggerated Caelius's friendship with Bestia (ambitious Roman politicians do not go places by turning *amīcī* into *inimīcī*); here, in turn, Cicero is very probably puffing up Herennius's remarks in order to increase the jury's skepticism at the prosecution's lack of witnesses.

Bestiae: L. Calpurnius Bestia was Atratinus's father; until Münzer showed this in 1909, the passage's full impact could not be understood. Recall that Cicero himself had no quarrel with Bestia (81–83;

932–934), and that, in fact, just seven weeks earlier (on February 11), he had successfully defended Bestia from prosecution by Caelius on a charge of *ambitus.* Note *meō necessāriō:* as the son at 25, so the father here. One of the most impressive aspects of this speech is how dexterously Cicero tries to balance the conflicting claims on his personal and political loyalties.

No other *Semprōniī Atrātīnī* are recorded after the fourth century B.C. Austin (pp. 154–155) believes that Bestia's son (whose *nōmen* and *cognōmen* also would have been "Calpurnius Bestia") "proba-bly...was adopted by some member of the Sempronian *gēns* who had himself revived the name of Atratinus and did not wish his branch of the family to become extinct" (p. 155). Until the time of Sulla, the person adopted assumed all the names of the adopter, plus his original *cognomen* with -*ānus* suffixed. Therefore, upon adoption by L. (presumably) Sempronius Atratinus, Calpurnius Bestia would have become L. Sempronius Atratinus Calpurnianus; the lack of Calpurnianus here may be because Atratinus was one of those who did not use the traditional formula, or because Cicero is being brief.

302. **cēnā(vi)sse: cēnō** (1), have dinner, dine
ventitā(vi)sse: ventitō (1), come or go often or habitually [freq. of **veniō**]. Cf. Cat. 8.4: *ventitābās quō puella dūcēbat,* "you always used to go wherever the girl led you."
domum: case and reason? Ben. 182.1b.

303. **praetūrae: praetūra, praetūrae,** *f.,* office of praetor, praetorship; bid or candidacy for the praetorship
perspicuē: perspicuus-a-um, *adj.,* clear, transparent; evident, plain, unmistakable

304. **etenim,** *conj.,* for truly, since indeed, for the fact is that
ūnā, *adv.,* in one group, together; at the same time, in concert [**ūnus,** one]
quī aut...aut quibus...: = *aut quī...aut quibus...*
necesse, *indecl. adj.,* compulsory, unavoidable, inevitable; indispensible, essential

305. **neque vērō...videantur** (311): Caelius and Herennius had been members of a *sodālitās* called the *Lupercī.* Whatever Herennius had said, Cicero insinuates that the Luperci had fallen to low estate, since its brothers not only attack one another, but do so by accusing one another of membership! Independent evidence confirms Cicero's allegation.

commovet: echoes *movēbat* above at 301.
quod: rel. pron. modifying *illud*
sibi: take with *sodālem.*

306. **Lupercīs: Lupercus, Lupercī,** a priest taking part in the *Lupercālia,* a festival (for promoting fertility and averting evil forces) held on the Palatine Hill on February 15 [perhaps **lupus,** wolf + **arceō,** protect]. During this festival, the Luperci, with painted faces and wearing only an animal skin, paraded about the Palatine Hill striking women with strips of goat skin in order to ensure their fertility (of which the goat is a symbol).

306–311. The structure of these lines is as follows:

Fera quaedam sodālitās et plānē pastōricia atque agrestis germānōrum Lupercōrum [est],

    quōrum   coitiō illa silvestris ante   est īnstitūta

                         quam hūmānitās atque lēgēs   [sunt īnstitūtae],

sī quidem nōn modo nōmina dēferunt inter sē sodālēs

        sed etiam   commemorant   sodālitātem in accūsandō,

ut, nē quis id forte nesciat, timēre videantur!

fera: ferus-a-um, *adj.,* wild, undomesticated, untamed, not tame, wild; barbarous, rough, uncivilized; aggressive, ferocious
quaedam: *quīdam* usually "tones down" an adjective it is used with ("a certain," "what might be called a"); here it is used in the secondary, intensifying sense "quite a," "a very" (Austin at 26.21); delimits *fera* (the preceding word, as usual).
sodālitās: sodālitās, sodālitātis, *f.,* brotherhood, companionship; association, society (for religious purposes, for feasting, or for illegal political activity). The *sodālitātēs* (more often *sodālicia*) were a serious problem in the late Republic, see 180n.

307. **plānē: plānus-a-um,** *adj.,* level, flat; clear, distinct; *hence adv.* **plānē,** distinctly, intelligibly; completely, thoroughly; *plānē pastōricia* = "utterly like a bunch of country bumpkins."
pastōricia: pastōricius-a-um, *adj.,* of or pert. to a shepherd, pastoral [**pastor,** shepherd]
agrestis: agrestis-is-e, *adj.,* of or pert. to the fields, rustic; countrified, rude
germānōrum: germānus-a-um, *adj.,* of or pert. to a brother and sister who have the same parents; real, genuine

308. **coitiō: coitiō, coitiōnis,** *f.,* a gathering, assembly; political combination, coalition, faction, conspiracy [**cum** + **eō**]; Austin (at 26.23) suggests "pack," which well-suits the context.

  silvestris: silvestris-is-e, *adj.,* of or pert. to woods, wooded; rural, pastoral

  ante...quam, *conj.,* before; the separation of a compound word into its component parts is called *tmēsis* [Gk. "a cutting," fr. **temnō,** to cut].

  est īnstitūta: īnstituō, īnstituere, īnstituī, īnstitūtum, put in place, set up, construct; establish, introduce, found; teach, educate, bring up [**in** + **statuō**]

309. **sī quidem,** *conj.,* if indeed; since, because

  nōmina: nōmen, nōminis, *n.,* name

  dēferunt: dēferō, dēferre, dētulī, dēlātum, bring or carry down or away; give, grant; report. Since there was no public prosecutor in ancient Rome, anyone who desired to prosecute someone else reported that person (*nōmen dēferre,* "to give information against"; the procedure is called the *nōminis dēlātiō*) to the official prescribed by the law under which the defendant was accused. In serious cases, the official would be the *praetor urbānus* (if both plaintiff and defendant were Roman citizens) or the *praetor peregrīnus* (if either plaintiff or defendant was not a Roman citizen); less often the official would be an aedile.

  The acceptance of the charge by the presiding magistrate (*nōmen accipere* or *recipere*), the assignment of attorneys to the case, and the setting of a date for a trial by jury constitute the indictment.

  inter, *prep. w. acc.,* between, among, amid

310. **commemorant: commemorō** (1), call to mind, recollect, recall; mention, relate; a free transl. of *etiam commemorant sodālitātem in accūsandō:* "they even mention their common membership as part of the indictment!"

  ut...: result clause (Ben. 284); take in the order *ut videantur timēre nē quis id forte nesciat.*

311. **nesciat: nesciō** (4), not know, be ignorant of; be unable to do, not to have learned; mood? Ben. 296.2.

  timēre: timeō, timēre, timuī, fear, be afraid

312–353 (chs. 27–30): Having dispensed in just a few minutes with Clodius's speech, Cicero returns to the arguments of Herennius Balbus.

312 (ch. 27). **omittō: omittō, omittere, omīsī, omissum,** disregard, put aside, release; omit mention of, pass over [**ob** + **mittō**]

A good ex. of the rhetorical device *praeteritiō* [**praetereō,** pass by], by which an orator deals with a matter by referring to it obliquely and saying he will not deal with it.

mē magis mōvērunt: answers *mē minus movēbat* in 301.

313.   **dēliciārum: dēliciae, dēliciārum,** *f.,* allurement, charm, delight; dissolute behavior, indulgence, dissipation; luxury, comfort; darling, sweetheart, beloved, "pet"

obiurgātiō: obiurgātiō, obiurgātiōnis, *f.,* reprimand, rebuke; a blaming, a scolding; cf. *obiurgāvit* above at 296n.

lēnior: lēnis-is-e, *adj.,* smooth, soft; gentle, calm, mild; the reading given is Clark's, as usual; he was trying to make sense out of P's *et eā lēnior.* Clark's text can suit the context only if *etiam* is ignored in translation and *lēnior* is taken as "rather calm," "rather subdued," "on the quiet side" (in comparison with Cicero's description of P. Clodius's harangue, to be described and dismissed below).

However, while "[a]n *obiurgātiō* does not necessarily imply violent anger" (Austin at 27.1), *lēnior* is hardly the word to go with the tenor of 291–300. Σ (the *Cluniacēnsis,* see Austin, pp. xvii–xx) read *et eā aliēnior* for *et eā lēnior,* which led Clark to propose (but not to admit to the Oxford text) *et ā causā aliēnior,* "and quite unrelated to our case," which gives excellent sense.

plūsque: *plūs* takes a genitive to complete its meaning when used as a noun.

314.   **disputātiōnis: disputātiō, disputātiōnis,** *f.,* discussion, debate, argumentation, fine reasoning

quō, *conj.,* for which reason; often, as here, with a comparative

315.   **nam:** introduces a sentence explaining the previous assertion.

P. Clōdius: one of the prosecutors (but not P. Clodius Pulcher; see 195n.).

amīcus meus: not, as English speakers might expect, a courteous "my friend" or "my colleague" directed toward a fellow member of the profession (for this Cicero would have used *vir optimus* or *vir clārissimus*), but a wry "my political supporter." While pointedly amusing, since this P. Clodius was a Clodian retainer, it also underscores the political background and implications of the trial (which are not to be ignored).

sē...iactāret: iactō (1), throw, hurl; *(with sē)* boast; gesticulate, make an extravagant display, conduct oneself wildly, behave boisterously; there is perhaps some contrast with the image of the youthful but controlled orator at 120.

316. **vehementissimē: vehemēns, vehementis,** *adj.,* energetic, vigorous; forceful, strenuous; furious, impetuous
īnflammātus: īnflammō, set fire to, set afire; excite, stir up

317. **tristissimīs verbīs:** Clodius's speech probably also moralized; for the special meaning of *tristis* in this context, see 149n.
tametsī, *conj.,* even if, although, even though
probābam: probō (1), make or find good, approve; show, demonstrate

318. **ēloquentiam: ēloquentia, ēloquentiae,** *f.,* speaking ability; eloquence [**ēloquor,** speak well]
pertimēscēbam: pertimēscō, pertimēscere, pertimuī, become very much afraid of, fear greatly
aliquot, *indecl. indef. num. adj.,* some; several; modifies *causīs.*

319. **frustrā,** *adv.,* in vain, pointlessly, to no avail; mistakenly, needlessly
lītigantem: lītigō (1), argue, dispute, quarrel; go to law, litigate, argue a case [**līs, lītis,** quarrel; legal case]; Cicero sneers that he is not afraid of Clodius's lawyering because he is so often an unsuccessful advocate.
Balbe: Herennius; it is not unusual for Romans to address and/or refer to an individual first by his *nōmen* (second or "gentile" name), as Cicero had referred to L. Herennius Balbus at 288, and then by the *cognōmen* (third name), or vice-versa; see Austin, p. 148, 148n1.

320. **precāriō: precārius-a-um,** *adj.,* obtained by request or entreaty; *hence adv.* **precāriō,** by entreaty, by permission, by one's leave [**precor,** beg]; *precāriō, sī licet, sī fās est* is melodramatic ("mock solemn," Austin, p. 165, at 27.8).
licet: licet, licēre, licuit *or* **licitum est,** it is allowed or permitted (+ *dat.*); "one may"
fās, *n. indecl.,* divine command, divine law; that which is right, fitting, not forbidden. In contrast to *fās* is *iūs, iūris,* human law; lack of conformity to *fās* is *nefās*; lack of conformity to *iūs* is *iniūria*; originally *fās* and *iūs* were separate spheres of Roman criminal law. For the distinction (and their later conflation), see Tellegen-Couperus, pp. 17–18; Wolff, pp. 50–52.

Cicero's comments here are humorous: Herennius Balbus had given such a tirade against sin and immorality that Cicero pretends it may be a *nefās* to defend Caelius.

321. **convīvium: convīvium, convīvī,** *n.,* dinner-party, banquet, feast [**vīvō,** live]

   renuerit: renuō, renuere, renuī, refuse by a motion of the head, decline, turn down [**re** + ***nuō,** nod]. The verbs *renuerit, fuerit, sūmpserit* and *vīderit* are subj. in rel. clauses of characteristic, Ben. 283. What figure of speech is *quī...quī...quī...quī?* Ben. 350.11b.

   hortīs: "grounds" of an estate, "gardens" of a manor house; cf. 443, 477, with Austin's note at 36.27.

   unguenta: unguentum, unguentī, *n.,* ointment, perfume [**unguō,** anoint]

   sūmpserit: sūmō, sūmere, sūmpsī, sūmptum, take, obtain [**sub** + **emō**]

322. **Bāiās: Bāiae, Bāiārum,** *f.,* Baiae, a town on an inlet of the *Sinus Cūmānus* (Bay of Cumae, the modern Bay of Naples), and probably the port of *Cūmae,* the oldest Greek settlement in Italy (ca. 740 B.C.). Baiae's temperate climate, natural beauty, and easy accessibility made it a kind of Monte Carlo for the ancient jet-set, and it was proverbially associated with excess and vice. During the imperial period, malaria (already noted as a problem in Cicero's time) and earthquakes (Aenaria, Prochyta, and Vesuvius are only a few miles away) diminished Baiae's appeal.

   vīderit: "has gone to see"

322–327. The structure of these lines is as follows:

Equidem multōs		et vīdī	in hāc cīvitāte
		et audīvī,	
	nōn modo	quī	prīmōribus labris gustāssent genus hoc vītae
		et	extrēmīs, ut dīcitur, digitīs attigissent,
	sed	quī	tōtam adulēscentiam voluptātibus dēdidissent,
			ēmersisse aliquandō
	et sē ad bonam frūgem, ut dīcitur,		recēpisse
	gravīsque hominēs atque inlustrīs		fuisse.

Austin (at 28.10) believes that this passage may obliquely allude to Julius Caesar's reputedly dissolute youth (so also 534–545).

(ch. 28). **multōs:** subject of *ēmersisse* in 325.

323. **prīmōribus: prīmōris-is-e,** *adj.,* the front part of, the surface of, the tip of
labrīs: labrum, labrī, *n.,* lip; here *prīmōribus labrīs* = "lightly," "superficially."
gustā(vi)ssent: gustō (1), taste a little of, enjoy; have a little knowledge
or experience of

---

324. **extrēmīs: extrēmus-a-um,** *adj.,* outermost, utmost; edge or tip of; final, last
ut dīcitur: Cicero almost asks for pardon for using a cliché like *extrēmīs
digitīs; prīmōribus labrīs, ad bonam frūgem* (324–326), and *diēs dēficiat*
(335) are also commonplaces.
digitīs: digitus, digitī, *m.,* finger
attigissent: attingō, attingere, attigī, attactum, touch, just barely touch;
reach, arrive at [**ad** + **tangō**]

325. **voluptātibus: voluptās, voluptātis,** *f.,* delight, enjoyment, pleasure
dēdidissent: dēdō, dēdere, dēdidī, dēditum, give up, surrender, yield;
(+ *sē*) give oneself over to or apply oneself to (an activity); devote
one's *acc.* to *dat.* [**dē** + **dō**]
ēmersisse: ēmergō, ēmergere, ēmersī, ēmersum, arise, emerge (from
water), come forth; extricate oneself from, get clear of
aliquandō: "at last" (Englert, p. 46)

326. **frūgem: frux, frūgis,** *f.,* fruit of the earth, crop, grain; maturity, fruition;
morality, virtue, excellence of mind
recēpisse: recipiō, recipere, recēpī, receptum, take or draw back, receive, accept; regain, recover; *ad [bonam] frūgem sē recipere* = "to reform oneself." Quintilian reports that this phrase was in Caelius's
speech in his own defense; and although it is a standard phrase,
Cicero may be echoing Caelius's own description of his youth.

327. **concessū,** *adv.,* by concession, with leave, by permission [**concēdō,** yield].
This word is formed from *concessum,* the supine of *concēdō;* the other
cases are wanting, as frequently in fourth decl. nouns formed from
participles, Ben. 57.1.
huic aliquī lūdus aetātī: chiastic. The term *chiasmus* describes an arrangement of words in which antithetical pairs (whether logical or
grammatical) are in reverse order, Ben. 350.11c. When written

huic   aliquī

X

lūdus   aetātī,

the parts that go together grammatically will connect to form the
Gk. letter *X,* or *chī.* See 383 for another ex.

aliquī: aliquī, aliquae *or* aliqua, aliquod, *indef. adj.,* some

328. lūdus: possibly "love-affair" (though not necessarily): *lūdum dare* + dat. is "to allow a person to enjoy himself," "to give a person indulgence," "to treat a person leniently."
profundit: profundō, profundere, profūdī, profūsum, pour forth, shed; spend, squander; discharge, bring forth, release; develop, produce

329. ita, *adv.,* thus, so, in this way, in such a way
ērumpunt: ērumpō, ērumpere, ērūpī, ēruptum, break open, cause X to burst forth; break out, rush forward
labefactent: labefactō (1), make unsteady, loosen; weaken, undermine; ruin, wreck [labefaciō, from labō, be shaky]

330. ēvertant: ēvertō, ēvertere, ēvertī, ēversum, upset, overthrow, overturn; destroy, ruin, wreck
tolerābilēs: tolerābilis-is-e, *adj.,* tolerable, bearable, endurable; passable, just acceptable
habērī: "to be considered," as *habitam esse* and *habērī* at 40–41 (ch. 29). tū: Cicero turns to Herennius Balbus.

331. vidēbāre: = *vidēbāris; -re* is commonly used as the second pers. sg. pass. personal ending, for *-ris.*

332. cōnflāre: cf. 139n.; here, with *invidiam,* it means "to engineer," "to trump up," "to manufacture prejudice against."
silentium: silentium, silentī, *n.,* stillness, silence, quiet; quiet; "silent attention" (Gardner). Through Cicero's repetition of the same theme several times, we can see how worried he was that Herennius's comments had been damaging, and we see further Cicero's methodical and highly rhetorical attempts to deal with this problem.
est...tribūtum: tribuō, tribuere, tribuī, tribūtum, divide out, allot, apportion; give, grant, confer; allow, concede

334. prōpositō: prōpōnō, prōpōnere, prōposuī, prōpositum, put forth, put on view, display; declare, relate, tell
vitiīs: vitium, vitī, *n.,* defect, fault, shortcoming; crime, moral failure, vice
cōgitābāmus: cōgitō (1), consider thoroughly, ponder, think *(here with dē)*; intend, plan

335. **dēficiat: dēficiō, dēficere, dēfēcī, dēfectum,** abandon, forsake, leave; fail, be wanting

dēficiat, sī...cōner: kind of condition? Ben. 303.

quae: not indefinite, as might be expected after *sī* (cf. 1), but rather a rel. pron. to be taken after *exprōmere.*

sententiam: sententia, sententiae, *f.,* opinion, thought; idea, notion, topic

336. **cōner: cōnor** (1), try, attempt, endeavor

exprōmere: exprōmō, exprōmere, exprōmpsī, exprōmptum, bring or take out (from a store), produce, display; disclose, reveal, state [**ex + prōmō,** bring out]

corruptēlīs: corruptēla, corruptēlae, *f.,* moral corruption or degeneracy; seduction, sexual misconduct; corruption, bribery [**corrumpō,** destroy, ruin]

adulteriīs: adulterium, adulterī, *n.,* illicit sexual activity, adultery [**adulter,** illicit lover]

337. **protervitāte: protervitās, protervitātis,** *f.,* outrageous conduct, impudence [**protervus,** impudent, shameless]

immēnsa: immēnsus-a-um, *adj.,* immeasurable, boundless, vast [**in + mētior,** measure]; a good ex. of *hyperbole,* as commonly with this word.

ut: "granted that," "even if" (*tamen* in the main clause shows that this *ut* must be concessive (not very common, but not rare either), Ben. 308, G&L 608.

reum nēminem: = *nūllum reum; nēmō* can be used as an adj. meaning "no," "not any," in place of *nūllus.*

338. **rēs...ipsa:** "the general topic itself," i.e., the *vitia,* and other associated evils, just mentioned.

cōpiōsē: cōpiōsus-a-um, *adj.,* well-supplied, abundant, rich; eloquent [**cōpia**]

339–344. The structure of these lines is as follows:

Sed vestrae sapientiae, iūdicēs, est nōn abdūcī ab reō

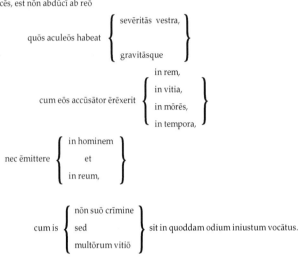

quōs aculeōs habeat {
  sevēritās vestra,
  gravitāsque
}

cum eōs accūsātor ērēxerit {
  in rem,
  in vitia,
  in mōrēs,
  in tempora,
}

nec ēmittere {
  in hominem
  et
  in reum,
}

cum is {
  nōn suō crīmine
  sed
  multōrum vitiō
} sit in quoddam odium iniustum vocātus.

339. **vestrae sapientiae:** case and reason? Ben. 198.2

340. **abdūcī: abdūcō, abdūcere, abdūxī, abductum,** lead or take away; distract, divert, sidetrack

nec: take with *ēmittere* in 342.

aculeōs: aculeus, aculeī, *m.,* sting (of an insect); something painful, a cutting remark [dim. of **acus,** a pin]; this word is common in judicial contexts in reference to oratory, testimony, or (as here) a jury's verdict; take *quōs aculeōs* as *aculeōs, quōs,* where *aculeōs* is object of *ēmittere* in 342.

habeat: mood and reason?

sevēritās: sevēritās, sevēritātis, *f.,* sternness, severity; austerity, self-discipline, sobriety

gravitās: gravitās, gravitātis, *f.,* weight, heaviness; sternness, strictness; dignity, seriousness, responsibility. Gaffney has interesting comments on the uses of *sevēritās* and *gravitās* in this section.

341. **eōs:** = *aculeōs.*

ērēxerit: ērigō, ērigere, ērēxī, ērēctum, set up, lift up, raise; excite, rouse, stimulate

in: "against"

rem: "a general topic," like *rēs* in 338

342. **ēmittere: ēmittō, ēmittere, ēmīsī, ēmissum,** send out or forward, dispatch; let fly, shoot (weapons); let go, free; *aculeum ēmittere* is another military image: "to send forth a projectile."

343. **sit:** take with *vocātus* in 344. Special meaning here?
iniustum: iniustus-a-um, *adj.,* unfair, unjust; undeserved, unmerited

344 (ch. 30). **tuae:** Cicero returns to Herennius Balbus.
oportet: oportet, oportēre, oportuit, it is proper, it is right, one *(acc.)* ought to or should; note mood of *ut oportet* before translating.

345. **erat...meum:** "it was mine" + inf., "I could be": *erat* is unusual and highly idiomatic: it basically expresses a present unreal condition (here the protasis or *sī*-clause goes unexpressed): "I could be doing this, if I wanted to." We would expect *esset* according to the usual rule for pres. unreal conditions, Ben. 304.
dēprecārī: dēprecor (1), try to avert by entreaty; ask for [**prex,** entreaty, prayer]
vacātiōnem: vacātiō, vacātiōnis, *f.,* freedom from duty, immunity; freedom from blame, excuse. Actually, Cicero will spend a large chunk of his speech doing exactly what he here says he is not going to do.

346. **perfugiīs: perfugium, perfugī,** *n.,* refuge, shelter; excuse, defence

347. **ūtor: ūtor, ūtī, ūsus sum,** use, employ *(+ abl.)*
iūra: "privileges," i.e., the sorts of things young men can do and have their elders look the other way.
dīmittō: dīmittō, dīmittere, dīmīsī, dīmissum, send in different directions, send away; let go, dismiss; give up, forgo
tantum: "only"
ut...nē...nē...noceant: "that neither X nor Y should harm"; for *ut nē* see also 86n.

348. **invidia commūnis:** "general prejudice."

349. **libīdinum:** "debauched ways" (Austin at 30.9)
quam: antecedent is *invidia* in 348.

350. **peccāta: peccō** (1), make a mistake, go wrong, err, sin; *hence subst.* **peccātum, -ī,** *n.,* error, mistake; moral offense, misdemeanor, sin

351. **īdem: īdem, eadem, idem,** *demon. pron. and adj.,* (the) same (one, person, thing); *ego īdem* = "I likewise."
    postulō: postulō (1), claim, demand, request; summon before a court, accuse, prosecute
    quīn...respondeam: take after *nōn recūsō,* for *quīn* with verbs of doubting, hindering, preventing, etc., see 5n., Ben. 298.

352. **propriē: proprius-a-um,** *adj.,* one's own, particular, peculiar; characteristic of one; *hence adv.* **propriē,** peculiarly, characteristically; properly, rightly; here "in person" (Austin at 30.14)
    cōnferuntur: cōnferō, cōnferre, contulī, collātum, bring or put together, collect; carry, convey

353. **recūsō: recūsō** (1), object to, protest against, oppose; decline, refuse

At this point, Cicero has dealt and dispensed with all the arguments of the prosecutor and his two *subscrīptōrēs* except those pertaining to Clodia. The audience would expect him to end the *praemūnītiō* and start the *narrātiō.*

354–619 (chs. 30.16–50). Cicero now appears to embark on the long-delayed *narrātiō,* or statement of the facts of the case, which would properly have been given at 30 (ch. 3), just after the *exordium;* actually he immediately preempts the *narrātiō* by sliding back into the *praemūnītiō,* in order to confront more directly the damning accusations Herennius had lodged the day before and which Cicero could not ignore. Given the uproarious humor of this part of the speech, no doubt the audience was more than compensated for the further postponement (and virtual abandonment) of the usual *narrātiō.* It is wise to keep in mind that while this speech is a masterly, and in the crucible of the courtroom, successful, demonstration of ancient oratorical techniques—not to mention of the benefits of outright slander and evasion!—it is nonetheless structurally a quite atypical work, for which see the introduction.

354–384 (chs. 30.16–32): Cicero finally mentions Clodia by name, and avers that the prosecution case stems from her alone.

354 (XIII). **duo: duo, duae, duo,** *card. num. adj.,* two
    crīmina: remember *not* to translate as "crime"; see 10n.
    aurī: aurum, aurī, *n.,* gold; thing(s) made of gold; gold ornaments. At 634, we find the items referred to as *ornāmenta,* "objects used for embellishment," "accoutrements." The prosecution had (probably) contended that these would be used for, or sold to raise money for, bribes.

venēnī: venēnum, venēnī, *n.,* poison; a use of poison, poisoning
in quibus...versātur: for the idiom, see note under *versētur* at 11.
Antecedent of *quibus*?

355. **eadem:** determine fully the form and function of this pronominal adj.;
see *īdem* at 7.
persōna: persōna, persōnae, *f.,* an actor's mask; actor, dramatic character, personage; be wary of translating this with the English word
"person," for which the Lat. word is *homo.* (The etymology of the
word is unclear, but the sometimes-mentioned derivation from *per,*
"through" and *sonāre,* "to sound," in reference to the mask worn
by the characters in Roman drama, which the actors would, so to
speak, "sound through" during their speaking, is fanciful.) Is the
use of this word a subtle comparison of this case to the theatrical
performances the jury was missing out on?
aurum...dīcitur: cf. 623.
ā: does not express agency here. How do we know? Who is the agent?
Clōdiā: Cicero's first direct mention. The reference marks the end of a
ten-second *narrātiō.*

356. **quod:** introduces a rel. clause of purpose (Ben. 282.2), inasmuch as one
could substitute *ut* with little change in meaning. The relative more
tightly binds the clause to its antecedent.
ut dīcitur: *ut* followed by the indic. means "as" or "when," cf. *ut...dedit*
at 96; the phrase is here a parenthetical remark.
omnia sunt alia: = *omnia alia sunt,* which = *omnia cētera sunt* (Austin at
30.19).

357. **crīmina:** this is the closest the word gets to "crimes."
iurgī...quaestiōnis: gen.'s of quality or characteristic (Ben. 203.1), used
like the abl. of quality, for an ex. of which see *ingeniō,* etc., at 13.
iurgī: iurgium, iurgī, *n.,* altercation, dispute, quarrel; abuse; Grant's
"shouting match" is close to the sense.

358. **quaestiōnis: quaestiō, quaestiōnis,** *f.,* a seeking, a searching; investigation, judicial inquiry (like its Engl. derivative, "inquest," which has
a narrower meaning; also cf. *dē...quaerī* at 7–10)
adulter, impudīcus, sequester: no doubt referred to in the prosecution
speeches; see 285–353 (chs. 25–30.15), 179-189 (ch. 16).
adulter: adulter, adulterī, *m.,* illicit lover, paramour; the word has a
wider meaning than our "adulterer."

impudīcus: impudīcus–a–um, *adj.,* immoral, indecent; sometimes this word means "homosexual" [**in-**priv. + **pudīcus,** decent, from **pudet,** it shames]; here subst., "pervert," in a broad sense. You be the judge of the exact coloring of the word!

sequester: sequester, sequestrī, *m.,* third party acting as a depositary or escrow agent; the middleman with whom a bribe promised to a third party is left; as Austin hints at 30.20, the word is here used to connote a third form of illicit activity.

convīcium: convīcium, convīcī, *n.,* a loud cry, shout; abuse, insult; reproach [prob. **cum**-intensive + **vox,** voice]

360. **sedēs: sedēs, sedis,** *f.,* seat; foundation, support, basis [**sedeō,** sit]. Repeats sense of preceding *fundāmentum* for emphasis; *OLD* notes that the pl. usage of this word with no difference in meaning from sing. is common; the MSS do not agree on *nulla* vs. *nullae.*

contumēliōsae: contumēliōsus-a-um, *adj.,* abusive, insulting, reviling, rude [**contumēlia,** insulting and abusive language]; Englert's "outrageous" (p. 48) is a nice translation, as it gets in two ideas that the word can have and probably does have here: "out of bounds" and "without substance."

temere, *adv.,* blindly, by chance; accidentally, without purpose or cause; heedlessly, recklessly

361. **accūsātōre:** who is this?

auctōre: auctor, auctōris, *m./f.,* the person with authority or power of some kind, "the principal," in a wide variety of senses: attestor, voucher; advocate, supporter; expert, authority; witness; author, originator; bringer (of an accusation)

(ch. 31). **hōrum:** picks up after the digression at the end of ch. 30, and refers to the first set of charges mentioned at 354; *hic* is used to refer the listener or reader back to the most important subject at hand (G&L 305.3).

362. **auctōrem:** in a different sense from previous occurrence. Note again that Latin does not mind such repetition, and in fact seems to have courted it; cf. *habeant,* etc. at 38.

certum: "particular," "identifiable"

videō...videō...videō: *anaphora,* or repetition of a key word or phrase for emphasis.

363. **opus fuit:** *opus est* + abl. = "there is a need," "it is requisite," "it is essential."

sūmpsit: who is the understood subject?

sine teste: a formal loan of this kind would be legally carried out with a prescribed formula and in the presence of witnesses.

364. **quamdiū,** *interrog. and rel. adv.,* how long?; as long as, so long as, until
maximum: "most impressive"

365. **ēgregiae: ēgregius-a-um,** *adj.,* "not of the common herd," most uncommon, outstanding, extraordinary, first-rate, admirable, exemplary, distinguished [**ex-,** out of + **grex,** flock]. The use here is ironical (Austin at 31.26) and sarcastic, a sense reinforced by *cuiusdam.*
Necāre...attulit: spoken deadpan, reinforcing the *parataxis* (110n.).
necāre: necō (1), kill

366. **sollicitāvit: sollicitō** (1), agitate, disturb, harass; rouse, importune, incite, urge to wrongdoing, inveigle [**sollicitus,** agitated, uneasy, from **cieō,** stir up]; Austin's more direct "bribed" (on 31.1) has the advantage of getting directly to the heart of the matter.
servōs: servus, servī, *m.,* slave, servant
pōtiōnem: pōtiō, pōtiōnis, *f.,* a drink, something to drink; a drink given for a purpose, as a restorative or poison [**pōtō,** drink]
parāvit: parō (1), provide, supply; buy, obtain, provide; prepare

367. **clam,** *adv.,* in secret, under cover, covertly, hidden [related to **cēlō** and **occulō,** conceal]
attulit: adferō, adferre, attulī, adlātum, bring or carry to a place
necāre (365)**...attulit:** *paratactic.*
rursus or **rursum,** *adv.,* back, backwards; on the other hand, then again
crūdēlissimo: crūdēlis-is-e, *adj.,* cruel, merciless; unfeeling [**crūdus,** raw, savage]

368. **discidiō: discidium, discidī,** *n.,* a tearing apart, a rupture, splitting; separation in feelings, disagreement, estrangement, separation [**discindō,** split, from **scindō,** tear]
exstitisse: exsistō, exsistere, exstitī, appear, arise, become; show oneself or prove oneself to be (a certain way), be

369. **muliere: mulier, mulieris,** *f.,* woman; "experienced" woman (as opposed to *virgō*). *Mulier* is the normal word for "woman" in Republican prose; *fēmina* is used to draw a distinction ("wife," "matron," etc.); cf. Cicero's use of *fēmina* at 412 and 783, which are complimentary and sarcastic, respectively (but see my note at 412).

nōbilī: nōbilis-is-e, *adj.,* well-known, celebrated, renowned; infamous, notorious; noble, of noble birth, esp. belonging to a family which had held curule magistracies [rel. to **nōscō,** learn, come to know]

nōtā: "well-known," "notorious." We can imagine the audience roaring at this; note also that *nōbilī...nōtā* form a *figūra etymologica* or *paronomasia,* a play on two words based on their common derivation: here both *nōbilī* and *nōtā* are derived from *nōscō.*

dē quā: = *et dē Clōdiā,* a connecting rel.

dē quā...causā: of course Cicero interprets this rather loosely, and in fact goes on to describe her excesses in great detail, as the crowd would have been anticipating.

370. **nisi:** "but for," "except"

dēpellendī: dēpellō, dēpellere, dēpulī, dēpulsum, drive off, push away; rebut, repel. Constr.? See *causā* at 32, Ben. 339.

(ch. 32) **prō,** *prep. w. abl.,* according to, by virtue of; in front of

371. **Cn. Domitī:** voc., Gnaeus Domitius Calvinus, a praetor serving as president (judge) of the court; he could have stopped Cicero from dragging Clodia into the case.

cum: here the prep.

rem esse nōbīs: what does this echo in the preceding chapter?

372. **quae:** = *et ea,* a connecting rel.

commodā(vi)sse: commodō (1), make fit, adapt, suit; oblige, serve; furnish, give, lend

nōn dīcit: in place of a more usual *negō,* but with no special emphasis.

373. **ab hōc:** constr.? Ben. 216. Who is referred to?

sibi: case? Ben. 187.

374. **mātrem familiās:** "a matriarch." *Familiās* is an archaic genitive, preserved in the classical period only in the expressions *pater familiās, māter familiās, fīlius familiās,* and *fīlia familiās.*

familiās: familia, familiae, *f.,* household

secus, *adv.,* differently, otherwise, in another way; poorly, wrongly, badly

mātrōnārum: mātrōna, mātrōnae, *f.,* married woman, matron, with overtones of "proper lady," "woman of quality" [**māter,** mother]; what is Cicero's angle in using this term?

sānctitās: sānctitās, sānctitātis, *f.,* sacrosanctity, inviolability; purity, chastity, probity; respectable status, respectability [**sānctus,** inviolate; upright]

376. **oppugnandum:** note the military language again; gerund expressing purpose after *ad*.

   illīs: identify the people about whom Cicero is talking.

   relinquuntur: relinquō, relinquere, relīquī, relictum, leave *(in a wide variety of senses)*; depart

   quid est aliud quod: "what else is there which..."

377. **patrōnī: patrōnus, patrōnī,** *m.,* protector, defender; advocate, counsel; in apposition to *nōs*.

   dēbeāmus: mood? See *pateat* at 88, Ben. 283.

   ut: introduces a purpose clause.

   eōs: dir. obj. of *repellāmus*.

378. **repellāmus: repellō, repellere, reppulī, repulsum,** drive away, repel

   quod: = *et id,* a connecting rel.

   quod...facerem: "And, indeed, I would be pressing this point [*id*]"; the protasis is put second. Mood? See *posset* at 59, Ben. 304.

   vehementius: identify this form in *-ius*.

379. **intercēderent: intercēdō, intercēdere, intercessī, intercessum,** come or go between, intervene; obstruct, oppose

   mihi: dat. w. the verb.

   inimīcitiae: inimīcitia, inimīcitiae, *f.,* hostility, enmity, unfriendliness, "bad blood"; the pl. is normal (like our "bad relations"), except when abstract.

380. **frātrem: frāter, frātris,** *m.,* brother

   hīc, *adv.,* in this place; in this way, under these circumstances

   modicē: modicus-a-um, *adj.,* of or pert. to measure, measured; modest, moderate; restrained, temperate [**modus,** measure]

381. **prōgrediar: prōgredior, prōgredī, prōgressus sum,** go forth, go out, advance. Is *prōgrediar* fut. indic. or pres. subj.?

   quam: take with *longius*.

   mē: acc.

   mea fidēs: i.e., Cicero's responsibility to his client.

   cōget: cōgō, cōgere, coēgī, coāctum, compel, constrain, force

382. **muliebrīs:** acc. pl.

   mihi: case? Ben. 189.1.

   gerendās [esse]: gerō, gerere, gessī, gestum, bear, carry; undertake, carry on, wage. Constr.? See *comprimendam* at 17.

383.   **cum:** the prep.

omnēs semper: note the mutual reinforcement created by position.

amīcam omnium...cuiusquam inimīcam: figure of speech? See above at 327n. Here there really are antithetical pairs.

amīcam: here a subst., "friend"; "lover," "mistress"

potius: "more," "rather"

384.   **inimīcam:** here a subst., "enemy"

385–415 (chs. 33–34): Cicero resurrects Appius Claudius Caecus to rebuke Clodia for her extravagant lifestyle.

385 (ch. 33). **utrum,** *adv. introducing dir. and (as here) indir. alternative questions, whether* [**uter,** which of two?]

sēcum: see *cum* at 38n.

386.   **sevērē et graviter et priscē...an remissē et lēniter et urbānē:** be sure your translation properly catches the antitheses set up in each of the three pairs; see Austin's notes on 6.25 and 33.23 for valuable comments on the components of *urbānitās*.

et...et...et: Latin usually connects three or more words with a series of *et*s or with no connectives at all.

priscē: priscus-a-um, *adj.,* old, ancient, antique, of yesteryear; old-fashioned, belonging to the good old times

mālit: mood? Ben 300.

an, *particle introducing the second possibility in an alternative indir. question,* or

387.   **urbānē: urbānus-a-um,** *adj.,* of or pert. to the city; refined, sophisticated, suave, "smart"

sī illō austērō mōre ac modō [māvult].

austērō: austērus-a-um, *adj., (of taste or smell)* bitter, sour, harsh; severe, stern, strict; *(of style)* plain-speaking [Gk. **austēros,** bitter]

mōre ac modō: case? Ben. 220.

īnferīs: īnferus-a-um, *adj.,* below, lower; of or pert. to the lower world, infernal; *hence pl. subst.,* **īnferī,** the dead; regions the dead inhabit

388.   **excitandus est: excitō** (1), stir up, set in motion; rouse, call up or raise (as spirits from the dead) [**ex-,** thoroughly + **citō,** set in motion]. Constr.? See *comprimendam* at 17.

barbātīs: barbātus-a-um, bearded [**barba,** beard]; used here to indicate men of antiquity ("antiquity" being relative to Cicero's own day), who wore full beards.

barbulā: barbula, barbulae, *f.*, little beard; abl. of quality, Ben. 224.
quā: abl. w. the verb *dēlectātur*
ista: = *Clōdia.*

389. horridā: horridus-a-um, *adj.*, bristly, prickly, rough, scruffy; dreadful, horrible [horreō, bristle]; here "unkempt" (Austin at 33.26) gives a nice effect.
quam: the rel. pron.
statuīs: statua, statuae, *f.*, statue [statuō, set upright]
antīquīs: antīquus-a-um, *adj.*, ancient, old; ancestral

390. imāginibus: imāgō, imāginis, *f.*, image, likeness. Aristocratic families made wax death masks of the faced of their dead, which were kept in the atrium of the house and were carried around Rome during funeral processions.
quī: the antecedent is *aliquis*; this person will do the job on Cicero's behalf. This figure of speech is called *prosōpopoiia* [Gk. prosōpon, theatrical mask; character + poiō, make]
obiurget: mood? Ben. 282.2.

391. suscēnseat: suscēnseō, suscēnsēre, suscēnsuī, *(w. dat.)* be angry or indignant with; bear a grudge; subj. in a negative clause of purpose, Ben. 282.
exsistat: a jussive volitive subj., expressing a wish, Ben. 275.

392. familiā: often refers to the household generally, here means family members, alive or dead.
ac potissimum: "and especially," "and in particular"
Caecus: Appius Claudius Caecus (the Blind), censor in 312 B.C. and consul in 307 and 296, was distinguished for a variety of political reforms and the construction during his censorship of the *Via Appia* (a major road going from Rome to Capua, later to Brundisium) and the *Aqua Appia* (Rome's first aqueduct). Clodia and her brother were members of the *gēns Claudia* (the Claudian clan). In 279 B.C., in advanced old age, Appius rebuked the Senate for even considering the peace proposals of King Pyrrhus while that adversary was on Italian soil; this speech soon became famous and was still circulated in Cicero's day. On Pyrrhus, see 412n.
ille: "that famous...," "that distinguished...," as often.
minimum: how can you tell whether adj. or adv.?

393. capiet: capiō, capere, cēpī, captum, *(in numerous senses)* take; here translate with *dolōrem*, "suffer," "endure."
sī exstiterit...aget...loquētur: identify the condition, Ben. 302.

394. quid...: a verb must be supplied; what is the effect of the ellipsis of the
verb?
quid...quid...quid: figure of speech? Ben. 350.11b.

395. adulēscentulō: adulēscentulus-a-um, *adj.*, youthful; *subst.*
adulēscentulus, young man, mere youth; perhaps one might translate "just a boy!" provided we remember that, as Austin points out
at 33.5, the appellation disparages Clodia, not Caelius.
cūr, *interrog. adv.*, why?
tam, *adv.*, so, to that degree, to such a degree

396. commodārēs, timērēs: mood? Ben. 284.

397. timērēs: timeō, timēre, timuī, fear, have cause to fear; be at risk from
Nōn...nōn...nōn...nōn...nōn: figure of speech? Ben. 350.11b.
avum: avus, avī, *m.*, grandfather; ancestor

398. proavum: proavus, proavī, *m.*, great-grandfather
abavum: abavus, abavī, *m.*, great-great-grandfather
atavum: atavum, atavī, *m.*, great-great-great grandfather
cōnsulēs: cōnsul, cōnsulis, *m.*, consul

399. fuisse: constr.? Ben. 314.1.
(ch. 34). dēnique: "to put the icing on the cake,..."
tē: tū, *2nd pers. sg. pron.*, you
Q. Metellī: Quintus Caecilius Metellus Celer, Clodia's deceased husband, whom she had been on bad terms with and was rumored to
have poisoned; see chs. 59–60. He was a *lēgātus* to Pompey in Asia in
66, praetor in 63, when he supported Cicero, and consul in 60, when
he vehemently opposed his brother-in-law, P. Clodius Pulcher. On
the Senate floor, Metellus once threatened to throttle Clodius if the
latter did not behave; see 744–747.
mātrimōnium: mātrimōnium, mātrimōnī, *n.*, matrimony, wedlock

400. tenuisse: mood? Ben. 314.1. What is the effect of the perfect tense here?
patriae: patria, patriae, *f.*, fatherland, homeland; gen. after *amantissimī*.

401. **amantissimi: amō** (1), love; when used as adj.'s, participles can be made into comparatives, as here: "most loving"; see also *ornātissimā* at 56.
     simul, *adv.,* at the same time, together; **simul ac,** as soon as
     pedem: pēs, pedis, *m.,* foot; step
     līminī: līmen, līminis, *n.,* doorway, threshold; *(by synecdoche)* house, home; *synecdoche* is the naming of a part of an object to refer to the entire object, e.g., in English, "a set of wheels" (= "car").
     omnīs...cīvīs: acc. pl.
     prope: here an adv., "nearly"

402 **virtūte: virtūs, virtūtis,** *f.,* manliness, courage; excellence, worth
     glōriā: glōria, glōriae, *f.,* universally recognized praise, honor, distinction
     superabat: superō (1), surpass, overcome; excel, outdo
     cum: translate "when," but the mood shows that some concession ("although") is present.
     amplissimō: amplus-a-um, *adj.,* large, spacious; eminent, distinguished

403. **nūpsissēs: nūbō, nūbere, nūpsī, nūptum,** marry

404. **cognātus: cognātus-a-um,** related, akin, kindred; *hence subst.* kinsman, blood-relative
     adfīnis: adfīnis-is-e, *adj.,* related by marriage; *hence subst.* **adfīnis,** a relation by marriage, an "in-law"
     familiāris: here a subst.
     nihil eōrum: "none of these." *Nihil* is frequently used where English speakers might expect *nēmō* or *nūllus.*

405. **temeritās: temeritās, temeritātis,** *f.,* chance, accident; rashness, recklessness, heedlessness [**temere**]
     nōnne: introduces a question expecting the answer "yes."

406. **sī:** identify the condition, Ben. 302.
     imāginēs: see the explanation above, at 390n.
     nē...quidem: "not even."
     prōgeniēs: prōgeniēs, prōgeniēī, f., offspring, descendant; race, stock, lineage

407. **Q. illa Claudia:** idiomatic for the more standard *Q. Claudia illa* (Austin at 34.18); note the similar arrangement *virgō illa Vestālis,* just below at 408. Cf. also *M. vērō Caelius* at 893.
     Claudia: The Roman historian Titus Livy (59 B.C.–A.D. 17 or 64 B.C.–A.D. 12)

is our source for her story (*Ab urbe conditā*, "From the Founding of the City," xxix.14.12):

P. Cornelius cum omnibus mātrōnīs Ostiam obviam īre deae iussus; isque eam dē nāve acciperet et in terram ēlātam trāderet ferendam mātrōnīs. Postquam nāvis ad ostium amnis Tiberīnī accessit, sīcut erat iussus, in salum nāve ēvectus ab sacerdōtibus deam accēpit extulitque in terram. Mātrōnae prīmōrēs cīvitātis, inter quās ūnīus Claudiae Quintae īnsigne est nōmen, accēpēre; cui dubia, ut trāditur, anteā fāma clāriōrem ad posterōs tam religiōsō ministeriō pudīcitiam fēcit. Eae per manūs, succedentēs deinde aliae aliīs, omnī obviam effūsā cīvitāte, tūribulīs ante iānuās positīs quae praeferēbātur atque accēnsō tūre precantibus ut volēns propitiaque urbem Rōmānam inīret, in aedem Victōriae quae est in Palātiō pertulēre deam prīdiē īdūs Aprīlēs; isque diēs festus fuit. Populus frequēns dōna deae in Palātium tulit, lectisterniumque et lūdī fuēre, Megalēsia appellāta.

"The consul Publius Cornelius Scipio was ordered to go to Ostia, the port of Rome, to meet a statue of the goddess, accompanied by the matrons of Rome; he was both to receive her from the ship and, once she had been taken onto shore, to hand her over to be carried by the women. After the ship reached the mouth of the River Tiber, he did as he had been ordered. Carried by ship into open sea, he received the goddess from her priests, and carried her onto the land. The leading women of the commonwealth received the goddess from him, among whom a distinguished name was that of one Claudia Quintia, whose earlier dubious reputation, it was said, made her virtue all the more celebrated by later generations because of so pious a service. These women carried the goddess in their hands, passing her hand-to-hand, since the whole community had poured out to meet her; incense-burners had been placed before the doorways which she was carried by, and, with the incense burning, all were praying that the goddess enter the city of Rome of her own accord and favorably-disposed. They carried her all the way to the Temple of Victory which is on the Palatine on April 12, 204 B.C.; and this was a festival day. The thronging crowd brought gifts to the goddess on the Palatine, and there were solemn feasting and games, and she was called 'The Great One.'"

aemulam: aemulus-a-um, *adj.,* emulous, vying with, rivaling; envious, jealous; *hence subst.* **aemulus** *or* **aemula,** a rival

408.   **admonēbat:** "wasn't she a reminder for you to...?" "didn't she suggest to you that...?"

virgō: virgō, virginis, *f.,* maiden; virgin

Vestālis: Vestālis-is-e, *adj.,* of or pert. to Vesta, goddess of the hearth (fireplace). The six *virginēs Vestālēs* were her priestesses, serving a minimum of thirty years, after which they were permitted to marry (although they rarely did so).

409.   **quae patrem complexa triumphantem:** a good ex. of *synchesis,* Ben. 350.11d, or interlocked word order.

complexa: complector, complectī, complexus sum, embrace, hug; seize, grasp; grip; cling to

triumphantem: triumphō (1), have a triumphal procession

tribūnō: tribūnus, tribūnī, *m.,* tribune, one of ten officials elected annually by the plebeians for the protection of their rights

plēbeī: plēbs, plēbis *or* **plēbēs, plēbeī,** *f.,* the commoners (opposite *patrēs;* the whole people is *populus*) [related to Gk. **plēthos,** the many]

410.   **currū: currus, currūs,** *m.,* chariot, triumphal chariot; triumph [**currō,** run]

frāterna: frāternus-a-um, *adj.,* of or pert. to a brother, fraternal; a smack at Clodius's notorious lifestyle

411.   **bona:** = *virtūtēs.*

paterna: paternus-a-um, *adj.,* of or pert. to a father, paternal

avīta: avītus-a-um, *adj.,* of or pert. to a grandfather; ancestral [**avus,** grandfather]

usque, *adv.,* as far as one can go, continuously, persistently, constantly

tum, *adv.,* then

cum...tum: virtually = *et...et,* with some slight emphasis on the second element ("both...and especially").

412.   **fēminīs: fēmina, fēminae,** *f.,* woman, wife; used instead of *mulieribus* to be complimentary (and because of *virīs,* with which *fēminīs* is here contrasted); see 369n.

ideōne: ideō, *adv.,* on that account, therefore, for that reason, for that purpose; note the *anaphora,* the strong first position at each recurrence, and the use of (emphatic and contrasting) nom. pers. pron.'s. *Anaphora* [Gk., a turning back, a reference] is the emphatic repetition of a word or phrase: "of the people, by the people, and for the people."

pācem: pāx, pācis, *f.,* pact, treaty; peace

Pyrrhī: Pyrrhus (319–272 B.C.), adventurer-king of Epirus (in northwestern Greece) and ally of Tarentum in southern Italy, who made war on Rome from 280–275 B.C.

dirēmī: dirimō, dirimere, dirēmī, dirēmptum, pull apart, part, separate, break up

413. **foedera: foedus, foederis,** *n.,* agreement, compact, treaty; bond, tie [related to **fidēs,** faith, and **fīdō,** trust]

ferīrēs: feriō, ferīre, hit, strike, blow; kill; *hence (from the sacrifice of animals at the making of a treaty)* **foedus ferīre,** to make a treaty, strike an agreement or bargain

aquam: aqua, aquae, *f.,* water; water supply, aqueduct

414. **addūxī: addūcō, addūcere, addūxī, adductum,** lead toward

eā: abl. with *ūterēre*; antecedent?

incestē: incestus-a-um, *adj.,* religiously unclean, unholy, profane; unchaste, lewd, defiled [**in**-priv. + **castus,** pure]

ūterēre: = *ūterēris* (see 331n.).

mūnīvī: mūniō (4), fortify; *(of roads)* build [**moenia,** defensive walls]; the terminology illustrates how the main impetus of early Roman road-building was military, not economic.

eam: antecedent?

415. **virīs:** case? Ben. 222.

comitātā: comitō (1), go along, accompany, attend, follow [**comes**]

416–431 (ch. 35): Cicero admits that a condemnation of Caelius's behavior is possibly implicit in the line of reasoning of "Appius Claudius Caecus," so he stops and restates his argument, underlining what Clodia has done wrong, and addressing her directly. This section serves as a transition to the second and far more daring prosōpopoiia in ch. 36.

416. **quid,** *adv.,* for what? why? [n. acc. sg. of **quis**]

indūxī: Austin notes at 35.28 that this word has a theatrical meaning, "to bring on stage"; note also *intrōductā* just below at 421.

ita...ut verear: kind of clause? Ben. 284.

417. **nē:** introduces what kind of clause? See 310n.

īdem: force?

repente: irreg. adv. of **repēns, repentis,** *adj.,* sudden, unexpected, completely new

convertat: **convertō, convertere, convertī, conversum,** turn, revolve; recoil, snap back

incipiat: **incipiō, incipere, incēpī, inceptum,** begin, start, set to work

418.   cēnsōria: **cēnsōrius-a-um,** *adj.,* of or pert. to a censor; austere, excessively moralizing, critical; see 296n.

vīderō: virtually = simple fut. *vidēbō* here: the difference is one of tone: *hoc vidēbō* = "I will see to it"; *hoc vīderō* = "When I (will) see to it, it will be *done*" (G&L 244; see also Austin at 35.2).

hoc: acc.

posterius: **posterus-a-um,** *adj.,* later, future; fully explain the *-ius* form.

419.   vel: adv. here, = "even," "one might go so far as to say."

disceptātōribus: **disceptātor, disceptātōris,** *m.,* arbitrator, judge [**disceptō,** arbitrate]

420.   vītam mē probātūrum esse: how does gender help to distinguish the subject and the object of the infinitive?

cōnfīdam: **cōnfīdō, cōnfīdere, cōnfīsus sum,** *(w. dat.)* trust in, be confident in [**cum-**intensive + **fīdō,** trust in]

tū vērō: a figure of speech called *apostrophē,* the sudden addressing of someone who is not present [Gk. **apo,** away, + **strophē,** a turning]. Apostrophe often produces a rapid shifting of gears, as here.

421.   tēcum: see *cum* at 38n.

nullā persōnā intrōductā: constr.? Be careful translating *persōnā*; see note at 355.

intrōducta: **intrōdūcō, intrōdūcere, intrōdūxī, intrōductum,** introduce, bring in or on (stage)

sī: *cōgitās* is the verb of the protasis; identify the condition, Ben. 302.

ea: object of *probāre* and antecedent of the five following *quae*s.

quae facis...: Note how Latin prefers the concrete and English the abstract; an acceptable English translation might be "deeds, allegations, claims, fabrications."

422.   īnsimulās: **īnsimulō** (1), accuse, charge, blame, allege; the word implies that the charge is false, as Engl. "claim" often does.

mōlīris: **mōlior** (4), labor to bring about, build [**mōlēs,** a mass, a burden]

423.   ratiōnem: "account," "explanation"

424.   **coniūnctiōnis: coniūnctiō, coniūnctiōnis,** *f.,* association, connection
       reddās: reddō, reddere, reddidī, redditum, give back, return
       expōnās: expōnō, expōnere, exposuī, expositum, put out, place out;
       put on display, explain; *reddās* and *expōnās* are subj.'s w. *necesse.*

425.   **necesse est:** it is necessary, followed by a subj. substantive clause with-
       out *ut,* as here, Ben. 295.8.
       libīdinēs: this and the following nouns are objects of *iactant;* the plurals
       of abstract nouns often describe specific instances or occurrences of
       the quality named by the abstract noun.

426.   **Baiās:** here "[wild] parties at Baiae," a colloquial use of a place name to
       describe the goings-on at that place (Austin at 35.10)
       actās: acta, actae, *f.,* seashore; seaside party [Gk. **aktē**]
       cōmissātiōnēs: cōmissātiō, cōmissātiōnis, *f.,* carousing, feasting, rev-
       elry, a Bacchanalian revel and nocturnal procession with torches
       and music [rel. to Gk. **kōmazō,** revel]
       cantūs: cantus, cantūs, *m.,* singing; song
       symphōniās: symphōnia, symphōniae, *f.,* agreement of sounds, har-
       mony; group of singers, performing band [Gk. **symphōnia**]

427.   **nāvigia: nāvigium, nāvigī,** *n.,* boat; here "boating parties"
       īdem: = *accūsātōrēs,* above at 425.
       significant: significō (1), indicate, signify; show, demonstrate [**signum,**
       sign + **faciō,** make]
       nihil sē: *sē* is subject, *nihil* object of the infinitive *dīcere.*
       tē invītā: construction? Ben. 227.

428.   **quae:** object of *voluistī* in 429.
       mente: mēns, mentis, *f.,* mind, intention
       nesciō: combines idiomatically with *quī, quae, quod* to form an adjective
       meaning "I know not who/what..." or "someone or other"; compare
       our "who knows?" in the middle of a sentence, as in "He sank who
       knows how much money into that perpetual motion machine." The
       expression is sometimes written as one word.
       effrēnāta: effrēnātus-a-um, *adj.,* unbridled, unrestrained, violent [**ex** +
       frēnum, bridle]
       praecipitī: praeceps, praecipitis, *adj.,* plunging down or ahead; impetu-
       ous, acting precipitously

429.   **dīluās: dīluō, dīluere, dīluī, dīlūtum,** dissolve & wash away; make
       clear, explain (away); rebut, refute [**dis-** + **luō,** wash]

430. **nihil:** = *nōn.*

431. **crēdendum esse: crēdō, crēdere, crēdidī, crēditum,** believe, trust in (+ *dat.*). Constr.? See *comprimendam [esse]* at 17. Strictly speaking the constr. here is slightly different, since, unlike *comprimō, crēdō* is intrans. and can only be used impersonally in passive constructions (Ben. 187.2a). Thus:

> **Huic crīminī et testimōniō crēdō,**
> *I believe (in) this charge and the testimony.*
> becomes in the passive:
> **Huic crīminī et testimōniō mihi crēditur,**
> *This charge and the testimony are believed in by me.*

If *crēdō* were trans., "this charge and the testimony" would be acc. in the first sentence, and nom. in the second (where *mihi* would be *ā mē*.).

fateāre: = *fateāris* (see 331n.)

dīluās, doceās, fateāre: subj.'s in a subst. clause after *oportet,* without *ut;* compare the construction with *necesse* at 425.

432–448 (ch. 36): In a second *prosōpopoiia,* Cicero brings on Clodia's brother to scold her for her behavior, playing maliciously on rumors of an incestuous relationship.

432. **sīn:** for the meaning and use of this word, see 1n.

urbānius: "in a more sophisticated way"; fully explain the form in *-ius. Urbānus* = "suave," "smart"; consider how Appius was described at 387ff.

mē: case?

agere: "proceed," "go on with my case"

māvīs: from *mālō,* Ben. 130.

agam: tense and mood?

433. **senem:** often used of the *paterfamiliās* of traditional comedy, "the old man," proverbially harsh and unsympathetic.

dūrum: dūrus-a-um, *adj.,* hard, solid; *(of demeanor)* rough, insensible, severe, unsympathetic

ex hīs: "from [among] these men [today]," i.e., Clodia's living relations, as opposed to *illum senem;* in contrast with the past, *hic* often refers to *present* time, circumstances, individuals, location, etc.

434.   **sūmam:** tense and mood? How does *removēbō* inform your answer?

minimum: "youngest." This would be P. Clodius Pulcher, who was such a thorn (and worse) in Cicero's side. Cf. also 315n., where (presumably) a different Clodius is mentioned.

in istō genere: "in that respect," "in that [your] kind of thing," i.e., in the sort of life Clodia leads; *in istō genere urbānissimus* focuses on the unsavory side of some people's self-styled *urbānitās* by referring to the baser and decadent aspects of upper-crust society.

435.   **quī:** what does the punctuation tell us about this (second) *quī*?

plūrimum: note balance with *minimum* above.

nesciō quam: on this expression, see 428n.; modifies *timiditātem*.

436.   **crēdō:** parenthetical, as often, and, as Austin notes at 36.20, ironical: "doubtless," "I suppose," "to be sure"

timiditātem: timiditās, timiditātis, *f.*, fear, fearfulness, cowardice

inānīs: inānis-is-e, *adj.*, empty, idle, without substance; groundless, unjustified, silly

metūs: metus, metūs, *m.*, alarm, apprehension, fear

437.   **pūsiō:** pūsiō, pūsiōnis, *m.*, boy, child, tyke [rel. to **puer**]; *pūsiō* is in apposition with the subject *tū*. Austin at 36.21 notes that this is a "low" word, but properly chosen.

maiōre sorōre: balances *minimum frātrem* above at 434.

sorōre: soror, sorōris, *f.*, sister

cubitābat: cubitō (1), be accustomed to lie, go to bed. From what word is *cubitō* derived, and how? Ben. 155.2. In addition to the more pedestrian meanings, *cubitō* can mean "go to bed with," "have sexual relations with"; Cicero's audience would not have missed the innuendo.

putātō: a fut. imp.; see 253n. Why does Cicero use this form here instead of a more workaday *putā* or a volitive subj. *putēs*? What figure of speech is repeated again in these lines? See 390n.

439.   **quid:** the interrog. adv., "why?"

tumultuāris: tumultuor (1), make a commotion or uproar, cause confusion [**tumultus**, great disorder]

īnsānīs: īnsāniō (4), be crazy, rave [**in**-priv. + **sānus**, healthy, sound]

440.   **quid...facis?:** this trochaic line is from a Roman comedy, author unknown, but suspected by some to be Caecilius Statius (d. 168 B.C.), well-known for his old grouches.

clāmōrem: clāmor, clāmōris, *m.,* a loud shouting, cry, outcry
exorsa: exordior, exordīrī, exorsus sum, start, begin [rel. to exordium]
parvam: parvus-a-um, *adj.,* little, small

441. vīcīnum: vīcīnus-a-um, *adj.,* nearby, neighboring [vīcus, village, neigh-
        borhood]; cf. Cicero's remarks at 213–216; Austin at 36.25 remarks
        that "possibly the intimacy only began after Caelius had moved
        house."
      adulēscentulum: on the use of this word, see above at 13n.
      aspexistī: aspiciō, aspicere, aspexī, aspectum, look at, notice, catch
        sight of [ad, towards + speciō, specere *(rare),* see]
      candor: candor, candōris, *m.,* brightness, radiance; dazzling white col-
        or, whiteness; healthy and radiant complexion, fairness [candeō, be
        shining white]. The desirability of a deep tan (= ability to be at lei-
        sure) is a mid-twentieth century development; to our predecessors
        paleness (= ability to avoid common field work) was a personal at-
        tribute to wished for.
      huius tē: how does this *juxtaposition* contribute to the meaning of
        Clodius's imagined question?
      prōcēritās: prōcēritās, prōcēritātis, *f.,* height [prōcērus, tall]

442. voltus: vultus, vultūs, *m.,* facial appearance, countenance; looks, fea-
        tures, "good looks"
      pepulērunt: pellō, pellere, pepulī, pulsum, strike, beat; force away, ex-
        pel; stir, enrapture
      saepius: comp. of saepe, *adv.,* often, many times, frequently
      nōn numquam: the double negative is frequent in good classical Latin
        style.

443. hortīs: "estate" (see 321n.); in īsdem hortīs = "in the same garden," i.e.,
        "in your garden *together.*"
      vīs: from *volō.*

444. familiās: = *familiae* (see 374n.).
      parcō ac tenācī: Austin suggests on 36.1 that these words recall the *senex*
        of comedy; cf. description of Caelius's father *(parum splendidus)* at 34.
      parcō: parcus-a-um, *adj.,* frugal, thrifty; stingy
      tenācī: tenāx, tenācis, *adj.,* grasping, tenacious; cheap, miserly, tight-
        fisted [teneō, hold fast]
      habēre: complementary inf.

dēvīnctum: dēvīnciō, dēvīncīre, dēvīnxī, dēvīnctum, bind, tie fast, attach, connect; *habēre...dēvīnctum* looks very much like the way English (as well as other modern European languages) forms its pres. perf. tense, and is fairly close in meaning to *esse dēvīnctum,* but more emphasis is put on the maintenance of the result than on the action.

445.   **calcitrat: calcitrō** (1), strike with the heel, kick; resist obstinately, balk, buck [**calx,** heel, with which one wearing open-toe sandals would kick!]
dōna: dōnum, dōnī, *n.,* gift, prize; benefit, bounty
tantī: the gen. and abl. are regularly used to indicate price or value.

446.   **cōnfer:** irreg. imp., for **cōnfere,* as usual in *ferō* and its compounds.
aliō, *adv.,* to another place, elsewhere; to another person or purpose
Tiberim: Tiberis, Tiberis, *m.,* Tiber River, on which Rome is situated
ac: "and in fact," "and even"; *atque* and *ac* aften introduce a term which strengthens or corrects the first item; see *OLD s.v. atque,* 4a,b.
eō locō: case and reason? See *hōc locō* at 97n., Ben. 228.

447.   **parāstī:** "you bought" (Austin at 36.4)
quō, *interrog. & rel. adv.,* to what place, to what purpose; in which place
natandī: natō (1), swim
vēnit: how do the surrounding verbs tell us the tense, though the spelling in the text is ambiguous? The problem is analogous to our problem with the word "read."
hinc, *adv.,* from this place
licet: has as subject a substantive *ut*-clause (Ben. 295.6, 295.8), though the *ut* is often omitted, as here.

448.   **condiciōnēs:** "marriage contracts," "love affairs," "matches."
huic: dat. after *molesta es,* "you are pestering."
spernit: spernō, spernere, sprēvī, sprētum, reject with scorn, contemn, disdain, spurn

449-482 (chs. 37–38): More comic fathers, one severe, one lenient, followed by a lecture at Clodia.

449 (ch. 37). **redeō: redeō, redīre, redīvī** or **rediī, reditum,** return, come or go back
vicissim, *adv.,* in turn, again [**vicis,** alternation]

450.   **auctōritātem: auctōritās, auctōritātis,** *f.,* authority, influence, leadership [**auctor,** originator]
       dubitō: dubitō (1), doubt, be uncertain; hesitate, waver; *dubitō* takes various constructions, depending on the author's style and the shade of meaning to be conveyed. Here it sets up an indir. question.
       quem: rel. adj.

451.   **potissimum:** part of speech?
       Caeciliānumne: Caeciliānus-a-um, *adj.,* of or pert. to Caecilius, see 440n. The *–ne* is a flag indicating that an indirect question follows or continues.

453.   **nunc...īrā:** another trochaic line from comedy.
       dēmum, *adv.,* at length, at last, finally
       mī: chiefly poetic form of *mihi.*
       ārdet: ārdeō, ārdēre, ārsī, burn, blaze; rage, be excited; be on fire with love
       cor: cor, cordis, *n.,* heart

454.   **cumulātur: cumulō** (1), heap up, pile up, pile on; fill up, increase, overload
       īrā: īra, īrae, *f.,* anger, rage, wrath; indignation, resentment.

456.   **ō,** *interj.,* O!
       īnfēlīx: īnfēlīx, īnfēlīcis, *adj.,* unhappy, unlucky, ill-fated, unprosperous [**in-**priv. + **fēlīx,** fortunate]
       sceleste: scelestus-a-um, wicked, villainous, accursed, infamous; unlucky; pernicious [**scelus,** crime]; Austin notes at 37.14 that the word is common in comedy but unusual for Cicero, who would normally use *scelerātus.*

457.   **ferreī: ferreus-a-um,** *adj.,* made of iron; hardhearted, harsh, inhuman, unyielding

458.   **dīcam:** the parallel *velim* will give the mood; explain it.
       quae: = *et ea,* a connecting relative.

459.   **foedīs: foedus-a-um,** *adj.,* foul, polluted; beastly, horrible, vile
       factīs: perf. pass. part. of *faciō* used as a noun.
       foedīs factīs facis: note two figures of speech.
       velim: mood?

nēquīquam, *adv.,* pointlessly, for nothing, to no purpose, without good
   reason, in vain

460. **vix,** *adv.,* scarcely, barely
      dīceret: "might have said," "could have said," potential subj.; cf. 78n.,
         Ben. 280 (but there is a better discussion at G&L 258). It may help to
         think of this as the apodosis of a contrary-to-fact condition with a
         suppressed protasis (and a slightly different transl.).
      vīcīnitātem: vīcīnitās: vīcīnitātis, *f.,* nearness, proximity; neighbor-
         hood, vicinity [**vīcus,** village; cognate to Engl. "-wick"]

461. **inlecebrīs: inlecebra, inlecebrae,** *f.,* an allurement, inducement, lure,
         enticement [**inlicio,** entice, allure]
      inlecebrīs cognitīs: construction? Ben. 227.
      refūgistī: refugiō, refugere, refūgī, run back or away; stay away from,
         avoid, shun; recoil

462. **nō(vi)stī.**
      dīde: dīdō, dīdere, dīdidī, dīditum, divide, distribute, scatter, spread
         round, strew [**dis-,** signifying dispersal + **dō,** give]
      dissice: disiciō, disicere, disiēcī, disiectum, throw in different direc-
         tions, cast asunder; break up, scatter; *(elliptical and fig.,)* squander
         money [**dis- + iaciō,** throw]

463. **per,** *prep. w. acc.,* through
      per mē: "for my part," "as far as I'm concerned"
      sī: kind of condition? Ben. 302.
      egēbīs: egeō, egēre, eguī, want, be in need; be without, lack *(w. abl.)*
      dolēbit: here impersonal

464. **sat:** short for **satis,** *n. indecl.,* enough, sufficient
      quī: "by which," an old abl. form, practically = *ut.*
      aetātis: partitive gen. w. *quod*
      relicuom: the *-om* form for *-um* is archaic, as might appear in comedy.
      oblectem: oblectō (1), amuse, delight; pass (time) pleasantly, [**ob- + lactō,**
         freq. of **laciō,** entice]
      meae: take with *aetātis.*

465 (ch. 38). **dērectō: dērigō, dērigere, dērēxī, dērēctum,** arrange, set straight;
         aim, direct, steer; *hence part.* **dērēctus** *as adj.,* direct, straight;
         straightforward, forthright, to-the-point, blunt [**dē + regō,** control]
      respondēret: mood? See *dīceret* at 460.

466.　**dēcessisse: dēcēdō, dēcēdere, dēcessī, dēcessum,** move away, depart, withdraw
　　Quid signī [est]?: case of *signī*? Ben. 201.

467.　**iactūra: iactūra, iactūrae,** *f.,* a throwing away (overboard), jettison, sacrifice; loss, squandering, wasting
　　quotus: quotus-a-um, *interrog. adj.,* which (in number)?, how many? [**quot,** how many?]; *quotus* asks for how many of something in relation to the total number.

468.　**quisque: quisque, quaeque, quidque (quicque)** *or* **quodque,** *indef. pron. and pronominal adj.,* each (one), every (one); **quotus quisque,** "how many are there who...?" i.e., "there are but few people who," or "how many?" i.e., "how few!"
　　effugere: effugiō, effugere, effūgī, flee, slip away, escape; keep away from, avoid
　　maledicā: maledicus-a-um, *adj.,* evil-speaking, slanderous, abusive; compare, but do not confuse with, the noun *maledictum.*

469.　**cīvitāte:** "city" is an acceptable translation, although "society" or "community" is closer to the Latin (*cīvitās* is never used for *urbs* in Republican Latin, though it is common in this usage later).
　　maledicā cīvitāte: spoken wryly; the sentiment is common Ciceronian fare.
　　mīrāris: takes an acc. and inf. construction here.
　　male audī(vi)sse: a conversational phrase (Austin at 38.2), difficult to turn into English: lit., "has ill-heard [with respect to himself]", i.e., "has been insulted or slandered," "[has] gained a bad reputation," see *OLD,* s.v. *audiō,* 5b.
　　cuius frāter: identify.

470.　**germānus: germānus-a-um,** of or pert. to a brother and sister who have the same parents; real, genuine; here intensifies *frāter,* "her very own brother."
　　sermōnēs: sermō, sermōnis, *m.,* conversation, talk; idle talk, gossip, rumor
　　inīquōrum: inīquus-a-um, unequal; unfair, unjust; hostile, adverse; *hence subst.* **inīquus,** ill-wisher, enemy [**in-**priv. + **aequus**]
　　vērō: see 19n. for a discussion of *vērus* and its adverbial derivatives.
　　lēnī...et clēmentī patre: abl. abs., Ben. 227

471. **clēmentī: clēmēns, clēmentis,** *adj.,* gentle, kind, mild; lenient, merciful, indulgent
ille: refers to the father from comedy who "speaks" the following two verses.

472. **forēs...resarciētur:** two lines from the comic poet P. Terentius Afer (195–159 B.C.), known to us as Terence, *Adelphī* [Gk. *The Brothers*], 120–121.
forēs: foris, foris, *f.,* door; *pl.,* double doors
ecfrēgit: effringō, effringere, effrēgī, effractum, break open, break down [**ex-,** thoroughly (*-ec* often before *f-*) + **frangō,** break]
restituentur: restituō, restituere, restituī, restitūtum, set up again, rebuild; renew, repair [**statuō,** set up]
dīscidit: dīscindō, dīscindere, dīscidī, dīscissum, cut up, cut into pieces, tear, shred [**dis-** + **scindō,** cut apart]

473. **vestem: vestis, vestis,** *f.,* clothing, clothes
resarciētur: resarciō, resarcīre, *resarsī, resartum, mend again, patch up; repair, restore [**sarciō,** mend]

474. **expedītissima: expediō** (4), free [the foot] from a snare, disentangle, extricate; *hence part.* **expedītus** *as adj.,* unimpeded, unencumbered, clear of difficulty. *Patrōnō facillima dictū,* comments Wageningen, "Awfully easy for his lawyer to say!"
esset: potential subj., Ben. 280.
in quō: "concerning which"

475. **facile:** part of speech?
dēfenderet: mood?
nihil: note strong first position.
nihil...dīcō: figure of speech? See 312n.
in: "against"
sī: sets up a contrary-to-fact condition, Ben. 304. The rest of the chapter (down to 482) is one long supposition. How does this suit Cicero's purpose at this point? Why is a "pretence of anonymity" (Austin at 38.9) used again here (Cicero had spoken directly to Clodia at 420–431)?

476. **aliqua:** although *qua* would be more common after *sī,* the longer forms are sometimes used, esp. when there is emphasis; thus *sī qua,* "if anyone," but *sī aliqua,* "if *someone*"; see G&L 315n1.

dissimilis: dissimilis-is-e, different (from), dissimilar (to), unlike (+ *gen. or dat.*)

istīus: = *Clōdiae;* case?

quae...quae...cuius...quae: figure of speech? Ben. 350.11b. Antecedent?

sē...pervolgāret: "made herself available to everyone," "prostituted herself"

477. **habēret:** takes *aliquem* as its obj.

palam, *adv.,* openly, publicly

dēcrētum: dēcernō, dēcernere, dēcrēvī, dēcrētum, decide, determine, resolve on; select, appoint; *dēcrētum aliquem,* "some man selected as her lover"

cuius in: "in whose"

hortōs: "estate" (see 321n.)

478. **Baiās:** "place at Baiae," a colloquialism (Austin at 35.10)

iūre: iūs, iūris, *n.,* law, rule, authority; *iūre suō,* "on their own authority," "at will," "freely"; *suō* here refers to the subject of *commeārent* (i.e., Clodia's lovers), not to the subject of the main sentence, Ben. 244.1.I.

libīdinēs omnium: = *omnēs libīdinōsī.*

commeārent: commeō, commeāre, commeāvī, commeātum, go or visit frequently, come and go [**meō,** go]; the word "suggests a regular flow of traffic" (Austin at 38.11).

479. **aleret: alō, alere, aluī, altum** *or* **alitum,** nurse, nourish, nurture; support, maintain

adulēscentīs: = *adulēscentēs,* acc. pl.

parsimōniam: parsimōnia, parsimōniae, *f.,* frugality, thrift; miserliness, parsimony [**parcō,** be sparing + suff. **-mōnia,** denoting a quality]

sūmptibus: "with her own expenditures," "at her own expense" (*sūmptibus* often has overtones of extravagance); case? Ben. 218.

480. **sustinēret: sustineō, sustinēre, sustinuī, sustentum,** hold up, support; sustain, withstand; here "compensate for" or "countervail" works nicely. *Sustineō* is from *sub(s)-* + *teneō,* "hold": we lift things *up,* reckoning according to the direction of motion; the Romans lifted *from below* (*sub*), reckoning from the starting point.

sī vidua līberē [vīveret], [sī] proterva petulanter [vīveret], [sī] dīves effūsē [vīveret], libīdinōsa meretrīciō mōre vīveret: the paired antitheses are not unlike 152–167 (on Catiline's paradoxical qualities).

vidua: viduus-a-um, deprived of a husband or wife, widowed; *hence subst.* **vidua,** widow

līberē: "in an uninhibited way," "loosely," "licentiously."

proterva: protervus-a-um, brash, reckless; forward, shameless, impudent

dīves: dīves, dīvitis, *adj.,* rich, wealthy

effūsē: effundō, effundere, effūdī, effūsum, pour out, shed; bring forth, produce abundantly; *hence part.* **effūsus** *as adj.,* relaxed, slack; unrestrained, extravagant, lavish

481. **libīdinōsa: libīdinōsus-a-um,** wanton, wilful, capricious; sensual, lustful [**libīdō**]

vīveret: vīvō, vīvere, vīxī, vīctum, live

[eum esse] adulterum.

putārem: impf. subj. in the apodosis of a contrary-to-fact condition, Ben. 304, but also deliberative in character (not "I would think," but "should I think?" "was I to think?"), Ben. 277

ego: force?

sī quis: the indef. *quis* emphasizes the anonymity, but needs to be translated "he" (i.e., Caelius); type of condition? Ben. 304.

482. **hanc:** = *Clōdiam.*

paulō līberius: the comparative often has the sense, "too much," so here "a little too loosely"; the adv. *paulō* is a fossilized abl. of degree of difference, Ben. 223.

salūtā(vi)sset: salūtō (1), greet, say hello; call on, visit

483–533 (chs. 39–42). Cicero becomes serious and grave again.

483 (ch. 39). **haec:** f., agreeing with *disciplīna*

tua: "your kind of"

484. **īnstituis: īnstituō, īnstituere, īnstituī, īnstitūtum,** put in place, set up, construct; establish, introduce, found; teach, educate, bring up [**in** + **statuō**]

adulēscentīs: acc. pl.

ob, *prep. w. acc.,* because of, on account of

puerum: puer, puerī, *m.,* boy

485. **trādidit: trādō, trādere, trādidī, trāditum,** hand over, deliver; commit, entrust [**trāns-,** across + **dō**]

ut: kind of clause? Ben. 282 (so also *ut* in 486).

ut in amōre atque in voluptātibus: a good ex. of *hendiadys* [Gk. **hen dia duoin,** "one through two"], a common stylistic feature of mature Latin prose in which an idea is expressed by two nouns joined by a conjunction rather than by a noun limited by a genitive or by an adj., Ben. 374.4. But for the hendiadys we would have here *ut in amōris voluptātibus.*

amōre: amor, amōris, *m.,* desire, love; love affair

voluptātibus: voluptās, voluptātis, *f.,* pleasure, delight, enjoyment; *pl.,* entertainments, shows; sexual adventures

486. **conlocāret: collocō** (1), put in place, set up, establish; occupy oneself with, spend time on, devote oneself to

hanc tū vītam: note the word order.

487. **studia: studium, studī,** *n.,* eagerness, zeal; affection, devotion; a pursuit or activity, course of study

dēfenderēs: mood? Ben. 282.

Ego...putō (494): a magnificent example of an ornate Latin period, which should be "mapped out" to reveal its logical and rhetorical structure. *Ego* is in strong first position, answering the accusatory *tua, tibi,* and *tūs* in the preceding clauses.

sī: governs a condition stretching to *coniūnctum* in 493.

rōbore: rōbur, rōboris, *n.,* oak or other hard timber; strength, endurance; strength of character, resolve

rōbore, indole: abl. of quality, Ben. 224.2.

488. **indole: indolēs, indolis,** *f.,* native character, one's "make-up," constitution; natural talent, genius, potential [rel. to *alō;* compare *prōlēs* and *subolēs*]; on this word, see Austin, p. 169, at 39.22.

hōc, hāc: refer to the qualities described by the fictitious speaker in the preceding quotation: "this kind of."

continentiae: continentia, continentiae, *f.,* a holding back, restraint; self-control, temperance [**teneō,** hold]

ut: governs both *respueret* and *cōnficeret;* kind of clause? Ben. 284.

respueret: respuō, respuere, respuī, spit out; refuse or reject contemptuously

omnīs: acc. pl.

489. **omnemque...cursum:** dir. obj. of *cōnficeret.*

cursum: cursus, cursūs, *m.,* a running, journey; course, path [**currō,** run]

corporis: corpus, corporis, *n.,* body

490. **contentiōne: contentiō, contentiōnis,** *f.,* a struggling or striving after;
      dispute, controversy [**contendō,** strive]; *in labōre corporis atque in
      animī contentiōne* is probably an oblique reference to the physical
      and mental stresses of an orator's training and work, a recurrent
      theme (see above at 96 and 120, also 554–568).

      cōnficeret: cōnficiō, cōnficere, cōnfēcī, cōnfectum, make, complete;
      exhaust, weaken

      quem: dir. obj. of *dēlectāret.*

      nōn...nōn...nōn: figure of speech? Ben. 350.11b.

      quiēs, quiētis, *f.,* rest; peace and quiet, tranquillity

491. **remissiō: remissiō, remissiōnis,** *f.,* a sending back, a returning; a re-
      leasing; relaxation, distraction [**remissus**]

      aequālium: aequālis-is-e, *adj.,* equal, comparable, uniform; of the same
      age; *hence subst.,* **aequālis,** one's contemporary, peer, friend

      lūdī: "love affairs" (Austin on 28.16)

492. **dēlectāret:** why singular? Ben. 254.3.

      [**sī quis**] **nihil in vītā expetendum** [**esse**] **putāret.**

      expetendum [**esse**]**: expetō, expetere, expetīvī, expetītum,** desire,
      strive after, seek to do; constr.? See *comprimendam [esse]* above at 17,
      Ben. 313; 337.8b.

      nisi...coniūnctum: take after *nihil* ("nothing except that which").

493. **hunc:** refers to the fictitious person Cicero is describing, and signals the
      start of the apodosis of the main condition (itself begun at 487).

      sententiā: sententia, sententiae, *f.,* opinion, thought; idea, notion, topic
      [**sentiō,** perceive]; a kind of abl. of manner (used, however, without
      a prep.: Ben. calls it an "abl. of accordance" at 220.3).

      > *Meā sententiā...putō* is a good ex. of *pleonasm* (for which see 154n.).

      dīvīnīs: dīvīnus-a-um, *adj.,* of or pert. to a deity, divine; godlike, super-
      human, superlative

494. **quibusdam: quīdam, quaedam, quiddam** *or* **quoddam,** *indef. pron. and
      adj.,* a certain (one), a particular (one)

      bonīs: n. subst. here: "good qualities," "virtues"; case? Ben. 218.

      īnstructum atque ornātum [**esse**]**.**

      īnstructum: īnstruō, īnstruere, īnstrūxī, īnstructum, arrange, set
      up; equip, fit out, prepare; *hence part.* **īnstructus** *as adj.,* furnished,
      prepared

      genere: "stripe"

495.   **arbitror: arbitror** (1), think, reckon, suppose

Camillōs, Fabriciōs, Curiōs: like "Washingtons, Jeffersons, and Lincolns." Cicero evokes these proverbial "types" to lend *exempla,* "precedents" (Austin at 39.6), and historical *gravitās,* "weightiness," to his speech. M. Furius Camillus captured the Etruscan-controlled town of Veii in 396 B.C. (a serious threat to the early Roman Republic), conclusively defeated a Gallic invasion in 387 B.C., and led Rome's subsequent recovery. His subsequent social and political success at home allowed him to campaign successfully against the Aequi and Volscians, beginning the steady acquisition and consolidation of power that would make Rome mistress of all Italy in just over one hundred years.

C. Fabricius Luscinus and M'. (Manius) Curius Dentatus campaigned throughout central Italy to consolidate Roman power there and were victors over Pyrrhus, the king of Epirus, in the 270s B.C. Both men were exaggerated into "types" for their distinguished careers and virtuous behavior.

omnīs: = acc. pl.

496.   **ex minimīs:** "from insignificant beginnings (to great estate)"

tanta: take with *haec,* which = *hoc imperium,* as often (Austin at 39.6).

496–497 (ch. 40). **Vērum...reperiuntur:** Austin at 40.7 amusingly notes that in the opinion of the ancient orators, obsessed as they were with "golden-age" notions of contemporary decline from an earlier era of bliss, Rome had been going down the drain for quite some time. On *vērum,* see 19n.

497.   **nōn sōlum [nōn]...sed vix:** the second *nōn* must be supplied from the negative idea in *vix.*

vix, *adv.,* not easily, hardly, with difficulty, scarcely

librīs: liber, librī, *m.,* inner bark of a tree; volume, book

reperiuntur: reperiō, reperīre, repperī, repertum, find (out), discover; acquire, get; devise, invent [**re-** + **pario,** give birth, bring forth]

498.   **chartae: charta** *or* **carta, chartae** *or* **cartae,** *f.,* sheet for writing on, ancient "paper," page; Gardner suggests (p. 457n.) that "[p]ossibly by *librī* Cicero refers to works in actual circulation, by *chartae* to the original parchments."

quoque, *postpos. adv.,* also, likewise, too

pristinam: pristinus-a-um, *adj.,* earlier, previous; antique, old-fashioned

continēbant: contineō, continēre, continuī, contentum, hold or keep together; check, restrain; contain, comprise [**teneō,** hold]

499. obsolēvērunt: **obsolēscō, obsolēscere, obsolēvī, obsolētum,** fall into
        disuse; sink into obscurity, go out of style
    neque sōlum...sed etiam (500): = *et nōn sōlum...sed etiam.*
    apud, *prep. w. acc.,* at; among
    quī: subject of *secūtī sumus*
    sectam: secta, sectae, *f.,* course of action; way of life; code of behav-
        ior; it is just possible that with *sectam* Cicero is referring to Stoicism
        (attractive to the Romans because of its practical hardheadedness),
        even though this sense of *secta* to refer to a philosophical school is
        rarely attested until after the Augustan period.

500. **rē, verbīs:** case and reason? Hint: not abl. of comparison. Ben. 226. An
        example of Roman chauvinism!
    secūtī sumus: sequor, sequī, secūtus sum, follow; here "act in accor-
        dance with"

501. **Graecōs: Graecus-a-um,** *adj.,* Greek; **Graecī,** *m. pl.,* the Greeks
    doctissimōs hominēs: omit *hominēs* in translation. Latin regularly
        avoids having an adjective modify a proper noun, and uses the
        construction found here, where we English speakers might expect
        Graecōs doctissimōs.
    quibus: dat. with *licēbat*
    cum: identify the kind of clause, Ben. 309.3. Hint: look at the mood and
        the *tamen* in the main clause.
    facere: here intrans., "to act"; *facere* and *loquī et scrībere* echo, and con-
        trast with, *rē* and *verbīs* above at 500: whereas the Romans are better
        doers than philosophers, the Greeks theorize because they are no
        longer free to act.

502. **scrībere: scrībō, scrībere, scrīpsī, scrīptum,** write (books)
    magnificē: magnificus-a-um, *adj.,* grand, splendid; noble, excellent;
        luxurious, sumptuous
    alia quaedam: take with *praecepta.*

503. **mūtātīs Graeciae temporibus:** constr.? Ben. 227.
    mūtātīs: mūtō (1), alter, change; transform, become different *(often for
        the worse)*
    Graeciae: Graecia, Graeciae, *f.,* Greece
    temporibus: tempus, temporis, *n.,* time; occasion; opportunity; here pl.,
        "the times"; Greek freedom of action—and hence her statesmen's
        capacity for statesmanlike actions—had been almost continuously

circumscribed from the middle of the fourth century B.C. on. First, Macedonia (Philip II, king from 359–336, Alexander the Great, king from 336–323, and their successors) established control over the Greek city-states in 338 B.C. Then the Romans were drawn into Greek affairs during the Second Punic War (218–201 B.C.); during the next half century they gained complete control of the Greek-speaking world.

praecepta: praecipiō, praecipere, praecēpī, praeceptum, instruct, teach; advise, warn; *hence subst.* **praeceptum, -ī,** *n.* "that which has been instructed," teaching, doctrine, precept

exstitērunt: "have sprung up"

504 (ch. 41). **itaque,** *adv.,* and so, consequently, therefore

aliī...aliī: "some...others"

aliī voluptātis causā: refers to the Epicureans, followers of the Athenian philosopher Epicurus (341–270 B.C.), who taught that people should live according to the dictates of *hēdonē,* "pleasure" (so Engl. "hedonism"), defined by Epicurus as avoidance of pain and disturbance. His doctrines were often misinterpreted in the ancient world, just as they are today (e.g., "Eat, drink, and be merry, for tomorrow we die" is often mis-cited as an Epicurean sentiment). At any rate, Cicero disapproved of the Epicurean position.

It is interesting to note that Cicero's contemporary, the Epicurean poet Lucretius (99 or 94 B.C.–55 B.C.), was just completing his philosophical poem *dē rērum nātūrā* ("On the Nature of the Universe") in Rome during this time (it would be published posthumously in 55 B.C.).

causā: the prep.

omnia: acc. obj. of *facere*

sapientēs: sapiō, sapīre, sapiī *or* **sapīvī,** taste; have good taste, be discerning, sensible, or wise; *hence part.* **sapiēns, sapientis** *as adj.,* intelligent, sensible, wise; subj. acc. of *facere.*

aliī...coniungerent: Academic and Peripatetic philosophers.

506. **coniungendam [esse].**

ut: here may introduce a clause of result or (less likely) purpose.

rēs: acc.

507. **inter,** *prep. w. acc.,* between, among, amid

repugnantīs: repugnō (1), fight against, resist; *(of abstract qualities)* be inimical to, be inconsistent with. *Repugnantīs* is acc. pl., to be taken with *rēs.*

dīcendī: take after *facultāte.*
facultāte: facultās, facultātis, *f.,* ability, skill, dexterity; perhaps "craftiness"? [**facilis,** easy]; case? Ben. 218.

508. **illud ūnum dērectum...quī probāvērunt:** *quī* is the subject both of its own clause and of the main clause. The entire sentence refers to the Stoics (see 499n.).
iter: iter, itineris, *n.,* way, road; journey
cum labōre: "through painstaking work"

509. **probāvērunt:** as usual, not "prove"
prope: here used as an adv.
scholīs: schola, scholae, *f.,* school; schoolroom; philosophical school or sect [Gk. **scholē,** leisure time given to discussion and learning]

510. **blandīmenta:** blandīmentum, blandīmentī, *n.,* flattery; allurement, pleasure, delight [**blandior,** flatter, from **blandus,** ingratiating, flattering]; this noun is usually found in pl., as here.
nātūra: nātūra, nātūrae, *f.,* nature; birth; character, temperament, innate abilities, one's "make-up" [**nāscor,** be born]
genuit: gignō, gignere, genuī, genitum, beget, bear, bring forth; cause, bring about
quibus: antecedent? Case? Ben. 219.
sōpīta: sōpiō (4), lull to sleep, overcome with sleep [**sopor,** sleep]

511. **cōnīvēret:** cōnīveō, cōnīvēre, cōnīvī *or* cōnīxī, close the eyes (in sleep); let pass unnoticed, overlook
interdum, *adv.,* sometimes, occasionally, now and then
adulēscentiae: dat.
lūbricās: lūbricus-a-um, *adj.,* slippery; uncertain, hazardous
ostendit: ostendō, ostendere, ostendī, ostentum *or* ostēnsum, show, display, reveal; tense? Hint: how does the tense of *posset* help? Think about sequence, Ben. 267.

512. **quibus:** case? Ben. 218; kind of clause?
illa: antecedent?
īnsistere: īnsistō, īnsistere, īnstitī, stand still, stand firm
ingredī: ingredior, ingredī, ingressus sum, step or walk forward, progress
cāsū: cāsus, cāsūs, *m.,* a falling down; accident, chance, mishap; moral failure, mistake [**cadō,** fall]

prōlapsiōne: prōlapsiō, prōlapsiōnis, *f.,* a slipping or sliding; slip up, mishap [**prōlabī,** slide forward]; this appears to be the only occurrence of this word in Republican Latin.

513. **iūcundissimārum: iūcundus-a-um,** *adj.,* pleasant, agreeable, delightful; congenial (to be with); agreeable (to the senses) [**iuvō,** please]
varietātem: varietās, varietātis, *f.,* variety, diversity; a motley, an assortment; fickleness, unpredictability, capriciousness [**varius,** manifold]
dedit: subject?

514. **quā:** "on which"
nōn modo haec aetās sed etiam iam [aetās] conrōborāta.
haec aetās: "this time of life," i.e., youth
conrōborāta: corrōborō (1), strengthen, reinforce, fortify [**con-** + **rōborō,** strengthen, from **rōbur**]; *aetās conrōborāta* is "a mature age," "maturity."

515–517: a good ex. of Ciceronian "padding."

515 (ch. 42). **ob,** *prep. w. acc.,* because of, on account of; **quam ob rem** (sometimes written as one word, *quamobrem*), *interrog. adv.,* for what reason?, why?; *rel. adv.,* for which reason, why; *causal,* for which reason, wherefore, therefore
sī: kind of condition? Ben. 302.
invēneritis: inveniō, invenīre, invēnī, inventum, encounter, come upon; procure, acquire, (manage to) get; find (out), discover
quī: governs *aspernētur, capiātur* (517), and *exclūdat* (517); kind of clause? Ben. 283.
aspernētur: aspernor (1), turn down, reject; despise, scorn

516. **pulchritūdinem: pulchritūdō, pulchritūdinis,** *f.,* attractiveness, beauty, handsomeness; *pulchritūdinem rērum* is "beautiful things."
nōn...nōn...nōn: figure of speech? Ben. 350.11.b.
odōre: odor, odōris, *m.,* smell, odor *(pleasant or unpleasant)*; aroma; sense of smell
tactū: tactus, tactūs, *m.,* touch; sense of touch or feeling [**tangō,** touch]
sapōre: sapor, sapōris, *m.,* flavor, taste; sense of taste

517. **exclūdat: exclūdō, exclūdere, exclūdī, exclūsum,** keep or shut out, bar, exclude [**ex-** + **claudō,** close]
auribus: auris, auris, *f.,* ear

suāvitātem: **suāvitās, suāvitātis,** *f.,* pleasantness, agreeability; attractiveness, charm [**suāvis,** pleasant, agreeable]; *omnem suāvitātem:* "every sweetness [of sound]," i.e., "every sweet sound"

hominī ego: juxtaposition

518.　**fortasse,** *adv.,* perhaps, possibly, "it may be that..." [rel. to **forte**]

paucī: paucī-ae-a, *adj.,* few, a few; subject with *ego*

deōs: deus, deī, *m.,* god

propitiōs: propitius-a-um, *adj.,* favorably inclined, well-disposed, kind(ly)

plērīque: plērīque, plēraeque, plēraque, *adj.,* most of, the greater part of, very many; *m. pl.,* the majority, many people; note that *-que* is part of the word, not the conj. Here *plērīque* is set in contrast with *ego et...paucī* (so also *īrātōs* with *propitiōs*).

519 (XVIII).　**ergō,** *adv.,* consequently, then, therefore

dēserta: dēserō, dēserere, dēseruī, dēsertum, leave, abandon; *hence part.* **dēsertus** *as adj.,* deserted, uninhabited; remote, secluded

inculta: incultus-a-um, *adj.,* not tilled, uncultivated; neglected

interclūsa: interclūdō, interclūdere, interclūsī, interclūsum, block, cut off; obstruct, prevent [**in + claudō,** close]

520.　**frondibus: frōns, frondis,** *f.,* a leafy branch; foliage, greenery. Do not confuse with *frōns, frontis,* the forehead, front.

virgultīs: virgulta, virgultōrum, *n.,* thicket, brushwood [**virga, virgula,** twig]

relinquātur, etc.: jussive subjunctives, Ben. 275.

520–533: an expansion of the parallel passage at 327–330.

521.　**nōn omnia...dēnegentur, nōn...superet...ratiō:** the usual negative in a jussive construction is *nē,* unless the negative is construed with a noun rather than with the verb: try to catch this in your translation.

omnia: "all facets of life"

522.　**vēra:** "honest," "upright," "true blue"

vēra illa: modifies *ratiō.*

vincat: vincō, vincere, vīcī, victum, conquer, defeat; be victorious, triumph

aliquandō, *indef. adv.,* at some time, once; at any time, ever; at times, occasionally

523. **dum,** *conj.,* while *(w. indic.)*; until *(w. subj.)*
    dum modo: = *dummodo,* "provided only that," "if only," "so long as," a clause of proviso, in which the subjunctive is regular, Ben. 310.
    illa: "the following," as often
    in hōc genere: "in this matter"

524. **praescrīptiō: praescrīptiō, praescrīptiōnis,** *f.,* a teaching, precept, rule
    moderātiō: moderātiō, moderātiōnis, *f.,* moderation, restraint; limitation, restriction [**moderor,** regulate, direct]
    parcat: parcō, parcere, pepercī, parsūrus, spare, be merciful to; refrain from; protect, be careful with
    iuventūs: here concrete, "a young man"
    pudīcitiae: "good name," but see 65n.

525. **nē:** the usual negative in a jussive expression (see 521n.)
    aliēnam [pudīcitiam].
    patrimōnium: patrimōnium, patrimōnī, *n.,* property of a *paterfamiliās,* estate; inheritance
    faenore: faenus, faenoris, *n.,* interest

526. **trucīdētur: trucīdō** (1), butcher, slaughter; destroy utterly, ruin [**caedō,** slaughter]
    incurrat: incurrō, incurrere, incurrī, incursum, rush upon, attack, invade; compare the Engl. noun "incursion." *...nē incurrat in alterīus domum atque familiam* refers to unwarranted prosecutions or obliquely to the factious street fighting of the kind led by (among others) P. Clodius Pulcher.
    nē probrum castīs [īnferat], [nē] lābem integrīs [īnferat], [nē] īnfamiam bonīs īnferat: note the carefully paired antitheses again (see 140–155).

527. **probrum: probrum, probrī,** *n.,* disgraceful or shameful act, misdeed; lewdness, unchastity; disgrace, shame
    lābem: lābēs, lābis, *f.,* spot, stain; a "blot" on one's reputation, disgrace, dishonor
    integrīs: integer, integra, integrum, *adj.,* untouched, untried; undamaged, whole; moral, upright [rel. to *tag-, root of **tangō,** touch]
    īnfāmiam: īnfāmia, īnfāmiae, *f.,* bad reputation, notoriety; discredit, disgrace, dishonor
    īnferat: īnferō, īnferre, intulī, illātum, bring or carry in; march forward, advance, attack; hurl, throw

528. **terreat: terreō, terrēre, terruī, territum,** terrify; terrorize
      intersit: intersum, interesse, interfuī, be present, be involved or take part in
      īnsidiīs: īnsidiae, īnsidiārum, *f. pl.,* ambush, trap; treacherous plot, conspiracy [**īnsideō,** lie in ambush, fr. **sedeō,** sit]
      scelere: scelus, sceleris, *n.,* utterly evil deed, crime, villainy
      careat: careō, carēre, caruī, lack, need, want; be free from, be without *(w. abl.)*
      postrēmō: postrēmus-a-um, last; *hence abl. as adv.,* at last, finally [superl. of **posterus**]

529. **pāruerit: pāreō, pārēre, pāruī,** obey; give way, submit, or yield to *(w. dat.)*
      (et) dederit: asyndeton, or lack of connectives, Ben. 346.
      temporis: partitive genitive with *aliquid,* Ben. 201.2.
      lūdum: "love affair" (see 491n.)

530. **inānīs:** acc. pl.
      hāsce: on -*ce,* see 3n.
      revocet: revocō (1), call back, recall

531. **cūram: cūra, cūrae,** *f.,* anxiety, concern, worry; attention, care, pains
      reī forēnsis: "activity in the law courts"

532. **ut:** kind of clause? Ben. 282.
      ea: object of the perf. inf. *abiēcisse* and *contempsisse*
      anteā, *adv.,* before this, earlier, previously
      dēspexerat: dēspiciō, dēspicere, dēspexī, dēspectum, look down on, despise, reject, scorn
      satietāte: satietās, satietātis, *f.,* overabundance, satiety, exhaustion created by excess [**satis,** enough]
      abiēcisse: abiciō, abicere, abiēcī, abiectum, throw away or down; give up, let go, renounce

533. **experiendō: experior, experīrī, expertus sum,** try, attempt; experience, undergo
      contempsisse: contemnō, contemnere, contempsī, contemptum, look down on, despise, disdain; value little, treat as unimportant [**temnō,** despise, scorn]

534–588 (chs. 43–47): Cicero asserts that many a fine Roman has had a rocky youth. At any rate, Caelius's whole career thus far is proof of his good character.

534 (ch. 43). **ac...quidem:** see 30n.

    et nostrā et patrum maiōrumque: the poss. pron. *nostrā* is the equivalent of a gen., and so the gen.'s that follow are parallel. Note use of *et...et...que,* like "*both* George *and* Jack '*n*' Jill," see 2n.

535.   **memoriā: memoria, memoriae,** *f.,* memory, recollection; case?

    summī: do not translate "highest"; the word is parallel with *clārissimī.*

    fuērunt: "there have been." Explain the kind of perfect used here, Ben. 257n2.

536.   **quōrum:** take with *virtūtēs.*

    dēfervissent: dēfervēscō, dēfervēscere, dēfervī *or* **dēferbuī,** stop boiling, simmer down; *(of passions)* cool or calm down, subside [**dē-,** expr. reversal of a process + **ferveō,** boil].

    eximiae: eximius-a-um, *adj.,* exceptional, uncommon, remarkable [**eximō,** take out]

537.   **firmātā iam aetāte:** = *conrōborātā iam aetāte* (see 514n.); construction? Ben. 227. What is the force of *iam?*

    firmātā: firmō (1), reinforce, strengthen, fortify [**firmus**]

    quibus: antecedent?

    nēminem: obj. of *nōmināre.* Note the alliteration.

538.   **libet: libet, libēre, libuit** *or* **libitum est,** it pleases, it is agreeable *(+ inf. as subject + dat. of person);* **mihi libet,** I want, I feel like

    vōsmet: case? Personal pronouns with the enclitic *-met* are intensive, Ben. 84.2.

    vōsmet vōbīscum: figure? See 134n., Ben. 374.3.

    recordāminī: recordor (1), recall, recollect, remember. This form is a plural present passive imperative ("Remember!"), unfortunately identical in form with the second person plural present passive indicative ("You are remembering"). The singular imperative would be *recordāre* ("Remember!"), which looks like a present active infinitive such as *amāre,* "to love."

        (The meaning is active because the verb is deponent. Passive imperatives occur most frequently with deponent verbs, although they are sometimes found with regular verbs, e.g., *monēre,* "Be warned!"; *monēminī,* "Be warned!")

    nōlō: nōlō, nōlle, nōluī, not wish, not want; be unwilling [**nē,** not + **volō,** wish]

539. **cuiusquam fortis atque inlustris virī:** take with *minimum errātum.*
      fortis: here has a certain moral import as well: "decent," "respectable,"
      "worthy."
      errātum: here a noun: "error," "mistake"; "moral offense," "slip up."
      nōlō...nē minimum quidem errātum...coniungere: one way to catch
      the emphatic effect of the double negative, common in Latin and
      older English, but alien to good usage today, is to translate "I do not
      want to commingle any infraction, not even the smallest, with..."

540. **maximā:** recall the difference in Lat. use of superlatives, 276n.
      coniungere: "connect," "juxtapose"
      quod sī: = *et sī id*; why is *quod* outside the *si*-clause? How do we know it
      is *not* just "but if"? (Hint: is *facere* trans. or intrans.?)
      sī: kind of condition? Ben. 304.

541. **ā mē:** ablative of agency, Ben. 216.
      praedicārentur: praedicō (1), make public, announce, state; cite (as an
      example or precedent) [**prae,** in front of + **dicō** (1), dedicate, set apart;
      the *-i-* is short in *(prae)dicāre,* long in the more common *(prae)dīcere*]

542. **partim,** *adv.,* in part, partly; **partim...partim,** (for) one part...(for) anoth-
      er part; (for) some...(for) others

542–543. Here we have yet another list of excesses.

      nimia: nimius-a-um, *adj.,* very great, very much; too great, excessive;
        immoderate, extravagant
      profūsa: profundō, profundere, profūdī, profūsum, pour forth, shed;
        spend, squander; discharge, bring forth, release; develop, produce
      luxuriēs: luxuriēs, luxuriēī, *f.,* lush growth of vegetation, fruitful-
        ness; excessively rich living, extravagance, dissipation [**luxus,**
        extravagance]

543. **magnitūdō: magnitūdō, magnitūdinis,** *f.,* size, magnitude; vast size,
        extensiveness [**magnus,** large]
      aeris: aes, aeris, *n.,* copper; bronze; coin; money; **aes aliēnum:** "anoth-
        er's money," i.e., a debt
      sūmptūs: here in pl. "expenses," with the implication of "excessive ex-
        penses," "extravagance."
      quae: "which things," *n.,* referring to and summing up the preceding
        list; and dir. obj. of *dēfenderet.*

544. **posteā,** *adv.,* afterwards, later, subsequently
virtūtibus: case? Ben. 218.
obtecta: obtegō, obtegere, obtexī, obtectum, cover, protect; cover up, conceal, screen; *obtecta* modifies *quae.*
adulēscentiae: take after *excūsātiōne* (and cf. 345: *dēprecārī vacātiōnem adulēscentiae*).
quī vellet: translate "he who so wished"; the entire clause is the subject of *dēfenderet*; mood of *vellet*? Ben. 283.

545. **dēfenderet:** mood? Ben. 304.
        We do not know to which noble Romans in particular (if any) Cicero was referring in this passage, but speculations include C. Valerius Flaccus and Caesar (both of Cicero's own day), as well as the great general of the Second Punic War, P. Cornelius Scipio Africanus Maior (236 B.C.–184/183 B.C.), each of whom had stories of youthful dissipation associated with him.

(ch. 44). **at vērō:** adversative, "but in fact," "on the contrary..."

546. **cōnfīdentius: cōnfīdō, cōnfīdere, cōnfīsus sum,** trust completely, be-lieve in; *hence part.* **cōnfīdēns, cōnfīdentis** *as adj.,* confident, daring [**fīdō,** trust]
audeō: audeō, audēre, ausus sum, dare, venture [**avidus,** eager]

547. **quaedam: quīdam, quaedam, quiddam** *or* **quoddam,** *indef. pron. and adj.,* a certain (one), a particular (one); acc. obj. of *cōnfitērī*; explain what this word refers to.
frētus: frētus-a-um, *adj.,* relying, trusting, or depending on (+ *abl.*); for *frētus vestrā sapientiā,* etc., see 218n.
sapientiā: sapientia, sapientiae, *f.,* good sense, soundness of judgment, prudence, wisdom [**sapiō,** be sensible]. Case? See *frētus* just above.
cōnfitērī: cōnfiteor, cōnfitērī, cōnfessus sum, admit, acknowledge; al-low, concede, grant; reveal, make known [**fateor,** confess]

549. **lustrōrum: lustrum, lustrī,** *n.,* bog, marshland, quagmire; *pl.,* **lustra,** brothel, den of iniquity; debauchery
quod quidem vitium ventris: *quod* is a connecting relative. Note the careful alliterations.
ventris: venter, ventris, *m.,* the belly, stomach; appetite, gluttony

550. **gurgitis: gurges, gurgitis,** *m.,* flood, whirlpool; a glutton; insatiable desire, gluttony
      minuit: minuō, minuere, minuī, minūtum, diminish, lessen, reduce
      hominibus: case? Ben. 188.

551. **auget: augeō, augēre, auxī, auctum,** increase, enlarge
      dēliciae: dēliciae, dēliciārum, *f.,* allurement, charm, delight; dissolute behavior, indulgence, dissipation; luxury, comfort; darling, sweetheart, beloved, "pet"; here "affairs" (Austin at 44.8).
      quae [in iūdicium] vocantur.

552. **praeditīs: praeditus-a-um,** endowed or equipped with, possessing *(w. abl.)* [**prae-** + **datum,** given]
      diūtius: compar. of *diū.*
      solent: soleō, solēre, solitus sum, be accustomed to, be usually [a certain way]
      mātūrē: mātūrus-a-um, ripe, mature; intellectually or morally mature; timely, quick; *hence adv.* **mātūrē,** quickly, in due time; early

553. **celeriter: celer, celeris, celere,** *adj.,* fast, quick, speedy
      dēflōrēscunt: dēflōrēscō, dēflōrēscere, *(of plants)* shed flowers, wither; lose vigor, decline, fade away [**dē-** + **flōreō,** flourish]; "flower and fade" (Austin at 44.10)
      occupātum: occupō (1), seize, grasp, lay hold of; engage, preoccupy [one's attention]

554. **impedītum: impediō, impedīre, impedīvī, impedītum,** entangle, ensnare; hinder, obstruct, prevent [**pēs,** foot]
      -ve, *enclitic conj.,* or
      audī(vi)stis.
      prō sē: i.e., as the first speaker at this, his own trial.

555. **audīstis:** what is the effect of the repetition?
      accūsāret—dēfendendī: note the juxtaposition.
      dēfendendī haec causā: take *haec* as dir. obj. of *loquor,* and *dēfendendī* w. *causā.*

556. **glōriandī: glōrior** (1), glory in, boast of, try to bring *glōria* to oneself; deponent verbs can have some active forms, such as gerunds, pres. and fut. act. participles and fut. act. infs. Why does Cicero feel it necessary to preface his remarks in this way?
      genus ōrātiōnis: see 299n.

557. **quae vestrā prūdentiā est:** Austin takes this as a compression for *prūdentiā* (abl. of means) *quae vestra est, = prūdentiā vestrā.*

558. **[et haec] perspexistis: perspiciō, perspicere, perspexī, perspectum,** inspect thoroughly, scrutinize; perceive fully, note thoroughly
in eō: = *in Caeliō.*
nōn sōlum: answered by *sed* below
ēlūcēre: ēlūceō, ēlūcēre, ēlūxī, shine forth, glitter; be clear, become apparent [**ē/ex,** out, forth + **lūceō,** shine]
eius: "of Caelius"; take w. *ingenium.*

559. **vidēbātis:** explain the tense.
quod: antecedent is *ingenium*
saepe, *adv.,* often
etiam sī: "even if"; kind of condition? Ben. 302.
industriā: abl. of means, Ben. 218.
valet: valeō, valēre, valuī, valitum, be strong, be well; be effective, avail, succeed

560. **ipsum:** "alone," "by itself"
vīribus: vīs, vīs, *f.,* force, power, violence; *pl.* **vīrēs, vīrium,** strength; *suīs vīribus,* "on one's own"
inerat: īnsum, inesse, īnfuī, be in or on; be contained in, be present in (+ *dat. or* **in** + *abl.*)
nisi mē...fallēbat: another formulaic clause, with impersonal verb ["unless it deceived me"]; kind of condition? Ben. 302.
mē: acc. obj. of *fallēbat*
benivolentiam: benevolentia, benevolentiae, *f.,* goodwill, kindness, friendship

561. **forte:** see 1n.
ratiō: modified by the two participles that follow.
et...et...et: the first two bind the participles; the third connects *cūrā* and *vigiliīs.*
bonīs artibus: "liberal arts," "cultural pursuits"; compare 100 and 279.
vigiliīs: vigilia, vigiliae, *f.,* wakefulness; watchfulness, vigilance; close attention, care [**vigil,** watchman]; here "burning the midnight oil"

562. **ēlabōrāta: ēlabōrō** (1), labor hard, strive, take pains; develop, perfect [**ex** + **labōrō,** take pains]

scītōte: for the form, see 437n.; but *scītōte* is used here because the pres. imper. of some words, such as *sciō,* was avoided: **scī* and **scīte* are unattested.

cupīditātēs: "lusts"; "dissipated tastes" (Grant); plural
Plural abstract substantives often have a concrete meaning.

eās cupīditātēs vs. **haec studia:** the quintessence of the contrast Cicero draws between appearances of excess and dissipation (and the case that the prosecution has built on these appearances), and what must have been at least part of the reality (that Caelius was a hard worker). The idea recurs in the peroration (chs. 70–80).

563. **disputō: disputō** (1), argue one's case, present a point of view, treat of [**dis-** + **putō**]; the word rarely (if ever) means "dispute" in its usual English meaning; compare Engl. "disputation" (which is an oral thesis defense).
facile: the adv.

564. **esse:** mood? Ben. 328.1.
posse: mood? Ben. 314.
fierī: fīō, fierī, factus sum, be made, become; *fīō* is used as the passive of *faciō.* A vowel before another vowel is usually short, and so *-īō* is unusual (so also *-ēī* in fifth declension nouns like *diēs*); *fierī (nōn) potest ut* + subj. is a common way of expressing "it is (not) possible that/to" (Ben. 297.2).
animus: subject of *possit* in 568.
libīdinī: case?

565. **dēditus: dēdō, dēdere, dēdidī, dēditum,** give up, surrender; dedicate or devote oneself to *(+ dat.)* [**dē,** thoroughly + **dō,** give]
amōre: this and the abl.'s that follow are governed by *impedītus* below.
dēsīderiō: dēsīderium, dēsīderī, *n.,* a longing for, desire, need; natural desire, lust. The word is derived from *sīdus, sīderis,* star: the ancients felt that the stars and constellations could help or afflict human health and destiny.
inopiā: inopia, inopiae, *f.,* lack (of wealth), poverty [**in-**privative + **ops,** wealth]; *cōpia, inopia:* figure of speech?

566. **nōn numquam:** "sometimes"; figure of speech? Ben. 375.1.
hoc: object of *sustinēre.*
quicquid: quisquis, quidquid *or* **quicquid (***adj.* **quodquod),** *generalizing rel. pron. and pron. adj.,* whoever, whatever
nōs: "we orators"

567.   **agendō...cōgitandō:** what is being compared or contrasted?

568.   **an:** usually used in alternative questions, but here introduces a rhetorical question that is designed to dispel an imaginary objection (so also at 576).
       vōs: i.e., the *iūdicēs*

569.   **praemiīs: praemium, praemī,** *n.,* booty, plunder, profit; reward, prize; distinction [**prae-** + **emō,** acquire]
       ēloquentiae: ēloquentia, ēloquentiae, *f.,* speaking ability; eloquence [**ē,** out, forth + **loquor,** speak]

570.   **voluptāte:** "pleasure," "delight," "satisfaction"
       dīcendī: "of oratory"
       honōre: "distinction," "prestige"

571.   **tam sint paucī semperque fuerint:** = *sint et semper fuerint tam paucī*; for the sentiment, see Cic., *dē ōr.* i.6–16.
       fuerint: mood and reason?
       quī...versentur: relative clause of characteristic after *tam*.

572.   **obterendae: obterō, obterere, obtrīvī, obtrītum,** crush underfoot, trample; destroy, wipe out; suppress [**ob-,** expr. opposition or confrontation + **terō,** wear down]

573.   **dēlectātiōnis: dēlectātiō, dēlectātiōnis,** *f.,* amusement, enjoyment, pleasure [**dēlectō,** delight in]
       lūdus: "amorous play"
       iocus: iocus, iocī, *m.,* joke, jest; love play

574.   **familiārium:** "with close friends"; but before translating in this way, be sure to identify the form.
       obterendae...dēserendus: cf. Seneca, *contrōversiae,* i.8.
       quā rē: = *quāre,* "for which reason," "therefore" (so also at 616)
       in hōc genere: "in this respect"
       offendit: offendō, offendere, offendī, offēnsum, dash or strike against, hit; drive away; displease, annoy

575.   **ā studiōque:** = *et ā studiō*; *-que* cannot attach to certain prepositions, particularly monosyllables.
       dēterret: dēterreō, dēterrēre, dēterruī, dēterritum, put off, discourage from, deter, discourage, ward off

nōn quō: "not because"

ingenia: "talents" taken as a whole is pl. in Engl. but sg. in Latin (*ingenium*); but the plural here must refer to more than one person: "intellects."

dēficiant: dēficiō, dēficere, dēfēcī, dēfectum, abandon, forsake, leave; fail, be wanting

aut doctrīna puerīlis [dēficiat].

576. **doctrīna: doctrīna, doctrīnae,** *f.,* teaching, instruction, training; learning, knowledge

puerīlis: puerīlis-is-e, *adj.,* of or pert. to a boy or child; in boyhood; childish, immature

an: the construction is the same as at 568.

hic: Caelius.

sī: kind of condition? Ben. 304.

sēsē: = *se,* with little difference in meaning or emphasis in Cicero.

istī vītae: "the life you describe."

577. **cōnsulārem: cōnsulāris-is-e,** *adj.,* of or pert. to a consul, of consular rank

cōnsulārem hominem: C. Antonius Hybrida (see 178n.)

admodum, *adv., (w. verbs)* very much, to a high degree; *(w. adj.'s)* very much, altogether, fully, quite *(esp. w. words denoting age).*

in iūdicium vocāvisset: on this expression, see 14n. (so also *hāc in aciē versātur* in the next line).

578. **sī:** kind of condition? Ben. 304.

fugeret: fugō, fugere, fūgī, fugitum, escape, flee; avoid, shun; a conative (Ben. 260.3) translation like "[if] he were trying to shirk..." catches the Latin nicely.

obstrictus: obstringō, obstringere, obstrīnxī, obstrictum, bind, oblige; constrain, hold in check, fetter [**stringō,** tie, bind]

voluptātibus: case?

579. **hāc in aciē:** = *in hāc aciē; hāc* would be accompanied by a wave of the hand: "this which is about and around us."

aciē: aciēs, aciēī, *f.,* a sharp edge; battle line; battle [***ac-,** root of **acuō,** "sharpen," and **acer**]. *OLD's* "the fray" gets it nicely. The metaphorical use of *aciēs, pugna,* and *certāmen* for the courts and politics is common (Austin at 47.9).

appeteret: appetō, appetere, appetiī *or* **appetīvī, appetītum,** seek to obtain, strive after; attack, assault [**petō,** seek]; *amīcitiam appetere* = "to court someone's friendship"; *inimīcitiās appetere* = "to risk bad blood."

inimīcitiās: see 379n.

580. **subīret: subeō, subīre, subiī** *or* **subīvī, subitum,** go up to, approach; undergo, endure, face

subīret perīculum capitis: see 185 for another ex. of this common construction, *subīre perīculum* + gen. of the charge.

perīculum: perīculum, perīculī, *n.,* experiment, test, attempt; danger, risk; a criminal trial, suit at law

capitis: "a capital case"

īnspectante: īnspectō (1), look at or on, view, watch; *special use w. pres. part. in an abl. absol.:* "with X *(abl.)* watching," "under the very eyes of X"

581. **tot,** *indecl. adj.,* as many; so many

mēnsīs: mēnsis, mēnsis, *m.,* month; case and reason? Ben. 181.

salūte: salūs, salūtis, *f.,* health, soundness; safety, welfare, well-being; greeting, salutation

582. **dīmicāret: dīmicō** (1), battle, fight; struggle, strive [**micō,** flash, flicker, move rapidly]

Nihilne: case and reason of *nihil*?

vīcīnitās: an echo of the *domus* theme, see 100n.

redolet: redoleō, redolēre, redoluī, emit an odor; smell of [**re-** + **oleō,** smell]

nihil...hominum fāma [redolet].

583. **illae:** = *Baiae.*

584. **nōn loquuntur sōlum:** = *nōn sōlum loquuntur.*

personant: personō, personāre, personuī, personitum, resound, ring out; proclaim loudly, cry out, bellow [**per** + **sonō,** sound out, resound; unrelated to *persōna,* see 355n.]

hūc, *adv.,* to this place; to this point, to this degree, this far

585. **esse prōlapsam: prōlābor, prōlābī, prōlapsus sum,** move forward, progress or proceed gradually; slip into a mistake, err; decline, degenerate [**prō-** + **lābor,** glide]; mood? Ben. 313.

ut: kind of clause? Ben. 284.

ea: the *ūnīus mulieris* above

sōlitūdinem: sōlitūdō, sōlitūdinis, *f.,* solitude, isolation; lonesomeness; *pl.,* a deserted place, wilderness [**sōlus**]

586. **tenebrās: tenebrae, tenebrārum,** *f.,* darkness; a dark place, "shadows"; obscurity, concealment

haec: color or significance? See 579n.

flāgitiōrum: flāgitium, flāgitī, *n.*, a disgraceful, scandalous, or shameful act, scandal [flāgitō, demand eagerly, fr. flāgitō, burn; in origin, a *flāgitium* was a contemptible act done in the heat of rage or passion; see also 191n.]

integumenta: integumentum, integumentī, *n.*, that which covers or protects, covering, protection; a means of concealment, cloak, disguise [integō, cover]

587. frequentissima: frequēns, frequentis, *adj.*, dense, crowded; repeated, constant, regular
   celebrītāte: celebrītās, celebrītātis, *f.*, crowd, multitude; crowded conditions [celeber, crowded]
   lūce: lūx, lūcis, *f.*, light

588. laetētur: laetor (1), rejoice, be delighted, revel in [laetus, cheerful]

589–619 (chs. 48–50): Cicero declares that the case boils down to the fact that Clodia is a meretrix, and that for this reason no blame can attach to Caelius for his affair with her.

589. sī: identify the condition, Ben. 302. Meaning and effect?
   sī [ali]quis est quī...putet: "if there is anyone who...thinks."
   interdictum (esse): interdīcō, interdīcere, interdīxī, interdictum, forbid, prohibit, stop (+ *dat. of person and abl. of the thing forbidden)*; here used impersonally. The word has a legal connotation (cf. the famous *aquā et ignī* (abl.) *interdīcō*, "prohibit from receiving fire and water," the formal Roman legal phrase for "banish").

590. putet: mood? Ben. 283.
   valdē, *adv.*, vigorously; exceedingly, extremely; intensely, very much [syncopated adv. fr. validus, strong]
   negāre: negō (1), say that...not, say no, deny

591. abhorret: abhorreō, abhorrēre, abhorruī, shudder at, shrink back from; be inconsistent with, deviate or differ from; be free from
   saeculī: saeculum, saeculī, *n.*, generation; an age, current times, era; a full century

592. concessīs: concēdō, concēdere, concessī, concessum, go away, withdraw; give place, yield; *hence part.* concessus-a-um *as adj.*, permitted, allowable, lawful; *hence (rare) subst.* concessum, -ī, *n.*, that which has been permitted, a thing permitted: "allowances" (Grant), "indulgences."

quandō, *adv.,* when; quandō...quandō...quandō...quandō: figure of speech? Ben. 350.11b.

593. hoc: subject; used generally and loosely: "this kind of behavior."
factitātum: factitō (1), make or do frequently or habitually, be accustomed to do, practice [freq. of facīō, do]
reprehēnsum [est], permissum [est]

594. permissum [est]: permittō, permittere, permīsī, permissum, let go, let loose; give up, surrender; allow, permit
hīc: the adv.

595. ipsam rem dēfīniam: compare 71–72; the asyndeton in this line is noteworthy.
mulierem nūllam nōminābō: echoes *nihil iam in istam mulierem dīcō* at 475 (the parallel passage).
tantum: "just so much"

596. mediō: medius-a-um, the middle of; *hence n. subst.* medium, -ī, the middle; a neutral or uncommitted state; *hence* in mediō, "in the middle position," i.e., "undecided"

596–606: The entire chapter (49) is composed of one long conditional period. The apodosis begins with utrum at 604:

Sī quae	nōn nupta mulier	domum suam	patefēcerit omnium cupiditātī
			palamque sēsē in meretrīciā vītā conlocā(ve)rit,
[sī]			virōrum aliēnissimōrum convīviīs ūtī īnstituerit,
	sī	hoc in urbe	[faciat],
	sī	[hoc] in hortīs	[faciat],
	sī [hoc] in Baiārum illā celebritāte	faciat,...:
sī dēnique ita sēsē gerat non incessū sōlum
sed ornātū atque comitātū,
nōn flagrantia oculōrum, nōn lībertāte sermōnum,
sed etiam complexū, osculātiōne, actīs, nāvigātiōne, convīviīs,
ut nōn sōlum meretrīx sed etiam proterva meretrīx procāxque videātur:
cum hāc sī quī adulēscēns forte fuerit,
utrum hic tibi, L. Herennī, adulter an amātor,
expugnāre pudīcitiam an explēre libīdinem voluisse videātur?

quae: indefinite ("some"), as usual after *sī*
nōn nupta: "not married," i.e., "widowed"

597.   **patefēcerit: patefaciō, patefacere, patefēcī, patefactum,** *(in various senses)* make visible; expose, uncover; open up, make available, "throw open" [**pateō,** lie open + **faciō**]
   omnium: "of all men"
   cupīditātī: case?

598.   **conlocārit:** mood? Ben. 302
   [sī] virōrum.
   ūtī: pres. inf. from *ūtor*
   īnstituerit: "has made a practice of" *(+ inf.)*

599.   **hoc:** object of *faciat*
   urbe: urbs, urbis, *f.,* city
   sī hoc in urbe [faciat], sī [hoc] in hortīs [faciat], sī [hoc] in Baiārum illā celebritāte faciat,...: figure of speech? Effect? Note the switch to the subj., Ben. 303.

600.   **incessū: incessus, incessūs,** *m.,* one's manner of walking, stride; bearing [**incēdō,** walk forward]; case and reason?
   ornātū: ornātus, ornātūs, *m.,* preparation; dress, "get up"; decoration, embellishment [**ornō,** adorn]

601.   **comitātū: comitātus, comitātūs,** *m.,* one's following, retinue, attendant crowd [**comitor,** accompany, fr. **comes,** companion]; here "the company she keeps"
   nōn...nōn: restate and reinforce previous *nōn sōlum;* omit in transl.
   flagrantiā: flagrantia, flagrantiae, *f.,* a blazing, burning, glittering, glow [**flagrō,** blaze with passion]; here "passionate glow" (of the eyes); Cicero referred to Clodia as *Boōpis* (Gk., "Ox-Eyed"), an epithet of Hera, because of her striking and expressive large brown eyes.

602.   **complexū: complexus, complexūs,** *m.,* embrace [**complector**]
   osculātiōne: osculātiō, osculātiōnis, *f.,* kissing [**osculum,** a kiss]. The word may have had an almost technical or mechanical ring to it ("kissifications"?; its only other occurrence in the classical period is at Cat. 48.6); if so, Clodia has a veritable assembly line of lovers. Cf. also Catullus's *bāsiātiōnēs.*
   actīs: from *acta,* "seashore" (as at 426); here refers colloquially to seaside parties (so also the next two words).
   nāvigātiōne: nāvigātiō, nāvigātiōnis, *f.,* sailing, navigation; a voyage [**nāvigō,** sail]; here "boating parties"

ut: identify the flag in the preceding clause(s) which shows what kind of clause this is.

603.   **meretrīx: meretrīx, meretrīcis,** *f.,* harlot, prostitute [**mereō,** earn (money)]

    procāx: procāx, procācis, *adj.,* impudent, shameless, licentious; demanding, importunate

604.   **videātur:** mood and reason? Ben. 303.

    cum hāc sī: = *sī cum hāc.*

    quī: the indef. *adj.*

    fuerit: fut. perf. indic. or pres. subj.? How does the verb in the apodosis help identify this form, and the type of condition?

    utrum: here an untranslatable particle which, with a following *an,* introduces an alternative question; in this case there are two parallel sets of alternative questions

    hic: the *quī* of the preceding clause

    tibi: "for your part"

605.   **amātor: amātor, amātōris,** *m.,* friend; lover, paramour [**amō,** love]

    expugnāre: expugnō (1), take by storm, capture, conquer, seize; overcome, subdue, wrest

    explēre: expleō, explēre, explēvī, explētum, fill up, make sufficient; assuage, satisfy *(an appetite or passion)*; achieve, fulfil

606 (ch. 50).   **oblīvīscor: oblīvīscor, oblīvīscī, oblītus sum,** forget; omit to mention, overlook, pass over in silence

    iniūriās: iniūria, iniūriae, *f.,* unlawful, injurious, or unjust treatment; injustice, injury, harm [**in-**priv. + **iūs**]; **iniūriās tuās:** cf. *dē domō* 62; *post red. in sen.* 18; *prō Sest.* 54.

    Clōdia: here named directly for the first time since 363.

607.   **dēpōnō: dēpōnō, dēpōnere, dēposuī, dēpositum,** lay aside

    dolōris meī: identify the reference (see intro., sec. 19).

    quae: subject of its own clause; antecedent is an understood *ea,* object of *neglegō.*

    abs: form of *ā, ab*; *abs tē* is slightly emphatic by position.

    in meōs: "against my family"

608. **mē absente:** constr.? Ben. 227.
nē sint haec in tē dicta quae dīxī: sarcasm is a ready product of what Austin calls Cicero's "elaborate pretence."

609. **et...et:** connects *crīmen* and *testem,* objects of *habēre.*
accūsātōrēs: see 32n. for the exact meaning of this word; it is the subject of *dīcunt.*

610. **quae:** indefinite, as usual after *sī*

611. **eius modī:** case and reason?
quālem: case and reason?
paulo: case and reason?
ante, *adv.,* beforehand, previously; *prep. w. acc.,* before, in front of
dēscripsī: dēscrībō, dēscrībere, dēscrīpsī, dēscrīptum, describe, delineate, portray, represent. Austin suggests "painted" and cautions that "no English word quite gives the meaning of *describo* in such a context, where an evil picture is meant...; it is particularly used of a repulsive appearance or of wicked morals" (at 50.18).
tuī: gen. with *dissimilis;* with *tuī dissimilis* compare *dissimilis istīus* at 476.
dissimilis: dissimilis-is-e, *adj.,* different from, unlike. Be sure to catch the humor.

612. **īnstitūtō:** perf. pass. part. of *īnstituō* used as a subst.: "custom," "way of life."
vītā īnstitūtōque: case?
aliquid: object of *habuisse;* take *ratiōnis* with it as a partive gen., Ben. 201.2.
hominem: subject of *habuisse*

613. **habuisse:** subject of *videātur*
num, particle introducing a question expecting the answer "no," of the form "you wouldn't..., would you?"
perturpe: perturpis-is-e, *adj.,* very base, very shameful, very disgraceful
perflāgitiōsum: perflāgitiōsus-a-um, *adj.,* very disgraceful, very scandalous
perturpe aut perflāgitiōsum: predicate adj.'s of the copulative phrase *esse videātur*

614. **ea:** "the woman"
sī: identify the condition. Ben. 302.
sīcut, *conj.,* just as, in the same manner as (+ *correl.*); just as *(for instance),* as indeed *(is the case)*

615. **volunt:** "they will have it"
   crīmen hoc: object of *pertimēscāmus*
   sī: identify the condition (Ben. 302) and the moods of *est, contemnis* and *pertimēscāmus* (Ben. 302, 300).

616. **pertimēscāmus: pertimēscō, pertimēscere, pertimuī,** become very scared of or frightened from
   quā rē: "for which reason"

617. **nihil:** subj. acc.
   Caeliō: case?

618. **impudentia: impudentia, impudentiae,** *f.,* shamelessness, immodesty *(in sexual conduct)*; impudence, lack of control; a strong word for a ringing conclusion
   cēterīs: these are her other lovers, who may have to endure the same travails as Caelius.

619. **magnam: magnus-a-um,** *adj.,* great, large
   ad sē dēfendendum: *ad sē dēfendendōs* would be more common; the construction of *ad* plus a trans. gerund is rare.

620–872 (chs. 51–69): finally, the **argūmentātiō**, postponed since ch. 31 (see the notes on pp. 109–110); it is a mixture of *cōnfirmātiō* (Cicero's analysis of the facts of the case) and *refūtātiō* (also called the *reprehēnsiō:* Cicero's rebuttal of the prosecution's analysis of the facts), plus a digression for a *miserātiō* (chs. 59–60); see intro. xxxi; Austin p. 112.

620–692 (chs. 51–55): Cicero addresses the charges against Caelius that pertain to his borrowing of gold from Clodia allegedly in order (1) to poison Dio of Alexandria via his host's (Lucius Lucceius's) slaves; and (2) to poison her.

620 (XXI, ch. 51). A nautical reference at this part of a speech was not unusual: cf. Hieronymus (St. Jerome), *Epistulae* 14.10.1:
   quia ē scopulōsīs locīs ēnāvigāvit ōrātiō et inter cavās spūmeīs fluctibus cautēs fragilis in altum cymba processit, expandenda vela sunt ventīs et quaestiōnum scopulīs transvadātīs, laetantium more nautārum, epilogī celeusma cantandum est.

"Because my speech has evaded the rocky places and the fragile boat has proceeded between the cliffs hollowed out by the foamy waves, the winds must spread open the sails, as the rocks of the case have been survived; in the custom of rejoicing sailors, the boatswain's call of the peroration must be sung."

ēmersisse: "to have come clear of"

vadīs: vadum, vadī, *n.,* a shallow, a shoal; *fig.,* shallows *(signifying safety or, as here, danger)*

scopulōs: scopulum, scopulī, *n.,* overhanging crag; projecting ledge; *fig.,* a hazard, danger [Gk. *skopelos*]

621.   **praetervecta...esse:** praetervehor, praetervehī, praetervectus sum, be carried past, travel past, get by

   ostenditur [esse].

   duo sunt enim crīmina: Cicero begins again where he had broken off at 365.

   ūna in mūliere: "pertaining to one woman"

623.   **summōrum facinōrum:** grammatically, a genitive of description (Ben. 203) with *crīmina* (see Austin, p. 170, at 51.2), but the phrase applies to the nearer *mūliere* (as a qualifying genitive) as well (hence Austin's confusion in his first edition); *aurī* and *venēnī* are in apposition.

   sūmptum [esse].

624.   **ēiusdem Clōdiae:** like *eadem persōna* at 355.

   necandae causā: constr.? Ben. 339; 198.1.

   parā(vi)sse.

625.   **aurum:** at 634 we find that this is in the form of *ornāmenta,* "jewelry" or "baubles."

   quod L[ūcī]. Luccēī servīs daret: rel. clause of purpose, Ben. 282.2.

   L. Luccēī: a senator of praetorian rank, Lucius Lucceius was a moderate optimate who called many *populārēs* friends, including Pompey and Cicero. A gentleman historian, during this period Lucceius was writing a history of Rome starting with the Social War (90–88 B.C.); he had no doubt graciously avoided Cicero's request (*ad fam.* 5.12) that he prepare a biographical history of the period from the Catilinarian conspiracy to Cicero's return from exile.

626. **daret, necārētur:** mood? Ben. 282.2.
      Alexandrīnus Diō: see chs. 18 and 23, esp. 205n.
      tum: perhaps fearing for his safety, Dio had moved from the house of Lucceius to that of Titus Coponius (see 279n.), where he was murdered.

627. **necārētur:** refers to Caelius's alleged attempts on Dio's life, not the murder that eventually took place; see 279n.
      magnum crīmen: acc. of exclamation, Ben. 183; there is no main verb in this sentence. On the sacrosanct status of *lēgātī*, see 262–284n.
      vel…vel: correlative ("either…or").
      lēgātīs: lēgātus, lēgātī, *m.,* ambassador, envoy; assistant to a provincial governor [**lēgō, lēgāre,** to appoint and send with a commission]
      īnsidiandīs: īnsidior, īnsidiārī, īnsidiātus sum (1), lie in wait (for); plot against (+ *dat.*) [**īnsidiae,** an ambush]; verbs that take the dat. are intransitive, and therefore cannot normally have gerundives (which normally have a "passive" sense): here translate actively.

628. **in servīs ad hospitem dominī necandum sollicitandīs:** *ad hospitem dominī necandum* is bracketed by *in servīs…sollicitandīs.*
      hospitem: hospes, hospitis, *m.,* host; guest, guest-friend, visitor; stranger, foreigner; the remarkably wide range of meanings for this word (and for the Gk. *xenía*) reflects the nexus of reciprocal relationships between guest and host in antiquity.
      dominī: dominus, dominī, *m.,* owner of a grand house or estate, master
      plēnum: plēnus-a-um, full of (+ *gen. or abl.*)

629. **sceleris, audāciae:** the uses of these words here echo their appearances and their cognates' in the section on Catiline, chs. 13–14.
      cōnsilium: in apposition with *crīmen* in 627.

      (ch. 52) **quō:** connecting rel. with *in crīmine:* "now then, as for this charge"

630. **requīrō:** see 221n.
      dīxeritne [Caelius]: the enclitic *–ne* here introduces an indir. question.
            (1) *dīxerit* expresses time prior to the main verb in primary sequence (since it depends on *requīrō*);
            (2) *sūmeret* expresses time concurrent with the main verb in secondary sequence (since it depends on *dīxerit*)

Compare the following sentences:

(1) *Rogat ubi fēminae sint,* "He is asking where the women are (will be)."
Rogat ubi fēminae fuerint, "He is asking where the women were."

(2) *Rogabat ubi fēminae essent,* "He was asking where the women were (would be)."
Rogabat ubi fēminae fuissent, "He was asking where the women had been."

See also 8n.

-ne...an: "whether...or"

quam ob rem: "for what reason?", "why?"

631.   **sī nōn [Caelius] dīxit, cur [Clōdia] dedit? Sī [Caelius] dīxit, [Clōdia]... dēvinxit.**

632.   **eōdem:** see 443n.
cōnscientiae: "complicity," "conspiracy"
tūne: Cicero turns to Clodia: "Or did you...", a good ex. of the use of the pers. pron. to contrast and emphasize; note also the anaphora (*tūne...tūne*).
armāriō: armārium, armārī, *n.,* cabinet, chest [**arma,** things that protect]

633.   **prōmere: prōmō, prōmere, prompsī, promptum,** take, give, or bring out; disclose, make known [**pro + emō,** issue]
Venerem: Venus, Veneris, *f.,* Venus, goddess of sexual love (Gk. *Aphrodite*); here a likeness or statue of Venus: Cicero imagines that Clodia has a statue of her favorite divinity on which she hangs gold presents and mementos (*ornāmentīs*) from her other lovers (*cēterōrum*). Note how *illam tuam* contributes to the humor: "that celebrated statue of yours."

634.   **ornāmentīs: ornāmentum, ornāmentī,** *n.,* adornment, jewelry; distinction, honor [**ornō**]; abl. of separation after *spoliāre.*
cum: concessive ["although"]
Spoliātrīcem: spoliātrīx, spoliātrīcis, *f.,* robber; in apposition to *Venerem,* on the model of cult titles such as *Venus Victrix, Venus Genetrix,* etc. Clodia's statue of Venus was the Robber of many men's gold; now she is despoiling the image, by daring to raid it in order to help support Caelius's schemes.

635.   **necem: nex, necis,** *f.,* (violent) death, murder

636. **sanctissimī: sanciō, sancīre, sanxī, sanctum,** make sacred, sanctify; confirm, ratify; *hence part.* **sanctus-a-um** *as adj.,* sacrosanct, inviolable; virtuous, upright

    lābem: Cicero has taken great pains to stress Lucceius's rectitude, a theme throughout chs. 54–55, with which Cicero's treatment of the prosecution witnesses at chs. 22 and 66, and of course also of Clodia throughout, should be carefully compared. "Character" was of even more importance in establishing the credibility of witnesses in ancient courts than in today's courts.

637. **sempiternam: sempiternus-a-um,** everlasting, permanent, perpetual

    huic facinorī tantō: "to this great a crime," dat. with *cōnscia, ministra, adiūtrīx.*

    līberālis: sarcastic. Note the tricolon crescens and anaphora:

    tua mēns līberālis cōnscia,
    tua domus populāris ministra,
    tua dēnique hospitālis illa Venus adiūtrīx.

638. **populāris: populāris-is-e,** of or pert. to the (common) people, democratic; open to everybody

    ministra: ministra, ministrae, *f.,* servant, subordinate; assistant, supporter

    hospitālis: hospitālis-is-e, of or pert. to a guest or host; friendly, hospitable

639. **adiūtrīx: adiūtrīx, adiūtrīcis,** *f.,* helper; another mock-cult title; the m. *adiūtor* often has an illicit feel ("aider and abetter [to a crime]," "co-conspirator") to it.

    esse nōn dēbuit: English puts the past-tense indicator ("have") of modal verbs like *dēbeō* with the inf., so translate "ought not to have been" or "should not have been," Ben. 270.2.

    (ch. 53) **vīdit hoc:** "took this into consideration" (Austin at 53.20), "understood this"

    Balbus: L. Herennius Balbus, for whom see 285–311n.

    cēlātam esse: cēlō (1), conceal, hide; keep in the dark, deceive

640. **ita:** "thus," "in the following way"

641. **ad ornātum lūdōrum:** "for the preparation of games," *i.e.,* for staging games; *ornātum* here implies expense. Caelius was not in or seeking office at this time—if he had been, Cicero would certainly have mentioned it in chs. 6–9 or 70–79; Caelius may have been trying to

help or may have been working for another politician (perhaps a creature of Pompeius?). The scenario Cicero composes, which has the young and relatively impecunious knight borrowing from the enormously wealthy Clodia, is plausible.

Clōdiae: dat. after *familiāris*

tū: Herennius Balbus.

642. **tū [eum] esse vīs:** see 726 and 861.
vīs: "you would have [him] be," see 615 and 721.
[Caelius] dīxit.

643. **profectō:** see 2n.
quō: "why?"

644. **vērum:** here a subst., "the truth"
ō, *interj.,* O
immoderāta: immoderātus-a-um, excessive, immoderate; unrestrained, outrageous [**in + moderor,** control]
sciēns: pres. part. used as an adj., but translate as an adv., "knowingly"; it picks up *cōnscientiae scelere* in 632.

645. **ad:** "for the purpose of"

646 (XXII) **quid:** "for what reason?", "why?"
argūmentīs: "deductions" (compare 259): the ancients regarded logical deductions (called variously *argūmenta, cōniectura, exempla, signa*; below at 658 they are referred to as *ōrātōris propria,* "the orator's toolbox") of more value than evidence and witnesses (*testēs*); Cicero dispenses with this principle when convenient (below starting at 658).

647. **innumerābilia: innumerābilis-is-e,** countless, innumerable
possum...possum (651)**...possum** (654): note the *anaphora* (rhetorical repetition); effect?
dīcere: governs the sentence down to 651.
mōrēs: note again the judicial importance of arguments from character established from the resume of a person's life.

648. **ā tantī sceleris atrōcitāte:** restates and echoes *tanta atrōcitās* in 3.
esse disiunctōs: disiungō, disiungere, disiunxī, disiunctum, keep apart, separate; distinguish, differentiate; *hence part.* **disiunctus** *as adj.,* different, distinct

minimē: "least of all," "not"

esse crēdendum: pass. periphrastic in indir. statement after *possum dīcere* in 724: "that it must not (*minimē*) be believed that...," "that it strains belief that...". An intransitive verb like *crēdō* can be used in pass. constructions only impersonally, Ben. 138.IV; 187.II.b; 256.3; for this kind of repetition of the same word, see 38n.

649.   **hominī:** take with *nōn vēnisse in mentem.*

    ingeniōsō: ingeniōsus-a-um, naturally clever, talented; see 767n.

    prūdentī: prūdēns, prūdentis, *adj.,* exercising foresight, intelligent, sagacious [contracted < **prōvidēns**]

    nōn vēnisse in mentem: sets up the indir. statement *rem...nōn esse crēdendum.*

650.   **ignōtīs:** see 25n.

    aliēnīs: "another master's"

651.   **alia:** dir. obj. of *perquīrere.*

    et: here twice, correlatively ("both...and"): coordinate conjunctions such as *et, sed, aut, vel,* etc. always join coordinate units. Note that the genitive case of a noun is grammatically equivalent to a possessive pron., as this ex. shows.

    cēterōrum patrōnōrum: Cicero stresses how eminently reasonable his position is.

652.   **perquīrere:** perquīrō, perquīrere, perquīsīvī, perquīsītum, inquire or search for carefully or thoroughly [**per** + **quaerō**, to seek]

    sit congressus: congredior, congredī, congressus sum: go near, approach

653.   **eī:** dat. of reference with *aditus.*

    aditus: aditus, aditūs, *m.,* approach, access; opportunity; "method of approach" (Grant)

    sī per sē [factum est], quā temeritāte [factum est]! sī per alium [factum est], per quem [factum est]?

654.   **omnīs:** acc. pl.

    latebrās: latebrae, latebrarum, *f.,* hiding place(s), recess; refuge

655.   **peragrāre:** peragrō (1), traverse, travel through; examine carefully, scrutinize

656.   **perficiendī: perficiō, perficere, perfēcī, perfectum,** accomplish, finish, complete [**per** + **faciō**]
       occultandī: occultō (1), conceal, hide [freq. of **occulō,** cover up]
       maleficī: maleficium, maleficī, *n.,* crime, misdeed [**malus** + root of **faciō**]

657.   **nōn ratiō ulla:** "no plan at all," a bit stronger than *nūlla ratiō*
       vestīgium: vestīgium, vestīgī, *n.,* footprint, track; remnant, trace

658 (ch. 54). **ōrātōris: ōrātor, ōrātōris,** *m.,* public speaker, orator; for *ōrātōris propria* see 646.
       mihi: take after *fructum aliquem ferre potuissent* in 660; Cicero frequently downplays his own oratorical powers in an effort to endear himself to a jury; note the contrast between *ingenium* and *exercitātiō ūsumque* (innate talents vs. diligent practice).

659.   **ūsum: ūsus, ūsūs,** *m.,* exercise, practice; benefit, profit

660.   **fructum: fructus, fructūs,** *m.,* yield, profit; enjoyment, pleasure [**fruor,** have use of, enjoy]
       ferre potuissent: "would have been able to bring forth," a potential subj.; this is the apodosis of a past unreal condition (see 18–24n.) whose protasis is implied ("if I had used them...").
       cum ā mē ipsō ēlabōrāta prōferrī vidērentur: the triple passive would be clumsy English but is fine in Latin: "they [the *ōrātōris propria*] would seem to be brought forward having been worked out by me myself" = "you would think that I had brought contrivances into the case."

661.   **prōferrī: prōferō, prōferre, prōtulī, prōlātum,** bring forward or out; display, show; invent
       brevitātis: brevitās, brevitātis, *f.,* brevity, conciseness [**brevis**]; *brevitātis causā relinquō omnia* is a *praeteritiō,* a figure of speech in which an orator brings up a topic through innuendo, by saying that s/he is not going to talk about it.

662.   **quem:** the antecedent is *L. Luccēium.*
       socium vestrae religiōnis iūrisque iūrandī: Cicero is keen to stress the juror's oath and to lay the foundation for Lucceius's testimony by asserting his fidelity to his own oath as a witness; note also the careful praise to come, some of it similar to that offered in ch. 24 for the Coponii.

663. **iūrisque iūrandi:** "oath"
      patiāminī: potential subj. (Ben. 280.2), the so-called "should-would"
          construction.
      in: "against"

665. **neque nōn audī(vi)sset:** "neither would not have heard," *i.e.,* "both
          would have heard"

666. **tulisset:** "would have tolerated"
      ille vir: subj. of *potuisset* in 669.

668. **illīus ipsīus:** Dio of Alexandria

669. **quod..., id...:** an elaborate structure repeated three more times and not
          easily reproduced in English: "[If it were directed] against a guest-
          friend, would he neglect [*ōmīsisset*] to take care of the very kind of
          crime which [*id...quod facinus,* loosely] he would not accept [if] di-
          rected against an unknown stranger?"

670. **intentum: intendō, intendere, intendī, intentum,** stretch out, extend;
          aim, direct; here circumstantial (see transl. above).
      cūrāre: cūrō (1), care for, watch over; be anxious about

671. **comperisset: comperiō, comperīre, comperī, compertum,** discover,
          learn; prove, verify

672. **temptātum: temptō** (1), try, attempt; certify, prove
      agrīs: ager, agrī, *m.,* (ploughed) field, farmland

673. **domī suae:** *domī* is locative; an adjective that modifies a locative will be
          in the gen. case.

674. **praetermitteret: praetermittō, praetermittere, praetermīsī, praeter-**
          missum, disregard, overlook, let pass
      doctissimī hominis: Dio of Alexandria
      dissimulandum [esse]: dissimulō (1), conceal the identity/fact of; hide,
          keep secret

676   (ch. 55). **diūtius:** comparative of *diū.*

677. **religiōnem auctōritātemque:** = *religiōnis auctōritātem,* an example of "hendiadys," a common stylistic feature even of early Latin oratory, in which two nouns are grammatically parallel but one logically delimits the other. Here *religiōnem* actually distinguishes what kind of *auctōritās* is in mind from the welter of *auctōritātēs* that could be. *Auctōritātem* here is a written statement or affidavit, as at 689.
      percipite: percipiō, percipere, percēpī, perceptum, acquire, collect; feel, perceive;   examine carefully [**per + capiō**]

678. **recitā: recitō** (1), read aloud (a document, esp. in public); this order is addressed to the clerk of the court. Lucceius's deposition (*testimōnium*) is in lieu of his personal testimony or that of his slaves.

679. **amplius:** take with *quid,* "What more?"

679–680. In this sentence, *ipsam prō sē causam et vēritātem* is subject of *mittere,* and *aliquam vōcem* is the object.

683. **quod actum esse dīcitur:** *i.e.,* what is said to have been carried out with Lucceius's slaves.

686. **domō:** the audience would have expected *muliere* (or perhaps *fēminā*); with *domō* ("House" or "dynasty"), Cicero is able to bring back the theme that the entire *gēns Clōdia* is rotten to the core.

687. **nefāriō: nefārius-a-um,** impious, irreligious; immoral [**nefās,** an irreligious act]
      integritātis: integritās, integritātis, *f.,* unimpaired condition, completeness; integrity, uprightness [**integer,** whole]

688. **quā:** connecting rel.
      iūre iūrandō dēvincta auctōritās: "an affidavit secured by a solemn oath"

689. **rēs minimē dubitanda:** "a matter hardly to be pondered for very long"
      pōnātur: mood? Ben. 284.

690. **utrum...an:** indirect alternative questions, to each of which the answer is "yes"
      temerāria: temerārius-a-um, accidental; reckless, rash
      finxisse crīmen [videātur]; *fingere* occurs 8x in this speech, to strengthen the notion that the prosecution's case has been "cooked up."

religiōsē: religiōsus-a-um, (religiously) conscientious; holy, sacred; according to one's bond

693–753. Cicero returns to the charge of poison.

693 (XXIII.56). **cuius:** connecting rel.

694. **nec principium invenīre neque ēvolvere exitum:** Van Wageningen notes that this is a metaphor from spinning wool.
principium: principium, principi, *n.,* beginning, origin
ēvolvere: ēvolvō, ēvolvere, ēvolvī, ēvolūtum, roll out; unravel, disentangle; explain, figure out
exitum: exitus, exitūs, *m.,* exit; end, close

696. **nē:** introduces a negative purpose clause, in response to the preceding question.
num, particle introducing a question expecting the answer "no," of the form "you wouldn't…, would you?"
crīmen haereat: *i.e.,* the murder of Dio; *cf.* 171–172, *in quō crīmen haerēbat.*

697. **num [ali]quis obiēcit:** *i.e.,* nobody was foreseeably going to try to prosecute him for Dio's death.

698. **mentiō: mentiō, mentiōnis,** *f.,* mention, reference [**mens**]
hic: the demonstrative pron., = Caelius.
nōmen dētulisset: the technical expression for "prosecute."
quīn, *adv.,* indeed, in fact; *hence* **quīn etiam,** "and furthermore," "yes, and"

699. **verbō:** "to put it briefly."
nōn futūrum fuisse: "would not have been," apodosis of a past contrary-to-fact condition within indir. statement:

"ORIGINAL":	"Ego molestum nōn fuisse Caeliō,	nisi…dētulisset."
	"I would not have been troublesome to Caelius,	if she had not brought an indictment."

SUBORDINATED:	Quīn etiam L. Herennium dīcere audīstis verbō	
	sē molestum nōn futūrum fuisse Caeliō,	nisi…dētulisset."
	Indeed, you heard Lucius Herennius say, to put it briefly, that	
	he would not have been troublesome to Caelius,	if she had not brought an indictment."

Note that the protasis is unchanged: see Ben. 321.A.2. For another ex., *cf.* 20n.
Caeliō: dat. with molestum.

700. **suō familiārī absolūtō:** abl. abs. This is L. Calpurnius Bestia.

701. **crēdibile: crēdibilis-is-e,** probable, plausible, believable

702. **fingī:** pres. pass. inf., "is being trumped up"
sceleris maximī crīmen...alterīus sceleris suscipiendī: *i.e.,* the prosecutors had invented the charge of trying to poison Dio in order to
give a reason why Caelius had undertaken the attempted poisoning
of Clodia (*alterīus*).

704 (ch. 57). **[rem] commīsit.**
adiūtōre: case? Ben. 218.1.

706. **servīsne mulieris:** dat., because it answers *cuī.*
dēmēns: dēmēns, dēmentis, *adj.,* crazy, insane

707. **vōs:** "you prosecutors"; everyone seems to have acknowledged Caelius's
brilliance.

708. **inimīca:** "hostile words," "vicious slander"
ōrātiōne [vestrā].
dētrahitis: "you drag out," "you say in disparagement," "slander," *s.v.*
OLD 8.

709. **rēfert: rēfert, rēferre, rētulit,** *impers.,* it is important, it makes a difference; it concerns, it matters [**rēs + ferō**]; *id ipsum* is the subject: Cicero
maintains that his harsh treatment of Clodia is necessary to his
defense, and not mere gossip: *cf.* 371n.
magnō opere: exceedingly, greatly; especially

710. **eīsne:** "was it to *these...*"
[Caelius] intellegēbat.

711. **servitūtis: servitūs, servitūtis,** *f.,* slavery, servitude
utī: pres. pass. inf.
licentius: licens, licentis, *adj.,* unrestrained, unbridled (in conduct);
hence adv. **licenter,** freely, without restraint; licentiously [pres. part.
of **licet**]
dominā: domina, dominae, *f.,* owner or mistress of a house

712. **videt** and **ignōrat:** set up indir. statement with *hīc servōs nōn esse servōs*
in 716.

ignōrat: ignōrō (1), not to know; take no notice of, fail to recognize

712–719. The structure of these lines is as follows:

Quis enim hoc nōn videt, iūdicēs,

    aut quis ignōrat,   in eius modī domō   in quā māter familiās meretrīciō mōre vivat,

                               in quā nihil gerātur quod forās prōferendum sit,

                                     inūsitātae libīdinēs,

                              in quā   luxuriēs   versentur,

                                   omnia dēnique inaudīta vītia ac flāgitia

            hīc servōs nōn esse servōs,   quibus omnia committantur,

                                 per quōs gerantur,

                                 quī versentur īsdem in voluptātibus,

                                 quibus occulta crēdantur,

                                 ad quōs aliquantum etiam ex cotīdiānīs sumptibus

                                        ac luxuriē redundet?

713.   **mater familiās:** see 374n.; compare *meretrīciō mōre vīveret* at 481.

714.   **forās,** *adv.,* (moving) out of doors, abroad; *(with prōferō)* make known publicly, reveal in public
      inūsitātae: inūsitātus-a-um, unusual, extraordinary

715.   **inaudīta: inaudītus-a-um,** unheard of, unusual

716.   **versentur:** "are present," "go on"
      hīc: the adv.

717.   **īsdem:** "together," see 443n.

718.   **aliquantum:** subj. of *redundet.*
      occulta: occulō, occulere, occuluī, occultum, hide, conceal; *hence n. pl. subst.* **occulta, occultōrum,** secrets

719.   **cotīdiānīs: cōtidiānus-a-um,** daily; ordinary, regular [**cotīdiē,** daily]
      redundet: redundō (1), pour over, overflow; abound in, have in excess [**re + unda**]; the slaves, whose status as mere slaves has already been called into question (*at quibus servīs* at 716), also share in the general sumptuous and lavish activities of the house.

720. **tam...quam:** "as...as"

721.   **vōs [eum esse] voltis** (= *vultis*); for the meaning see 615n.; *vōs* are the
prosecutors.
familiārīs: acc. pl.

722.   **eī:** Caelius; case? Ben. 190.
tanta…quanta ā vōbīs indūcitur: "as much as is alleged by you";
indūcitur has a theatrical tint, as *indūcere* can = "to bring a character
onto a stage": see 290 and 416, with notes, and 466.

724 (XXIV). **quem ad modum:** "how?", "in what way?"

725.   **pactō: paciscor, pasciscī, pactus sum,** make an agreement; *hence subst.*
pactum, pactī, *n.,* agreement, contract; manner, way; *hence abl.*
pactō, in some way; *hence* **quō pactō,** "by what means?"

726.   **[Caelium] habuisse [venēnum] āiunt:** on the clipped, conversational
style, seee 642n.
domī: loc.
eius: = *venēnī.*
vim: "potency"
vimque eius esse expertum in servō: it is remarkable to a modern reader that Cicero does not appear to blanche at the idea of this.

727.   **parātō:** "purchased," as at 373.
percelerī: perceler, perceleris, percelere, very quick
interitū: interitus, interitūs, *m.,* (violent) death or destruction [**intereō,**
perish]

728–753 (chs. 59–60): with the thought of quick-acting poisons, Cicero makes
a sudden and dramatic switch to a *miserātiō* ("appeal to pity") on
the mysterious death of Clodia's husband Q. Metellus Celer, a fairly
pedestrian but important optimate aristocrat; vicious tongues had
gossipped that Clodia had poisoned him, and Cicero plays that
card here. Ornate, formal periods mark this section of the speech—
studied preparation being no bar to theatricality and emotion (his
thought of Metellus *vōcem meam flētū dēbilitāvit,* "made [his] voice
crack with tears"). On Metellus's death, see *In Clodium et Curionem*
(Appendix A, with notes on his career). A considerable amount of
the vocabulary of this section recurs in the *perōrātiō,* as if Cicero
wished to suggest that the jury should not condemn Caelius to political death as Clodia had (allegedly) condemned Metellus to actual
death; see chs. 70–80.

728.   **ab hōc:** = *ab Caeliō*
       comprobātum: comprobō (1), approve heartily; confirm, prove
       prō, *interj., of wonder or lamentation,* oh! ah! alas!
       dī: = *deī.*
       immortālēs: immortālis-is-e, immortal, undying

729.   **cōnīvētis: cōnīveō, cōnīvēre, cōnīvī** *or* **cōnīxī,** close the eyes (in sleep);
       let pass unnoticed, overlook

730.   **praesentīs:** take with *poenās.*
       fraudis: fraus, fraudis, *f.,* deceit, deception; error, mistake; crime
       poenās: poena, poenae, *f.,* penalty, punishment
       in diem: "until later"
       reservātis: reservō (1), save up

730–736. A mapping of this period is given below:

vīdī enim, vīdī et illum hausī dolōrem vel acerbissimum in vītā,

cum Q. Metellus abstraherētur ē sinū gremiōque patriae,
cumque ille vir quī sē nātum huic imperiō putāvit

| tertiō diē | { quam in cūriā, quam in rostrīs, flōruisset, quam in rē publicā } | { integerrimā aetāte, optimō habitū, maximīs vīribus } | ēriperētur indignissimē | { bonīs omnibus atque ūniversae cīvitāte. } |

731.   **hausī: hauriō, haurīre, hausī, haustum,** drink in, absorb; exhaust, weaken
       vel: + superl. = "the most X possible"

732.   **abstraherētur: abstrahō, abstrahere, abstraxī, abstractum,** draw, drag,
       or pull away from; deprive
       sinū: sinus, sinūs, *m.,* a bending, a fold; bosom, lap; embrace
       gremiō: gremium, gremī, *n.,* bosom, lap; center, heart
       cum: governs *ēriperētur* in 735.

733.   **nātum huic imperiō:** a common phrase used of "worthies."
       tertiō: tertius-a-um, third; *tertiō diē post* actually means "on the second
       day after," as the Romans counted inclusively.
       cūriā: cūria, cūriae, *f.,* senate house [**cūra,** concern]

734.   **rostrīs: rostrum, rostrī,** *n.,* bird's beak; ship's prow; *(pl.)* elevated speak-
       ers' platform in the Forum Romanum, called *Rostra,* "the Prows" be-
       cause the prows of vessels captured in the battle of Antium in 338 B.C.
       had been added to the original platform [prob. from **rōdō,** gnaw]

flōruisset: flōreō, flōrēre, flōruī, bloom, flower; be in one's prime; be distinguished or eminent **[flōs]**
integerrimā aetāte: "in the full flower of his life"

735.   **habitū: habitus, habitūs,** *m.,* condition, state, health; manner, bearing; style
vīribus: see 9n.

ēriperētur: ēripiō, ēripere, ēripuī, ēreptum, seize or pull out or away; deprive, strip, steal

indignissimē: indignus-a-um, undeserving *(in either a good or bad sense);* unworthy

bonīs omnibus atque ūniversae cīvitātī: dat. of separation after *ēriperētur,* Ben. 188.2.d.

ūniversae: ūniversus-a-um, *(sg.)* the whole of, entire; *(pl.)* all together; general, universal **[ūnus + vertō,** turned into one]

736–744. A mapping of this exquisite period is given below; note especially the anaphora *mihi...me...me* and *reī publicae...cīvitātī...rem publicam... patriam:*

Quō quidem tempore ille moriēns,
    cum iam cēterīs ex partibus oppressa mēns esset,

        extrēmum sēnsum ad memoriam reī publicae reservābat,   ⎧ quanta inpendēret procella mihi, ⎫
                                                                                                                      ⎨   ⎬
        cum mē intuēns flentem significābat interruptīs ac morientibus vōcibus   ⎩ quanta tempestās cīvitātī   ⎭

                                                                                                                      ⎧ crēbrō Catulō   ⎫
        et cum parietem saepe feriēns eum quī cum Q. Catulō fuerat eī commūnis   ⎨ saepe mē   ⎬ nōminābat,
                                                                                                                      ⎩ saepissimē rem publicam ⎭

        ut nōn tam sē morī   ⎧ cum patriam   ⎫
            quam spoliārī suō praesidiō ⎨   ⎬ dolēret.
                                                  ⎩ tum etiam mē ⎭

quō: connecting rel.

737.   **moriēns: morior, mori, mortuus sum,** die
cum: concessive ("although")
cēterīs ex partibus: "in other respects"
oppressa...esset: opprimō, opprimere, oppressī, oppressum, press on or against; crush, overpower, subdue

738.   **sēnsum: sēnsus, sēnsūs,** *m.,* sensation, feeling; judgment, perception, understanding

739. **intuēns: intueor, intuērī, intuitus sum,** look at attentively, watch carefully or plaintively

flentem: fleō, flēre, flēvī, flētum, cry, weep; lament, weep for

interruptīs: interrumpō, interrumpere, interrūpī, interruptum, break in two; disturb, interrupt; *hence partic.* **interruptus-a-um** *as adj.,* disconnected, "halting"

740. **quanta inpendēret mihi:** a reference to Cicero's exile (see intro. 19).

inpendēret: inpendeō, inpendēre, tower over, threaten; be imminent; carefully distinguish from *inpendō, inpendere, inpendī, inpēnsum,* expend.

procella: procella, procellae, *f.,* storm, tempest; *(fig.)* civil unrest, commotion

tempestās: tempestās, tempestātis, *f.,* season; (stormy) weather

741. **parietem: pariēs, parietis,** *m.,* wall of a house, party wall (between two houses; the two politicians evidently lived next-door to each other).

Q. Catulō: Quintus Lutatius Catulus Capitolinus was the leader of the optimates from his consulship in 78 until the mid-60s; the *lex Lutātia dē vī* that he carried as consul was a precursor of the law under which Caelius was tried. *Miserātiōnēs* do not get any more theatrical, emotional, and contrived than this one, with a dying man remembering a dead man.

742. **crēbrō: crēber, crēbra, crēbrum,** crowded together; repeated, frequent; *hence adv.* **crēbrō,** often, repeatedly

crēbrō Catulum, saepe mē, saepissimē rem publicam: note tricolon and parallel structure (adv. followed by noun each time).

743. **praesidiō: praesidium, praesidī,** *n.,* defense, protection; guard, garrison, encampment; case? Ben. 214.

cum...tum: "both...and."

744 (ch. 60). **quem:** connecting rel.

745. **repentīnī: repentīnus-a-um,** sudden, unexpected; quick-working

sustulisset: tollō, tollere, sustulī, sublātum, lift, raise up, elevate; remove, carry off; English-speakers "lift things *up,*" reckoning from the finishing point; the Romans "lifted things *down,*" reckoning from the starting point.

quōnam modō: "can you tell me (*-nam*), in what way...?"; *-nam* intensifies questions, adding liveliness or wonder.

furentī: furō, furere, rave, be crazy, be in a rage; a political term, see 105n.

frātrī: = *frātrī patruēlī,* a cousin on the father's side of one's family, here P. Clodius Pulcher; his mother was the sister of Metellus Celer's father, making Clodia and her husband first cousins—not common, but also not taboo.

746.   **quī...dīxerit:** *dīxerit* sets up an indir. statement: *sē* is the subj. acc., *interfectūrum [esse]* the infinitive (= direct *interficiam*), and *[frātrem patruēlem] incipientem furere atque cōnantem* the dir. obj. of the infinitive.
cōnsul: modifies *quī* ("who, as a consul,...").
cōnsulāris: modifies *ille* in 745.

747.   **tonantem: tonō, tonāre, tonuī,** thunder; Clark's conjecture (for MSS *cōnantem*) is a clever suggestion.
interfectūrum [esse]: interficiō, interficere, interfēcī, interfectum, kill, murder
audiente senātū: abl. absol.

748.   **celeritāte: celeritās, celeritātis,** *adj.,* speed, swiftness; a play on Q. Metellus *Celer*: the Romans (and Greeks) liked these verbal games; see also 889n.

749.   **metuet: metuō, metuere, metuī, metūtum,** fear, be afraid [**metus,** fear]
nē [domus] [ali]quam vōcem ēiciat: note the *domus* theme again.

750.   **ēiciat: ēiciō, ēicere, ēiēcī, ēiectum,** send, drive, or throw out, eject; utter (words)
nōn[ne].
noctem: nox, noctis, *f.,* night
fūnestam: fūnestus-a-um, dismal, mournful; grief-causing; fatal, deadly

751.   **luctuōsam: luctuōsus-a-um,** sad, mournful, disconsolate [**luctus,** grief]

753.   **flētū: flētus, flētūs,** *m.,* weeping, lamentation
dēbilitāvit: dēbilitō (1), cripple, enfeeble, weaken [**dēbilis,** feeble, weak]
mentem impedīvit: not just "clouded my mind" but also "burdened my conscience" (see R.G.M. Nisbet on *In Pīsōnem* 43)

754–872 (chs. 61–69): in this continuation of the poison section of the *argūmentātiō,* Cicero returns to a paratactic, conversational style for the "Battle of the Baths." Note especially the mock-reverence with which he asks for particulars from the prosecution about how the poison was tranferred—details which we must assume were lacking. For a contrary view, see Gotoff's cautious paper. On the other hand, most commentators (including this one) agree that there must have been some truth to the story, however exaggerated by the prosecution. Geffcken (2003) sees this passage as the culmination in the *Pro Caelio* of "a common sequence of dramatic forms—from tragedy [ch. 18] to comedy [chs. 33–38] to mime [chs. 61–69]."

754 (XXV, 61). **tamen:** "to continue" ("resumptive *tamen,*" see Austin).

755. **āiunt:** governs down to 758.
    huic P. Liciniō: otherwise unknown; *huic* here and *hunc...quem vidētis* at 839 indicate that he was present in court; perhaps *imbēcillum* at 827 explains the surprising fact that he was apparently not asked to give testimony.

756. **pudentī: pudet, pudēre,** it causes shame; *hence part.* **pudēns, pudentis** *as adj.,* proper, decent; see also 65–101n., 77n.
    bonō: a political term, see 105n. Latin is fond of word order like *pudentī adulescentī et bonō* (compare *castrēnsis ratiō et militāris* at 122).
    cōnstitūtum esse: impersonal construction)"that it was agreed," "that there was an agreement") in indir. statement after *āiunt.*

757. **venīret:** mood? Ben. 295.4. The secondary sequence results from the perfect tense *cōnstitūtum esse* rather than *āiunt.*
    balneās: balneum, balneī, *n.,* bath, bathing place; *(f. pl.)* **balneae, balneārum,** (public) baths; the pl. is heteroclite (declined in a different paradigm from the sg.).

758. **Seniās:** "Senian," "of Senia (or perhaps a Gk. *Senias*)"; this person (who probably built or operated the baths) is otherwise unknown; Cousin's emendation *Seniānās* is small but attractive.
    eōdem, *adv.,* "to the same place or point"
    [Licinium] esse ventūrum, [esse] traditūrum: "[they assert that Licinius] was to come, was to hand over…"

758. **pyxidem: pyxis, pyxidis,** *f.,* a little box (used for perfumes, medicines, and poisons) that was often made from boxwood, a very close-grained, heavy wood; the word is Greek and a bit exotic.

hīc: the adv.

759.　quid: "why?"
　attinuerit: attineō, attinēre, attinuī, attentum, stretch out to, reach to;
　　impers., it is important, it matters
　[venēnum] ferrī: acc. + inf. after *attinuerit.*
　cōnstitūtum: take this perf. pass. part. as an adj. modifying *locum.*

760.　ad Caelium domum: lit., "to Caelius, to home" = "to Caelius's home."
　manēbat: maneō, manēre, mānsī, mānsūrus, stay, remain; wait for, await

761.　cōnsuētūdō: "familiarity," "friendship" (so also 763).
　suspiciōnis: partitive gen. with *quid.*

762.　quid...esset, sī...vīsus esset: mixed contrary-to-fact condition, Ben. 304.

763.　suberat: there is a hint of concealment implied in this verb.
　simultās: simultās, simultātis, *f.,* hostile meeting; grudge, animosity
　　[simul, at the same time]
　exstincta erat: exstinguō, exstingere, exstinxī, exstinctum, put out, ex-
　　stinguish; destroy, kill

764.　"hinc illae lacrimae": a proverbial quotation from Terence's (see 472n.)
　　comdey *Andria* ("The Woman From Andros"), line 126.
　nīmīrum, *adv.,* certainly, surely, truly; often ironic, as here.

765 (ch. 62). immo, *adv.,* on the contrary; Austin suggests "oh no!"
　inquit: "it is said"—or perhaps "Herennius says" (with a gesture to
　　the prosecution bench): in a speech filled with Cicero's imperson-
　　ations, one wonders to what extent Cicero "acted out" this part as
　　Herennius.

767.　ingeniōsa: here of Clodia, as so often of Caelius (who is *ingeniōsus* at
　　649; his *ingenium* is spoken of at 13, 558, 575, and 707).
　praecēpit: praecipiō, praecipere, praecēpī, praeceptum, direct, give in-
　　structions to (+ *dat.*)
　pollicerentur: subj. in a jussive noun clause after *praecēpit ut.*

768.　manifestō: manifestus-a-um, clear, evident; detected, caught red-
　　handed; *hence abl. as adv.,* clearly, plainly, undeniably

769. **cōnstituī:** pres. pass. inf.
   locum: "as the place" (in apposition to *balneās Seniās*).
   [Clōdia] iussit.
   eō, adv., to that place, there; for that purpose

770. **dēlitīscerent: dēlitīscō, dēlitīscere, dēlituī,** hide or conceal oneself, lie
   hid/hidden; also spelled *–ēsco* [**dē** + **latēscō,** hide or conceal]; mood?
   Ben. 282.2.

771. **prōsilīrent: prōsiliō, prōsilīre, prōsiluī,** spring up, leap out [**prō** + **saliō**]

772 (XXVI). **quae:** connecting rel.

773. **reprēndendī:** "of refutation."
   potissimum: "most of all," "in particular"

774. **in quibus:** connecting rel., "and in these baths."
   togātīs: "in togas," "fully-clothed"

775. **posset:** the subj. is used rather than the indic. because as a rhetorical question it represents an "original" deliberative subjunctive.
   Compare the following cases:

   DIRECT: "Quae latebra togātīs hominibus esse potest?"
                     "What hiding place can there be for men wearing togas?"

   INDIRECT: Nōn inveniō quae latebra togātīs hominibus esse possit.
                     I cannot discover what hiding place there can be for men wearing togas.

   DIRECT: "Quae latebra togātīs hominibus esse possit?"
                     "What hiding place could there be for men wearing togas?"

   INDIRECT: Nōn inveniō quae latebra togātīs hominibus esse possit.
                     I cannot discover what hiding place there could be for men wearing togas.

   sī: kind of condition? Ben. 304. The contrary-to-fact condition stresses the improbability of the whole scenario put forward by the
   prosecution.
   vestibulō: vestibulum, vestibulī, *n.,* an entrance courtyard, forecourt

776. **latērent: lateō, latēre, latuī,** lie hid / hidden; be concealed; skulk, keep
   out of sight

intimum: intimus-a-um, innermost; most secret; *hence subst.* **intimum, intimī,** *n.,* the inmost part, interior, "the deepest recesses or shadows" [superl. of **interior,** inner]

cōnicere: cōniciō, cōnicere, cōniēcī, cōniectum, throw together; conjecture, guess; hence **sē…cōnicere,** flee, hurry away

commodē: commodus-a-um, fit, suitable; convenient, easy

777.   **calceātī: calceō, calceāre, calceāvī, calceātum** (1), put shoes on; the word picks up *togātīs* from 774; like *togātīs, calceātīs* is a part. formed from a noun (*calceus,* "shoe"), and the verb *calceō* is a good ex. of "back-formation" from the part.

vestītī: vestiō (4), dress, clothe

778.   **quadrantāriā: quadrantārius-a-um,** of or pert. to a quarter of an *as,* a copper coin or "penny" [**quadrāns,** a quarter]. In his defense speech, Caelius had dubbed Clodia *quadrantāria Clytemnēstra,* "a farthing Clytaimestra"; see Appendix C. Clytaimestra (the transliteration from what is likely the most correct Greek form), queen of Mycenae, murdered her husband Agamemnon upon his triumphal return from the Trojan War; the reference is to Clodia's alleged poisoning of her own husband. Skinner points out that Clytaimestra's killing of her husband Agamemnon in a bathtub (Aeschylus, *Agamemnon* 1331 ff.), has extra point here in the "Battle of the Baths"; note also *potēns,* "imperial."

779.   **permūtātiōne: permūtātiō, permūtātiōnis,** *f.,* a complete change or alteration; exchange

facta erat: fīō, fierī, factus sum, become, be made; *facta erat* is vivid for *facta esset,* Ben. 304.3.

balneātōrī: balneātōr, balneātōris, *m.,* keeper of a bath, bathman; dat. with *familiāris.*

780 (ch. 63). **equidem:** "for my own part," "as for me"

781.   **dīcerentur:** mood? Ben. 300.

782.   **adhūc:** "yet," "up to this point"

quīn, *conj., following negative verbs of doubt, hesitation, or surprise,* that, but that, that…not (+ *subj.)* [**quī + ne**]

pergravēs: pergravis-is-e, very weighty, important, or impressive; compare *gravēs erunt hominēs* at 234, the shadowy witnesses.

783. **fēminae:** not *mulier* (see 369n., 412n.): effect here?

   prōvinciae: prōvincia, prōvinciae, *f.*, official duty, charge; sphere of office; the better-known meaning of the word comes from the idea that a "province" is an administrative district over which a magistrate performs state duties; the official and military tone of the word is useful here.

784. **contrūderentur: contrūdō, contrūdere, contrūsī, contrūsum,** push together, stuff in, crowd in

   quod: "a thing which"

   illa: Clodia

785. **quam velit sit potēns:** for "direct" *quam vis sit potēns.*

786. **impetrāvisset: impetrō** (1), get, obtain (by asking); effect, bring to pass [**patrō,** father; achieve, accomplish]

788. **Testīs ēgregiōs! :** acc. of exclamation (so also *Ō magnam vim* in 889): "What outstanding witnesses!"

   dein: = *deinde.*

   temerē: "too quickly," "before they should have"

789. **temperantīs: temperō** (1), be moderate, practice self-control; regulate, temper

   fingitis: governs, in indir. statement, *ēvolāsse* in 791, *retraxisse* in 793, and *coniēcisse* in 794.

   cum: governs down to *trādidisset* in 791.

791. **ēvolāsse: ēvolō** (1), fly or rush out; spring forward

   praeclārōs: praeclārus-a-um, very clear or bright; very distinguished or famous

   sine nōmine: "nameless"

793. **porrexisset: porrigō, porrigere, porrēxī, porrectum,** reach out, extend [**prō** (with metathesis of **r** and **ō**) + **regō**]

   retraxisse: retrahō, retrahere, retraxī, retractum, draw or drag back; hold back; withdraw

794. **fugam: fuga, fugae,** *f.*, a flight, a running away

795. **calliditātem: calliditās, calliditātis,** *f.,* cleverness, skill; artifice, cunning [**callidus,** clever, skilful; sly]
       sol(l)ertiam: sol(l)ertia, sol(l)ertiae, *f.,* dexterity, ingenuity [**sol(l)ers,** adroit]

796. **ipsa:** modifies *quae* in 794; note the order *sē per sē ipsa* (reflexive before intensive), which is invariable.
       (XXVII, ch. 64) **velut** *or* **velutī,** *adv.,* even as, just as when

797. **fābella: fābella, fābellae,** *f.,* a little story; small play, trivial drama [dim. of **fābula**]
       veteris: vetus, veteris, *adj.,* old, longstanding; experienced in *(+ gen.)*
       poētriae: poētria, poētriae, *f.,* poetess
       quam...quam: "How...! How...!"

798. **argūmentō:** "plot"; compare Shakespeare's or Milton's use of "argument" at the start of a play or long poem.

800. **Licinius:** note the considerable number of repetitions of vocabulary that begin with this line and continue to 822.
       oculīs: dat. of reference

801. **testātior: testor, testārī, testātus sum** (1), speak as a witness, declare, assert; *hence part.* **testātus-a-um** *as adj.,* clear, proven, well-attested.
       āmīsērunt: āmittō, āmittere, āmīsī, āmissum, send away, dismiss; lose, let slip away
       quī: "why?", "how"

803. **quam:** completes the expectation set up by *minus.*

806. **quōs...nōn reperiō** (808): translate as if *et ego quidem quam ob rem (=cur) tū eōs temerē atque ante tempus prōsiluisse dicās nōn reperiō;* note that *atque* connects the two adverbial expressions *temerē* and *ante tempus* ("too early").

807. **ante tempus:** "(too) early"

808. **fuerant...rogātī, fuerant...conlocātī:** the "double" pluperfect, while practically equivalent to *erant...rogātī, erant...conlocātī,* stresses completion and finality.
       ad hoc: "for this [purpose]"

809. ut venēnum [comprēnderētur], ut īnsidiae [comprēnderētur], ut
      (moved) facinus dēnique ipsum ut manifestō [comprēnderētur].

812 (ch. 65). quae: refers to *pyxidem.*
      sī: this word is italicized because of an editorial move:
           MSS: *quae sī cum iam erat trādita servīs ēvāsissent...*
           Clark: *quae cum iam erat trādita servīs, sī ēvāsissent...*
      ēvāsissent: ēvādō, ēvādere, ēvāsī, ēvāsum, escape, evade, flee

813. subitō: subitus-a-um, sudden, unexpected; *hence abl.* subitō *as adv.,*
      suddenly, unexpectedly

814. inplōrāret: inplōrō (1), beseech, invoke, entreat [plōrō, beg]
      fidem: "good faith," "innocence"; Austin suggests *inplōrāret hominum*
           fidem = "protest his innocence"
      trāditam [esse].

815. pernegāret: pernegō (1), deny flatly, deny altogether
      quem: refers to *pyxidem.*
      quō modō: "how?"

816. [Quod sī fēcissent,] prīmum ad sē revocārent.

817. id...quod: "that...which"

819. expedīret: "was unwrapping the box"

820. mīmī: mīmus, mīmī, *m.,* farce, slapstick comedy, mime, very popular at
      Rome.
      exitus [est].

821. clausula: clausula, clausulae, *f.,* (fitting) end, conclusion
      deín scabílla cóncrepánt: the sense and pronounced iambic rhythm
           suggest that these words may be a (presumably well-known) quota-
           tion from Roman comedy.
      scabilla: scabillum, scabillī, *n.,* small footstool; (foot) castanet or clap-
           per [dim. of scamnum, bench]

822. concrepant: concrepō, concrepāre, concrepuī, concrepitum, rattle
      loudly, creak; sound out; crash; make a noise by slapping together

aulaeum: aulaeum, aulaeī, *n.,* embroidered tapestry; stage curtain: the curtain was actually lowered down from the ceiling into a slot at the front of the stage to begin the performance, then raised at the end.

823 (XXVIII, ch. 66). **haesitantem: haesitō** (1), move hesitatingly or falteringly; be uncertain or undecided; be at a loss [**haereō,** stick]
cēdentem: cēdō, cēdere, cessī, cessum, go away, depart; give in, yield

824.   **mulierāria: mulierārius-a-um,** of or pert. to a woman, womanly: "controlled by a woman"
manus…manibus: note the play on the two senses of this word.

825.   **ipsīus cōnfessiōne, multōrum oculīs, facinoris dēnique vōce:** note the tricolon.
cōnfessiōne: cōnfessiō, cōnfessiōnis, *f.,* an admission, acknowledgement [**confiteor,** confess]

826.   **expresserint:** "has chiseled out," a metaphor from statuary, *OLD s.v.* 6b.
an: "or perhaps," sarcastically and ironically.

827.   **tot ūnum [superāre non possent], valentēs imbēcillum [superāre non possent], alacrēs perterritum [superāre non possent].**
imbēcillum: imbēcillus-a-um, weak, feeble, frail
alacrēs: alacer, alacris, alacre, quick, lively, spirited

830.   **coniectūra: coniectūra, coniectūrae,** *f.,* inference, guess [**cōniciō**]
inlustrārī: inlustrō *or* **inlustror** (1), light up, illuminate; make clear or known (+ *dat.*)

831.   **tōta:** take with *haec causa* in 829.
trāducta est: trādūcō, trādūcere, trāduxi, trāductum, lead over or across, transfer; give over to, pass [**trāns + dūcō**]
quōs…testīs: = *et eōs testēs.*

832.   **timōre: timor, timōris,** *m.,* anxiety, dread, fear

833 (ch. 67). **praegestīs: praegestiō** (4), be very eager, desire greatly
animus [meus].
lautōs: lavō, lavāre, lāvī, lautum, wash, bathe; *hence part.* **lautus-a-um** *as adj.,* washed; refined, elegant, foppish

834. **iuvenēs: iuvenis, iuvenis,** *m./f.,* young person (esp. between the ages of 20 and 40)
     beātae: beātus-a-um, blessed, fortunate; opulent, rich
     familiārīs: acc. pl.
     fortīs: acc. pl.

835. **imperātrīce: imperātrīx, imperātrīcis,** *f.,* a female commander or general
     praesidiō: "suggests both the protection that the baths afforded and that it was the 'station' that the men had to occupy as 'garrison'" (Austin).

836. **conlocātōs:** a military term, = "garrisoned"

837. **alveusne: alveus, alveī,** *m.,* a hollow; hold of a ship; belly, stomach [**alvus,** belly, abdomen]
     ille: "that famous," "that well-known"
     equus: equus, equī, *m.,* horse
     Trōiānus: Trōiānus-a-um, of or pert. to Troy, Trojan; Cicero uses this most famous scene from Greek epic frequently in the speeches.
     invictōs: invictus-a-um, unconquered; invincible, unconquerable

838. **bellum: bellum, bellī,** *n.,* war; reinforces *quadrantāria Clytemnēstra* and perhaps echoes once more Aeschylus's comment on the murderous queen, portrayed in *Agamemnon* as having assumed manly roles.
     gerentīs: acc. pl.
     texerit: tegō, tegere, texī, tectum, cover; conceal, keep secret, hide
     [eōs] respondēre.

839. **hunc…quem vidētis:** Licinius, see 755n.

841. **in istum locum:** "into the witness box"; *istum* is deictic and would have been accompanied by a gesture.

842. **prōcesserint: prōcēdō, prōcēdere, prōcessī, prōcessum,** go forward, proceed; turn out okay, prosper; kind of condition? Ben. 302.

     explicābunt: explicō (1), uncoil, disentangle; explain, expound
     quam volent: "as witty as they please"

843. **dicācēs: dicāx, dicācis,** *adj.,* witty, entertaining; sarcastic, sharp-tongued
     nōn numquam: "sometimes"
     vīnum: vīnum, vīnī, *n.,* wine; *ad vīnum* = "over their cups of wine"

dīsertī: diserō, disserere, disseruī, dissertum, discuss; speak about, treat of; *hence part.* **disertus-a-um** *as adj. (note the irreg. spelling)*, eloquent, well-spoken; glib, slick-talking [**serō,** link, join]

alia forī vīs est, alia trīclīnī [vīs est], alia subselliōrum ratiō [est], alia lectōrum [ratiō est]; nōn īdem iūdīcum cōmissātōrumque cōnspectus [est]; lux dēnique longē alia est sōlis, alia [est] lychnōrum; note the sympotic decadence—rather ironic given Cicero's Hellenizing tendencies, but here he vogues as a steadfast, hard-headed Roman lawyer.

844. **trīclīnī: trīclīnium, trīclīnī,** *n.,* dining couch (for formal meals); dining room

   subselliōrum: subsellium, subsellī, *n.,* courtroom bench (for jurors); law court

   ratiō: "idea," "meaning," "implications"

   lectōrum: lectus, lectī, *m.,* couch for reclining at meals; bed

845. **cōmissātōrumque: cōmissātor, cōmissātōris,** *m.,* partier, reveller [**cōmissor, cōmissārī,** make a joyous procession]

   cōnspectus: cōnspectus, cōnspectūs, *m.,* sight, view; appearance, look

846. **sōlis: sōl, sōlis,** *m.,* sun

   lychnōrum: lychnus, lychnī, *m.,* light, lamp

   excutiēmus: excutiō, excutere, excussī, excussus, shake or throw out; examine, investigate [**ex + quatiō,** shake]

   omnīs: acc. pl.

847. **dēliciās:** "affectations," "foppery"

   ineptiās: ineptiae, ineptiārum, *f. pl.,* foolish behavior, silliness, nonsense

   audiant...parcant: mood of these 10 verbs? Ben. 274.

   nāvent aliam operam: *nāvāre operam* is "to busy oneself with" something; *aliam* is "something else."

   ineant grātiam: *grātiam inīre* is "to curry favor successfully," "to win favor."

849. **vigeant: vigeō, vigēre:** bloom, thrive; be in high esteem, have a good reputation

   venustāte: venustās, venustātis, *f.,* beauty, charm, elegance [**venus**]

   dominentur: dominor (1), rule over, govern (+ *abl.*) [**dominus**]; *dominentur sumptibus* = "let them rule over their banquets"

850. **iaceant: iaceō, iacēre, iacuī,** be situated, lie; be inert or inactive
dēserviant: dēserviō (4), be a slave; be devoted
capitī: "life," as often
innocentis: innocēns, innocentis, *adj.,* harmless, inoffensive; blameless, upright

852 (ch. 68). **dē:** "according to"
cognātōrum sententiā: at some sort of family council, as a woman *in tutēlā* ("under guardianship," as virtually all were) would require her relatives' consent for a property transaction such as the emancipation of slaves.

853. **manū missī:** "emancipate"; to be *in manū* of someone = to be "under the legal control" of someone.
tandem, *adv.,* at length, at last

855. **propinquōrum: propinquus-a-um,** near, neighboring; *hence subst.* **propinquus, propinquī,** relative, kinsman

856. **cupiō: cupiō, cupere, cupīvī** *or* **cupiī, cupītum,** wish for, long for
quid...argūmentī: constr.? Ben. 201.2.

857. **manūmissiō: manūmissiō, manūmissiōnis,** *f.,* manumission, freeing (of a slave)
in quā [manūmissiōne].

858. **quaestiō:** "investigation," "interrogation"
sublāta [est]: from *tollō,* "free from," "avoid"
multārum rērum: gen. with *cōnsciīs.*

859. **cum causā:** "with [good] reason"
persolūtum [est]: persolvō, persolvere, persolvī, persolūtum, loosen; explain; pay, discharge *(a debt)*
propinquīs [meīs].

860. **tūte:** intensive form of *tū* (Clodia).

861. **adlātam, compertam:** modify *rem.*
[tē] dēferre: see 642n.
(ch. 69) **hīc:** the adv.

862. **sī:** does not introduce a condition here: take after *mirāmur:* "should we wonder if / that"

commentīciam: commentīcius-a-um, devised, invented; imaginary, *ben trovato* (= a story that is not true but is so good it should be!) [**commentus < comminiscor,** contrive]

obscēnissima: obscēnus-a-um, morally repugnant, indecent; we do not know what was in the pyxis that Caelius presented to Clodia, but it was so indecent (*obscēnissima*) and the story so well-known (*illam, percelebrāta*) that Cicero does not tell us. There have been many suggestions, perhaps the most likely being Skinner's depilatory resin (associated with prostitutes).

864. **cadere: cadō, cadere, cecidī, cāsum,** fall, collapse; fall in line with, suit (+ *in* + acc.)

percelebrāta: "talked about everywhere"

865. **dūdum,** *adv.,* some time ago; *hence* **iam dūdum,** some while ago now.

867. **quid enim attinēbat?:** "For how did it attach to him?"

868. **insulsō: insulsus-a-um,** unsalted; insipid, tasteless; dull, unimaginative [**in**-priv. + **salsus,** salty; witty]

inverēcundō: inverēcundus-a-um, shameless, immodest

869. **modestum: modestus-a-um,** mild, moderate; honest, moral, virtuous

870. **infacētum: infacētus-a-um,** dull, unwitty; coarse, rude

872. **quadrāre: quadrō** (1), make square; fit exactly, agree with, square, suit [**quadrum,** a square]

aptē: aptus-a-um, appropriate, fitting; *hence adv.* **aptē,** suitably, perfectly

873–991 (chs. 70–80): With the social and legal destruction of Clodia now complete, Cicero turns serious and hypotactic again in the perōrātiō or conclūsiō, which includes a careful, detailed vita (ēnumerātiō) of Caelius's career and another commiserātiō. The start of this section echoes the early part of the exordium (esp. chs. 70 and 72).

875. **dē vī:** for the charges, see intro. sec. 31: only charges (1) and (2) could be construed as matters falling under the *lex Lutātia dē vī* (*vis* = "political street battles"), and Cicero claims that these were brought in purely to supply a reason to prosecute Caelius in this particular court.

Catulus had carried the *lex Lutātia dē vī* during his consulship in 78–77 B.C. in order to deal with political street gangs; its provisions were modified or augmented by a *lex Plautia dē vī* probably passed around 70 B.C.; for discussion of the related problem of *sodālicia* (society or gang organized for political bribery), a political issue at the time of Caelius's trial, see ch. 16 esp 179n., 180n.

quae…pertinet: *pertinēre ad* = "pertain to," "apply to"

lex: lex, lēgis, *f.,* law; rule, regulation, stipulation

māiestātem: māiestās, māiestātis *f.,* greatness, grandeur; the sovereign power; treason. Originally, *māiestātem laedere / minuere* = "to injure or diminish the greatness of the Roman people"; *crīmen māiestātis* = "high treason," but the term *māiestās* alone came to mean "high treason."

statum: status, statūs, *m.,* placement, position; condition, state; this section echoes the very start of the speech.

876. **pertinet: pertineō, pertinēre, pertinuī, pertentum,** stretch out, reach, extend; concern, pertain to

877. **dissēnsiōne: dissēnsiō, dissēnsiōnis,** *f.,* difference in feeling, disagreement, incompatibility
     extrēmīs: "most desperate"

878. **sēdātā: sēdō** (1), settle, assuage, calm; *hence part.* **sēdātus-a-um** *as adj.,* calm, composed, tranquil
     flammā: flamma, flammae, *f.,* flame, blazing fire

879. **fūmantīs** (acc. pl.): **fūmō** (1), smoke, smolder [**fūmus,** smoke]
     reliquiās: reliquiae, reliquiārum, *f. pl.,* remains, remnants, "embers"

880. **libīdinēs et dēliciās:** hendiadys (see above at 677).

881. **dēposcitur: dēposcō, dēposcere, dēpoposcī,** demand, require, request earnestly; here = "is invoked."

(XXX, ch. 71). **M. Camurtī et C. Caesernī:** we know nothing about these men; evidently the prosecution had adduced their convictions as precedents (*entechnoi pisteis*) in this case. But Cicero implies that larger than their cases's use as shaky precedents, the prosecution had brought them up in order to make mention of Vettius and (889) *illa vetus aerāria fābula* connected with him. The details are sketchy.

Austin (at 71.10, p. 172) has a list of several Vettiī, but we cannot identify this Vettius securely; on the possible identification with the Victius of Catullus 98, see Appendix B. *C* is italicized because Clark added it to the text on the assumption that *praenōmina* always appear on a person's first or only mention and a C would have been absorbed easily during the transmission of the text into following Caesernī.

damnātiō: damnātiō, damnātiōnis, *f.,* condemnation; conviction

praedīcātur: praedīcō (1), declare publicly, publish; honor, speak highly of

882. **stultitiam: stultitia, stultitiae,** *f.,* folly, foolishness, stupidity; case? Ben. 183.

884. **singulārem: singulāris-is-e,** alone, single; unique, extraordinary

cum ab eā muliere veniātis: "since you are creatures of that woman."

flagiti: flagitium, flagitī, *n.,* disgraceful act or thing, shame

886. **exstinctam illam [memoriam].**

repressam: reprimō, reprimere, repressī, repressum, keep back, check, curb; limit, restrain

vetustāte: vetustās, vetustātis, *f.,* old age; long passage of time

887. **periērunt: pereō, perīre, periī** *or* **perīvī, peritum,** perish, die; be ruined; be convicted or condemned

nempe, *adv.,* to be sure, truly, certainly

quod: "because"

888. **Vettiānō: Vettiānus-a-um,** of or pertaining to Vettius

stuprō: stuprum, stuprī, *n.,* disgrace, dishonor; (sexually) perverse crime

sunt…persecūtī: persequor, persequī, persecūtus sum, follow, pursue hotly; take vengeance on; seek restitution for

889. **vetus:** note the play on *Vettius.*

aerāria: aerārius-a-um, of or pert. to bronze, copper, or money; a copper coin; *illa vetus aerāria fābula* = "that old tale about the copper coin": see 881n.

890. **referrētur: referō, referre, rettulī, relātum,** bear or carry back; restore, renew; pay back, return; compare *rēfert* at 709.

idcirco, *adv.,* on that account, for that reason

891.   **eō:** either the adv. ("to such an extent," "so," with a result clause following), or abl. of *is* (to be taken with *maleficiō*).

892.   **nullīus:** gen.
laqueīs: laqueus, laqueī, *m.,* noose; net, trap, snare
implicātī: implicō (1), entwine
eximendī: eximō, eximere, exēmī, exemptum, take away, remove, banish; free, release; consume, waste

893 (chs. 72–75): In this part of the *perōrātiō* (see the beginning at 873: *Dicta est
ā mē causa, iūdicēs, et perōrātā.*), Cicero restates the material of chs.
6–16 by giving another selective summary of Caelius's youth; the
performance is careful, controlled, and restrained.
in hoc iūdicium vocātur: see 12n.

894.   **proprium:** "appropriate."
quaestiōnis: "of this court."

895.   **sēiunctum:** see 277n.

896.   **cuius:** "of Caelius."
prīmā aetās: another *locus dē pudicitiā;* see above at 65.
ēdita fuit: ēdō, ēdere, ēdidī, ēditum, put forth, give out; make known,
publish; divulge

897.   **quibus:** abl. of means.

898.   **capessendam: capessō, capessere, capessīvī** or **capessīī, capessītum,**
seize, get hold of (eagerly); take upon oneself, undertake; *rem publicam capessere:* "to become involved in politics."
honōrem, glōriam, dignitātem: what a triad of significant words!

899.   **maiōrum nātū:** presumably men like Crassus (sec. 9), Lucceius (sec. 55),
and Pompeius Rufus (sec. 73); cf. *dē Off.* II.46:

> *facillimē autem et in optimam partem cognōscuntur adulēscentēs, quī sē ad
> clārōs et sapientēs virōs bene cōnsulentēs reī publicae contulērunt, quibus-
> cum, sī frequentēs sunt, opīniōnem afferunt populō eōrum fōre sē similēs,
> quōs sibī ipsī dēlēgerint ad imitandum.*

"But young men, if they attach themselves to the famous and saga-
cious men who give good counsel to the Republic, become known
even in the best party; and if they are the frequent campanions of
those men, they make people think that they would be similar to
those whom they themselves chose to imitate."

autem: "also," "moreover."
imitārī: imitor (1), imitate, copy; depict, be like, act like

902 (ch. 73). **cum iam rōboris accessisset aetātī:** "when he had reached a more
balanced stage of life...."

903.　**Q. Pompeiō:** praetor in 63, proconsular governor of *Africa* in 61; see intro. sec. 28. Caelius certainly went to Africa for the reasons Cicero
states in this speech (*i.e.*, to gain administrative experience, to make
connections, and to administer his father's property there); but is it
not possible that he went also in order to lie low after his brush with
the Catilinarians and their downfall?
contubernālis: contubernālis, contubernālis, *m.,* tent-companion,
comrade: a young man who accompanied a general (in his "train"
or cohort) to learn the art of war [**contubernium,** tent]

904.　**castissimō hominī:** note again how Caelius's mentor's chastity and upright morals are stressed.

905.　**possessiōnes: possessiō, possessiōnis,** *f.,* a getting possession of; oc-
cupation; a possession or property

906.　**prōvinciālis: prōvinciālis-is-e,** of or pert. to a province, provincial

907.　**illinc,** *adv.,* from that place, on that side.

909.　**exemplō: exemplum, exemplī,** *n.,* a sample; an example, general character; model, precedent

911.　**ex aliqua inlustrī accūsātiōne:** Van Wageningen compiles a nice list of
those relatively youthful orators Cicero praises, including Crassus,
M. Antonius (the father of the *triumvir*), Caesar, Asinius Pollio, and
C. Licinius Calvus (Catullus's lawyer-poet friend).
(XXXI, ch. 74) **aliō:** "to another place," to another person," "to another
topic."

912. **cūpīdō:** "thirst."

913. **querēlae: querēla, querēlae,** *f.*, a complaining or complaint [**queror,** lament]
conlegam: conlega, conlegae, *m.*, colleague, associate

914. **beneficī: beneficium, beneficī,** *n.*, kindness; favor, service
prōfuit, nocuit: another example of Cicero's selective memory on behalf of his client; on Antonius, see intro., sec. 29.

916. **negōtiīs:** "court cases."

918. **vigilantes: vigilō** (1), be awake, keep awake, watch; be attentive or alert;
hence part. **vigilāns,** watchful, wakeful, vigilant
sōbrii: sōbrius-a-um, not drunk, sober; moderate, reasonable, sensible
industriī: industrius-a-um, diligent, industrious, hardworking

920 (ch. 75). **flexū: flexus, flexūs,** *m.*, a bending or turning; transition, turning
point (esp. in horse and foot racing: note the metaphor)
quasi: quasi, *adv.*, as if, just as; "so to speak"

921. **paululum: paululus-a-um,** very little, very small; *hence subst.* **paululum, -ī,** n., a little bit, a trifle; *hence adv.* **paululum,** a little; some-
what; for a short while [dim. of **paulus,** little, small]
mētās: mēta, mētae, *f.*, a post or mark on a race course, turning point; a
place of danger, a critical moment

922. **nōtitiā: nōtitia, nōtitiae,** *f.*, state of being known, fame, celebrity; idea,
notion
novā: novus-a-um, new
insolentia: insolentia, insolentiae, *f.*, inexperience; lack of moderation,
extravagance; arrogance [**insolēns,** contrary to custom]

923. **inclūsae: inclūdō, includere, inclūsī, inclūsum,** shut in, enclose; block,
obstruct

924. **cōnstrictae: cōnstringō, cōnstringere, cōnstrinxī, cōnstrictum,** bind,
restrain

925. **vel dīcam:** a "corrective," as Austin notes.

926. **nēquāquam,** *adv.*, by no means, not at all; in no way; do not confuse
with *nēquīquam,* "in vain"

928. **tantum abesse...ut...:** "it is so far from...that...", *i.e.,* "he is so far from the disgrace of her intimacy (= intimacy with her) that he is now adverting from himself her enmity and hatred."

930 (chs. 76–77): Caelius is stable and sane; whatever flaws he has are either trifling or the understandable result of exuberant youthful ambition.
interpositus: interpōnō, interpōnere, interposuī, interpositum, introduce, insert between; put in the way, intervene
dēsidiae: dēsidia, dēsidiae, *f.,* a sitting idle or still, idleness, apathy

931. **hercule,** *interj.,* by Hercules!

932. **amīcī meī:** L. Calpurnius Bestia.

933. **īnsequitur: īnsequor, īnsequī, īnsecūtus sum:** follow, succeed; pursue with hostile intent, hound; attack, assail
nostrum: gen. pl.
obtemperat: obtemperō (1), comply with, conform to (+ *dat.*)

934. **violentior: violentus-a-um,** violent, vehement, boisterous [**vis**]
vellem: potential subj.

935. **cadit in:** "pertains to."

936. **vincendī: vincō, vincere, vīcī, victum,** conquer, overwhelm
ardōre: ardor, ardōris, *m.,* flame, fire; ardent desire, passion (of love)

937. **contractiōra: contrahō, contrahere, contraxī, contractum,** draw together, make tight; *hence part.* **contractus** *as adj.,* narrowed, limited

938. **tamquam,** *conj.,* as, just as
herbīs: herba, herbae, *f.,* stalk, grass, herb; another example of a vegetation metaphor. The elaborate, ornate, and studied metaphors and extended imagery of this entire section (through 947) should not be missed.
mātūritās: mātūritās, mātūritātis, *f.,* ripeness, maturity; the right moment or proper time [**mātūrus,** ripe]

940. **refrēnandī [fuērunt]: refrēnō** (1), hold with a bridle; rein back, check
incitandī: incitō (1), spur, urge on

941. **amputanda: amputō** (1), prune, cut off excess growth; remove, curtail
      efflōrescit: efflōrescō, efflōrescere, efflōruī, blossom, bloom; spring
      up or flourish in youth, beauty, *etc.*

942. **īnserenda [sunt]: īnserō, īnserere, īnsēvī, īnsitum,** sow or plant in,
      graft, implant
      (ch. 77) **effervisse: effervescō, effervescere, effervī,** boil up, boil over;
      become greatly excited

943. **inimīcitiīs:** "political quarrels."

944. **ferōcitās: ferōcitās, ferōcitātis,** *f.,* wild or untamed fierceness or cour-
      age; arrogance
      pertinācia: pertinācia, pertināciae, *f.,* perseverance; obstinacy, stub-
      bornness [**pertināx,** tenacious]
      minimōrum hōrum: "of these very minor offenses" [Englert]; partitive
      gen. w. *aliquid*

945. **purpurae: purpura, purpurae,** *f.,* purple; a purple garment, esp. as a
      sign of wealth or power

946. **nitor: nitor, nitōris,** *m.,* brilliance, luster, brightness; beauty, elegance
      [**niteō,** shine, be bright]
      deferverint: fut. perf. indic.

947. **mītigārit: mītigō** (1), make mild or soft; assuage, mitigate [**mītis,** mild +
      agō]; *mītigārit = mītigāverit.*

948–972. Cicero carefully pledges himself as the guardian of Caelius's continued good behavior. This entire section is replete with deft use of purposeful
illogical statements for very logical ends; it is written in elaborate, "high"
style. This section partially echoes fragments of *In Clodium et Curionem,*
Appendix C.

948 (XXXII). **cōnservāte:** note use at 973 as well.
      reī publicae: used 6x in this section. Effect?

949. **bonārum artium, bonārum partium, bonōrum virōrum:** on the politi-
      cal connotations of *bonus,* see 105n.; the *tricōlon crescēns* makes a nice
      jingle; while parallel, the phrases form a kind of "adjectival zeug-
      ma," since the genitives form three different kinds of grammatical
      relationship with *cīvem:* "a citizen who is trained in the liberal arts,
      who is a Tory partisan, and who counts only solid patriots as his
      friends." *Bonārum artium* is a genitive of description; *bonārum par-
      tium* is a genitive of possession; on the troublesome *bonōrum virōrum*
      see Austin at 77.19.

950. **prōmittō: prōmittō, prōmittere, prōmīsī, prōmissum,** promise, assure
      X *(dat.)* of Y *(acc.)*
      spondeō: spondeō, spondēre, spopondī, spōnsum, promise solemnly,
      pledge
      nōs...nostrīs...nostrā: "I...my...my."

951. **ā nostrīs ratiōnibus:** "from my way of thinking" (so Austin).

952. **sēiunctum fore:** = *sēiunctūrum esse.*
      quod: = *et id; id* is "the fact that Caelius won't stray from the straight and
      narrow path."
      cum...tum: "both...and."
      nostrā familiāritāte: abl. w. *frētus.*

953. **sē ipse:** good Latin, but omit *ipse* in translation; compare 123.
      obligāvit: obligō (1), bind, tie up; oblige, put under obligation

954. (ch. 78). **Nōn enim potest [is,] quī...vocārit[,]...ipse esse...:** "For he who
      has indicted...cannot himself be...."; the structure of the following
      sentence is similar.
      hominem cōnsulārem: a reference to Caelius's successful prosecution
      of C. Antonius Hybrida; see 178n. and 577n.

955. **violātam esse: violō** (1), mistreat, violate; infringe upon, transgress
      in iūdicium vocā[ve]rit: see 12n.

956. **turbulentus: turbulentus-a-um,** full of trouble or commotion; agitated,
      disturbed; troublesome, troublemaking, seditious [**turba**]; a politi-
      cal term (see 105n.).

ambitū: abl. of the charge (a variant of the more common gen. of the charge) with *absolūtum;* the reference is to Caelius's prosecution of L. Calpurnius Bestia. *Ambitus* sounds very much like the modern American term WAM or "Walk Around Money," cash quasi-legally dispensed to political operatives to help "get out the vote."

nē...quidem: "not...even"

957. **impūne,** *adv.,* with impunity, without (fear of) punishment; safely [**pūniō,** punish]

largītor: largītor, largītōris, *m.,* one who spends liberally; one who bribes; for the charge, see 179-189.

958. **duās accūsātiōnēs:** Caelius's prosecutions of C. Antonius Hybrida and L. Calpurnius Bestia (intro. secs. 29 and 31).

vel...vel: "either...or"

959–972: An elaborate section that can be "mapped" as follows:

Quā rē ōrō obtestorque vōs, iūdicēs, ut

quā in cīvitāte paucīs hīs diēbus Sex. Cloelius absolūtus sit,

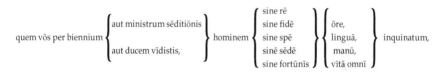

quī aedīs sacrās [incendit],
quī cēnsum populī Rōmānī [incendit],
quī memoriam publicam suīs manibus incendit,
quī Catulī monūmentum adflixit,
[quī] meam domum dīruit,
[quī] meī frātris incendit,
quī in Palātiō atque in urbis oculīs servitia ad caedem et ad īnflammandam urbem incitāvit;

in eā cīvitāte nē patiāminī illum absolūtum muliebrī grātiā,
 M. Caelium libīdinī muliebrī condōnātum,

Sextus Cloelius was a very bad man, to judge from Cicero; he seems to have been one of Clodius's most active henchmen, unsuccessfully prosecuted by Milo in March 56 B.C. This excursus on the recent Cloelius case serves (1) as an example of what bad behavior is really like; and (2) as an exercise in relative ethics ("if we have acquitted a really bad man, we cannot convict someone less bad if not wholly good").

959. **obsidēs: obses, obsidis,** *m./f.,* hostage; a security, guarantee (against danger *from Caelius*)
      pignora: pignus, pignoris, n., something with which a promise is guaranteed, a security, surety; assurance, proof
      ōrō: ōrō (1), beg, entreat
      obtestor: obtestor, obtestārī, obtestātus sum (1), call as a witness; beseech, implore

960. **quā in cīvitāte:** the antecedent is *in eā cīvitāte* in 968.
      paucīs hīs diēbus: "just a few days ago"

961. **biennium: biennium, biennī,** *n.,* a period of two years [**bis** + **annus**]; this refers to the political confusion and street violence of 58–56 B.C.
      ministrum: ministrum, ministrī, *n.,* servant, subordinate; supporter, assistant, accessory [**minor**]

962. **ducem: dux, ducis,** *m.,* leader, ruler; commander

963. **sēde:** "a proper political home"
      ōre, linguā, manū, vītā omnī inquinātum: compare Cicero's earlier comment on Cloelius (addressed to P. Clodius Pulcher, a double-whammy *double entendre*): *qui suā linguā etiam sorōrem tuam ā tē abaliēnāvit,* "a man who with his own tongue has separated even your sister from you"; the expression here implies sexual vice as well as inadequacy (Cloelius had to resort to oral sex to satisfy women, a common trope of Roman invective).

964. **aedīs: aedēs, aedis,** *f., (pl.)* house; shrine, temple
      sacrās: sacer, sacra, sacrum, sacred; *sacrās aedīs* is the *Nymphārum Aedēs,* "Temple of the Nymphs," probably located in the Campus Martius; various government records were kept there.
      cēnsum: cēnsus, cēnsūs, *m.,* written records of the census, the census-roll

965. **incendit: incendō, incendere, incendī, incēnsum,** burn, set fire to; incite, excite
      Catulī monumentum: a portico constructed by Q. Lutatius Catulus in 101 B.C.

966. **adflixit: adflīgō, adflīgere, adflīxī, adflīctum;** strike one thing against another; crush, destroy, ruin

dīruit: **dīruō, dīruere, dīruī, dīrutum,** demolish, destroy, ruin [**dis** + **ruō**] [domum] meī frātris.

967. servitia: **servitium, servitī,** *n.,* slavery; *(pl.)* a body of slaves
caedem: **caedēs, caedis,** *f.,* slaughter, massacre

968. in eā cīvitāte: picks up 960 *quā in cīvitāte.*
nē patiāminī: = *nōlīte patī.*

969. condōnātum: **condōnō** (1), present as a gift; hand over, give over; forgive, overlook

970. coniuge: **coniunx, coniugis,** *m./f.,* spouse, husband, wife; *i.e.,* Clodius (see 379–380)

971. lātrōnem: **lātrō, lātrōnis,** *m.,* bandit, highwayman; thief
ēripuisse...oppressisse: the same collocation occurs in the Metellus Celer *miserātiō* (735–737).

973–991 (chs. 79–80): In these last minutes of the speech, Cicero includes a (com)miserātiō or "appeal to pity," a part of the overall perōrātiō. Such devices were a common feature of Cicero's defense speeches; this one is a masterpiece of mournful histrionics.

973. quod: here a conjunction: "but."
huius: "of this man" or "of my client"; take with *adulēscentiam.*
vōbīs: reflexive; note how it is flanked by *hūius...adulēscentiam.*
prōposueritis: **prōpōnō, prōpōnere, prōposuī, prōpositum,** put forth, display; expose, hold up to (the mind); imagine, put to oneself, picture to oneself; tense, mood and reasons? Position? See *sī* at 18 and *cōnstituētis* at 20.

974. cōnstituitōte: the fut. imp. (see 253n.) lends *gravitās* to the last moments of the speech.
etiam: force?
senectūtem: **senectūs, senectūtis,** *f.,* old age, a person in old age
huius miserī senectūtem: Caelius's father, who is *miser* because of what Caelius is enduring (see 47–49). *Huius* is deictic.
miserī: **miser, misera, miserum,** wretched

975. **ūnico: ūnicus-a-um,** *adj.,* one, only, sole; matchless, peerless, singular, unique
      quī...pertimēscit: figure of speech?
      huius...huius...hōc...huius...huius: figure of speech?

976. **quem:** = *et eum,* dir. obj. of *sustentāte.*
      vōs: nom., subject of *sustentāte;* note the enveloping in *quem vōs supplicem.*
      supplicem: supplex, supplicis, *adj.,* humbly entreating, supplicating, suppliant; *hence subst.,* a suppliant [**sub** + **plācō** *or* **placeō,** please]
      misericordiae: misericordia, misericordiae, *f.,* pity, compassion, tender-heartedness [**miser** + **cor,** heart, feelings]; objective gen. after *supplicem*

977. **potestātis: potestās, potestātis,** *f.,* ability, power; office, magistracy
      abiectum: perf. pass. part. of *abiciō* used as an adj., "dejected," "downcast"
      non tam...vestrōs: delimits *abiectum.*
      tam...quam: "so much...as"
      pedēs: pēs, pedis, *m.,* foot
      sēnsūs: sēnsus, sēnsūs, *m.,* sense, sensation, feeling; judgment, perception, understanding

978. **vel...vel:** "either...or"
      recordātiōne: recordātiō, recordātiōnis, *f.,* a recollection, remembrance [**recordor,** recollect]
      līberōrum: līberī, līberōrum, *m.,* children

979. **iūcunditāte: iūcunditās, iūcunditātis,** *f.,* pleasantness, agreeableness, delightfulness, charm, pleasure [**iūcundus,** delightful, from **iuvō,** please]
      sustentāte: sustentō (1) hold up, support, sustain, maintain [freq. of **sustineō,** support]
      iūcunditāte, sustentāte: a figure of speech called *homoeoteleuton* [Gk. **homoios,** similar + **telos,** end].
      ut: what kind of clause does this introduce? Ben. 284.
      alterīus: gen. sg., regularly used as the gen. of *alius*
      vel...vel: why not "either...or" here?

980. **indulgentiae: indulgentia, indulgentiae,** *f.,* leniency, indulgence, kindness, lenience *(esp. by a superior)* [**indulgeō,** be forbearing]
      vel pietātī vel indulgentiae: cf. *vel recordātiōne parentum vestrōrum vel līberōrum iūcunditāte* at 978.
      serviātis: serviō (4), serve *(as a slave);* be at the service of; be devoted to, gratify

nōlīte: the usual way of expressing a negative command; *nōlīte...velle* is pleonastic.

aut...aut: connects *exstinguī* and *pervertere,* each depending on *velle.*

hunc: = *patrem Caelī*

hunc...occidentem: subject of *exstinguī.*

981.   **nātūrā ipsā:** case? An adverbial translation like "quite naturally" works nicely.

occidentem: occidō, occidere, occidī, occāsum, fall, fall down; die, perish; be ruined [**ob-** + **cadō,** fall]; do not confuse this verb with the equally common trans. *occīdō, occīdere, occīdī, occīsum,* slay (fr. *caedō,* "slaughter").

mātūrius: part of speech? (fr. **mātūrē)**

exstinguī: exstinguō, exstinguere, exstīnxī, exstīnctum, put out, extinguish; kill; abolish, destroy, annihilate

volnere: vulnus, vulneris, *n.,* a hurt, injury, wound; blow, misfortune; character flaw, defect

982.   **fātō: for, fārī, fātus sum,** speak, say; *hence subst.* **fātum, fātī,** "that which has been spoken," "prophetic statement," fate; *fātum* is derived from a pass. usage of this otherwise deponent verb (cf. *nōtīs* at 36n.).

hunc...flōrēscentem: object of *pervertere,* whose subject is contained in *nōlīte.*

flōrēscentem: flōrēscō, flōrēscere, begin to blossom, come into flower; begin to flourish, increase in renown, prosperity, status, etc. [**flōs, flōris,** a flower]

firmātā iam stirpe virtūtis: construction?

983.   **stirpe: stirps** (or **-is** or **-ēs**), **stirpis,** *f.,* stem/stock of a tree/plant; stock, source, origin; root, foundation, origin

tamquam, *conj.,* as, just as

turbine: turbō, turbinis, *m.,* whirlwind, tornado, whirlpool

subita: subitus-a-um, *adj.,* sudden, unexpected

tempestāte: tempestās, tempestātis, *f.,* season; weather, stormy weather, storm [**tempus,** season (of weather)]

984.   **pervertere: pervertō, pervertere, pervertī, perversum,** turn thoroughly upside down, overturn, overthrow, upset; Cicero had his choice of active or passive inf. here (*hunc...flōrentem* could be subject or object): why did he choose this? Hint: think about style more than about grammar.

cōnservāte: cōnservō (1), preserve, save

nē: here introduces what kind of clause?

985. dēspērātam: dēspērō (1), give up hope, despair; *hence part.* **dēspērātus-a-um** *as adj.,* desperate, hopeless

986. plēnam: plēnus-a-um, full of *(+ gen.)*

vōs: case?

987. perculisse: percellō, percellere, perculī, perculsum, beat, strike or knock down, overturn, shatter; knock down, overthrow, destroy

adflīxisse: adflīgō, adflīgere, adflīxī, adflīctum, strike or dash one thing against another; crush, destroy, ruin

quem: Caelius

sī nōbīs [cōnservātis], sī suīs [cōnservātis], sī reī publicae cōnservātis: figure of rhetoric? Effect? Case and reason?

988. nōbīs: "to me," as often.

addictum: addīcō, addīcere, addīxī, addictum, dedicate, devote, assign

addictum, dēditum, obstrictum...habēbitis: almost a periphrastic future perfect: this construction puts great emphasis on the permanent result of the action; translate "you will possess him...," then follow with the participles as adjectives.

989. omniumque: the *-que* connects the clause containing *habēbitis* with that containing *capiētis*.

huius: i.e., of Caelius

990. nervōrum: nervus, nervī, *m.,* sinew, tendon; *pl.,* strength, vigor, efforts; energy, verve

vōs: subject

fructūs: fructus, fructūs, *m.,* output, yield, profit, reward; pleasure, satisfaction [fruor, have use of, enjoy]

ūberēs: ūber, ūberis, *adj.,* abundant, plentiful, fruitful; rich, fertile

991. diūturnōs: diūturnus-a-um, *adj.,* long-lived, lasting; durable, permanent

SELECT BIBLIOGRAPHY

Austin has an extensive bibliography (to 1959) on pp. xxviii–xxxii and p. 162 of his edition. The bibliography below includes (1) all sources that are referred to in this edition regardless of their dates of publication; (2) all *Caeliana* known to me that were published after 1959 or are otherwise not contained in Austin's bibliography; and (3) a few other items of *Ciceroniana* that may be of interest to the student or teacher.

ABBREVIATIONS:

AJP	*American Journal of Philology*
CJ	*Classical Journal*
CP	*Classical Philology*
CQ	*Classical Quarterly*
HSCP	*Harvard Studies in Classical Philology*
PCPS	*Proceedings of the Cambridge Philological Society*
TAPA	*Transactions of the American Philological Association*

Ben. Bennett, Charles E. *New Latin Grammar.* Allyn and Bacon, 1908. Repr. Wauconda: Bolchazy-Carducci Publishers, Inc., 1995.

G&L Gildersleeve, B. L., and Gonzales Lodge. *Latin Grammar,* 3rd ed. Scarborough, Ontario: Nelson Canada, 1992.

L&S Lewis, Charlton T., and Charles Short. *A Latin Dictionary.* Oxford: Oxford University Press, 1879.

OLD Glare, P. G. W., ed. *Oxford Latin Dictionary.* Oxford: Oxford University Press, 1982.

References to Austin that appear in his 1933 commentary (pp. 41–143 in the 1960 edition) are cited by Oxford chapter and line number; references to his notes from 1960 ("Additional Notes," pp. 162–175) are cited with the page number as well.

I. EDITIONS

Austin, R. G., ed. *M. Tulli Ciceronis Pro M. Caelio Oratio,* 3rd. ed. New York: Oxford University Press, 1960. This masterly volume is the *sine qua non* of *pro Caelio* study and scholarship, with commentary on everything from manuscript transmission to historical background.

Clark, Albert Curtis, ed. *M.T. Ciceronis Orationes pro Sex. Roscio, etc.* Oxford: Oxford University Press, 1905.

Crawford, Jane W., ed. *M. Tullius Cicero: The Fragmentary Speeches,* 2nd ed. Atlanta: Scholars Press, 1994. Pp. 227–263 contain a useful discussion of the fragmentary *in Clodium et Curionem,* which may be read profitably with *pro Caelio,* and which is also discussed in Geffcken.

———. *M. Tullius Cicero: The Lost and Unpublished Orations.* Göttingen: Vandenhoeck und Ruprecht, 1984. Sections 20, 21, 26–30, 36, 37, 42, 45–52, and 55 may be of interest.

Cousin, Jean, ed. *Cicéron. Discours 15: Pour Caelius, Sur les prov. cons., Pour Balbus,* 2nd ed. Paris: Société d'édition Les Belles Lettres (Budé), 1962.

Englert, Walter, ed. *Cicero, Pro Caelio.* Bryn Mawr, PA: Thomas Library, Bryn Mawr College, 1990. A Bryn Mawr Commentary.

Gardner, Robert, ed. and trans. *Cicero. The Speeches, pro Caelio, de provinciis consularibus, pro Balbo.* London: Loeb Classical Library, 1958. There is much useful information in the essays on pp. 398–405.

Grant, Michael, transl. *Cicero: Selected Political Speeches.* London: Penguin Books, Ltd., 1989.

Klotz, Alfred. *M.T. Ciceronis scripta,* fasc. 23. Leipzig: Bibliotheca Teubneriana, 1915.

Klotz, Alfred, and Schoell, F. *M.T. Ciceronis scripta,* vol. vii. Leipzig: Bibliotheca Teubneriana, 1919.

Maslowski, Tadeusz, ed. *Orationes in P. Vatinium testem, pro M. Caelio.* Stuttgart: Bibliotheca Teubneriana, 1995.

II. BIOGRAPHICAL, HISTORICAL AND LEGAL

Alexander, Michael C. *"Praemia* in the *Quaestiones* of the Late Republic,*"* *CP* 80 (1985) 20–32.

Allen, Jr., Walter, "Claudius or Clodius?" *CJ* 33 (1937) 107–110.

Bailey, D. R. Shackleton, transl. *Cicero, Back From Exile: Six Speeches Upon His Return.* Atlanta: Scholars Press, 1991. This volume includes felicitous translations and brief notes for *post reditum in senatu, post reditum ad quirites, de domo suo, de haruspicum responsis, pro P. Sestio* and *in P. Vatinium,* and might be used to advantage by students who want rapid exposure to Cicero's oratory as well as to the politics and personalities of the period 57–56 B.C.

———. *Cicero: Epistulae ad Familiares,* vol. 1 (62–47 B.C.). Cambridge: Cambridge University Press, 1977.

Boissier, Gaston. *Cicero et ses amis.* Paris: Librarie Hachette, 1905. Esp. 167–219. Transl. A. D. Jones, *Cicero and His Friends* (New York: Cooper Square, repr. 1970) 159–208.

Broughton, T. Robert S. *The Magistrates of the Roman Republic,* vol 2. New York: American Philological Association, 1952.

Brunt, P. A. "'*Amicitia*' in the Late Roman Republic." *PCPS* 191 (1965): 1–20.

——. *The Fall of the Roman Republic and Related Essays.* Oxford: Clarendon Press, 1988.

Clarke, M. L. *Rhetoric at Rome: A Historical Survey.* London: Cohen and West, 1953.

Classen, C. J. *Recht, Rhetorik, Politik: Untersuchungen zu Ciceros rhetorischer Strategie.* Darmstadt: Wissenschaftliche Buchgesellschaft, 1985.

Clauss, James J. "The Ignoble Consistency of M. Caelius Rufus." *Athenaeum* 68 (1990) 531–540.

Crownover, Emma. "The Clash between Clodia and Cicero," *CJ* 30 (1934) 137–147.

Dane II, Nathan. "*Rufus Redolens*," *CJ* 64 (1968) 130.

Dixon, Suzanne. "A Family Business: Women's Role in Patronage and Politics at Rome 80–44 B.C.," *Classica et Mediaevalia* 34 (1983) 91–112.

Epstein, David F. "Cicero's Testimony at the *Bona Dea* Trial," *CP* 81 (1986) 229–235.

Fuhrmann, Manfred. *Cicero and the Roman Republic.* Oxford: Blackwell Publishers, 1990.

Greenidge, A. J. H. *The Legal Procedure of Cicero's Time.* Oxford: Oxford University Press, 1901.

Gruen, Erich S. *The Last Generation of the Roman Republic.* Berkeley: University of California Press, 1995. Gruen persuasively explores sources of stability in the late Republic. Along with Wiseman (1985), Gruen, pp. 305–309, is a compelling alternative to Austin's reading of *pro Caelio* as principally a society trial. Both demonstrate the political struggles that gave rise to the case.

Hayes, J., and Gilbert Lawall, edd. *Teacher's Guide to Cicero.* Amherst, MA: CANE Instructional Materials, 1994.

Hillard, Tom. "Republican Politics, Women, and the Evidence," *Helios* 16 (1989) 165–182.

Kennedy, George. *The Art of Rhetoric in the Roman World.* Princeton: Princeton University Press, 1972.

——. "The Rhetoric of Advocacy in Greece and Rome," *AJP* 89 (1968) 419–436.

Leen, Anne. "Teaching Two Speeches of Cicero," *CJ* 85 (1990) 350–356.

May, James M. "Patron and Client, Father and Son in Cicero's *Pro Caelio*," *CJ* 90 (1995) 433–441.

McDermott, William C. "The Sisters of P. Clodius," *Phoenix* 24 (1970) 39–47.

Mulroy, David. "The Early Career of P. Clodius Pulcher: A Reexamination of the Charges of Mutiny and Sacrilege," *TAPA* 118 (1988) 155–178.

North, John. "Politics and Aristocracy in the Roman Republic," *CP* 85 (1990) 277–287.

Pomeroy, Sarah B. "The Study of Women in Antiquity: Past, Present and Future," *AJP* 112 (1991) 263–268.

Rankin, H. D. "Clodia II," *L'Antiquité Classique* 38 (1969) 501–506.

Rieks, Rudolf. "Prosopographie und Lyrikinterpretation," *Poetica* 18 (1986) 249–273.

Rothstein, M. *"Catull und Lesbia,"* *Philologus* 78 (1923) 17.

Salzman, Michele Renée. "Cicero, the *Megalenses* and the Defense of Caelius," *AJP* 103 (1982) 299–304.

Skinner, Marilyn B. "Clodia Metelli," *TAPA* 113 (1983) 273–287.

———. "Pretty Lesbius," *TAPA* 112 (1982) 197–208.

Stockton, David. *Cicero: A Political Biography.* New York: Oxford University Press, 1971.

Stroh, Wilfried. *Taxis und Taktik: die advokatische Dispositionskunst in Ciceros Gerichtsreden.* Stuttgart: B. G. Teubner, 1975.

Syme, Ronald. *The Roman Revolution.* Oxford: Clarendon Press, 1939. See esp. 149–161 on invective and political lampoon.

Tatum, W. Jeffrey. "Catullus' Criticism of Cicero in Poem 49," *TAPA* 118 (1988) 179–184.

———. "Cicero and the *Bona Dea* Scandal," *CP* 85 (1990) 202–208.

———. "Cicero's Opposition to the *Lex Clodia de Collegiis*," *CQ* 40 (1990) 187–194.

Taylor, Lily Ross. *Party Politics in the Age of Caesar.* Berkeley: University of California Press, 1949. For a critique of Taylor's view that Cicero achieved praetorian seniority rights in the senate through his prosecution of Verres, see Alexander, *supra.*

Tellegen-Couperus, Olga. *A Short History of Roman Law.* New York: Routledge, 1993

Treggiari, Susan. *Roman Marriage: Iusti Conjuges From the Time of Cicero to the Time of Ulpian.* Oxford: Oxford University Press, 1991. See esp. 173–190.

Tyrrell, Robert Y., and Louis C. Purser, edd. *The Correspondence of M. Tullius Cicero,* vol. 3. Dublin: Dublin University Press, 1914. Has dated but still useful essays on the life of Caelius and his correspondence with Cicero.

Wiseman, T. P. "Clodia: Some Imaginary Lives," *Arion* n.s. 2 (1975) 96–115.

———. *Catullus and His World: A Reappraisal.* New York: Cambridge University Press, 1985. Ch. 4, "The Trial of Marcus Caelius" is required reading, esp. along with Gruen (1995).

Wolff, Hans Julius. *Roman Law: An Historical Introduction.* Norman, Oklahoma: University of Oklahoma Press, 1951.

Zarker, John W. "Lesbia's Charms," *CJ* 68 (1973) 107–115.

III. STYLE, DICTION, CONSTRUCTION, ETC.

Buller, Jeffrey L. "Cicero's *Pro Caelio:* Text and Context," *Classical Outlook* 71 (1994) 121–128.

Bush, Archie C., and Steven Cerutti. "The Term *Frater* in *Pro Caelio*," *CJ* 82 (1986) 37–39. See Wilson, *infra*, for a vigorous dissent.

Classen, C. J. "Ciceros Rede für Caelius." In H. Temporini, ed., *Aufstieg und Niedergang der römischen Welt*. Berlin: Walter DeGruyter, 1973.

Craig, Christopher P. "Reason, Resonance, and Dilemma in Cicero's Speech for Caelius," *Rhetorica* 7 (1989) 312–328.

——. *Form as Argument in Cicero's Speeches: A Study of Dilemma*. Atlanta: Scholars Press, 1993.

——. "Teaching Cicero's Speech for Caelius," *CJ* 90 (1995) 407–422.

Dorey, T. A. "Cicero, Clodia, and the *Pro Caelio*." *Greece and Rome* 27 (2nd ser., 5) (1958) 175–180.

Duckworth, G. E. *The Nature of Roman Comedy: A Study in Popular Entertainment*. Princeton: Princeton University Press, 1952. Repr. Norman, OK: University of Oklahoma Press, 1994. See esp. ch. 9 for useful background on the *adulescentes, senes, meretrices, etc.*, of Roman comedy.

Gaffney, G. Edward. "*Severitate Respondere:* Character Drawing in *Pro Caelio* and Catullus' *Carmina*," *CJ* 90 (1995) 423–431.

Geffcken, Katherine A. *Comedy in the Pro Caelio*. Leiden: E. J. Brill, 1973. Repr. Wauconda: Bolchazy-Carducci Publishers, Inc., 1995. Geffcken examines Cicero's uses of comedy in light of ancient comedy and modern psychological theories about comedy.

Gotoff, Harold C. "Cicero's Analysis of the Prosecution Speeches in the *Pro Caelio:* An Exercise in Practical Criticism," *CP* 81 (1986) 122–132.

Jocelyn, H. D., ed. *The Tragedies of Ennius: The Fragments*. Cambridge: Cambridge University Press, 1967.

May, James M. *Trials of Character: The Eloquence of Ciceronian Ethos*. Chapel Hill–London: University of North Carolina Press, 1988. See esp. pp. 106–116 for *pro Caelio*.

Prill, Paul. "Cicero in Theory and Practice: The Securing of Good Will in the *Exordia* of Five Forensic Speeches." *Rhetorica* 4 (1986) 93–109.

Vasaly, Ann. *Representations: Images of the World in Ciceronian Oratory*. Berkeley: University of California Press, 1993.

Volpe, M. "The Persuasive Force of Humor: Cicero's Defense of Caelius," *Quarterly Journal of Speech* 63 (1977) 311–323.

Wilson, Joseph P. "Three Non-Uses of *Frater* in *Pro Caelio* 32," *CJ* 83 (1988) 207–211.

IV. TEXTUAL CRITICISM, LEXICOGRAPHY, ETC.

Bailey, D. R. Shackleton. "On Cicero's Speeches," *HSCP* 83 (1979) 237–285.

——. "On Cicero's Speeches *(Post Reditum),*" *TAPA* 117 (1987) 271–280.

——. "Sex. Clodius - Sex. Cloelius," *CQ* n.s. 10 (1960) 41–42.

Kinsey, T. E. "*Pro Caelio* 31," *Hermes* 94 (1966) 253–254.

Maslowski, Tadeusz. "Cicero: *Pro Caelio* 31," *AJP* 112 (1991) 507–511.

——. "Cicero's *Pro Caelio:* The First Collation of the *Vetus Cluniacensis* in Italy." In Fidel Fajardo-Acosta, ed., *The Influence of the Classical World on Medieval Literature, Architecture, Music, and Culture: A Collection of Interdisciplinary Studies.* Lewiston, NY and Queenston, Ontario: The Edwin Mellen Press, 1992.

McDermott, William C. "*In Caelianam,*" *Athenaeum* 48 (1970) 408–409.

Palmer, L. R. *The Latin Language.* London: Faber and Faber, 1954.

Ramage, Edwin S. "Clodia in Cicero's *Pro Caelio.*" In David F. Bright and Edwin S. Ramage, *Classical Texts and their Traditions: Studies in Honor of C. R. Trahman* (Atlanta: Scholars Press, 1984) 201–211.

Reynolds, L. D., ed. *Texts and Transmission: A Survey of the Latin Classics.* Oxford: Oxford University Press, 1983.

Watt, W. S. "*Enim Tullianum,*" *CQ* 74 (1980) 120–123.

Wiseman, T. P. "Cicero, *pro Caelio* 47: a matter of punctuation," *Liverpool Classical Monthly* 9.1 (Jan., 1984) 12.

APPENDIX A

CAELIUS, *PRO CAELIO*, AND CATULLUS

On the basis of vocabulary or overall content, ten poems from the corpus of Catullus (49, 58a, 59, 69, 71, 77, 79, 83, 98, and 100) may be relevant to Caelius and *prō Caeliō*:[1]

The situations described in poems 77 (addressed to a Rufus) and 58a (addressed to a Caelius; 58b is a fragment (?) unconnected with 58a) make identification of the addressee in each with M. Caelius Rufus probable if not certain:

Poem 77:

> Rūfe mihī frustrā ac nēquīquam crēdite amīce
>   (Frustrā? Immō magnō cum pretiō atque malō),
> sīcine subrēpstī mī atque intestīna perūrēns
>   —ei !— miserō ēripuistī omnia nostra bona?
> Ēripuistī. Ēheu nostrae crūdēle venēnum
>   vītae; ēheu nostrae pestis amīcitiae.[2]

> My friend Rufus, I trusted you in vain and to no purpose
>   (Did I say "In vain?" No, rather at great cost and great evil),
> was it in this way that you have crept up on me and, thoroughly churning
>   up my guts
>   —alas! oh!—, in this way you have stolen everything that is good to
>   me, in love?
> You have stolen it. Alas! you cruel poison
>   of my life; alas! you plague of my friendship.

Poem 58a:

> Caelī, Lesbia nostra, Lesbia illa,
> illa Lesbia, quam Catullus ūnam
> plūs quam sē atque suōs amāvit omnēs,
> nunc in quādriviīs et angiportīs
> glūbit magnanimī Remī nepōtēs.

---

[1] This statement excludes the poems purely of the Lesbia cycle, which I take to be principally 2, 2b, 3, 7, 8, 11, 13, 36, 43, 51, 58a, 60 (possibly), 70, 72, 75, 76, 77, 79, 83, 85, 86, 87, 92, 104, 107, and 109.

[2] The verbal echoes of this poem in the somber elegy 76 are striking.

Caelius! Our Lesbia, that Lesbia,
that very Lesbia, whom alone Catullus
loved more than himself and all his own—
now on corners and in alleys
she services the descendants of great-souled Remus.

Poem 100 mentions a Caelius, but, as Austin notes (p. 148), he is from Verona and it is hard to imagine how this fact (as well as thematic considerations) can be made to square with ch. 5 of *prō Caeliō.*

Poem 69 (and by extension 71, no doubt referring to the same person) is addressed to a Rufus whose love life suffers from the *trūx caper* ("rough goat," = body odor) that lives under his armpits. Austin feels (pp. 148–149) that the coarse content of the poem militates against its referring to our M. Caelius Rufus, but this is exactly the kind of treatment one would expect in what is essentially a mild invective. Dane's clever suggestion that *bestia* ("the beast," = "the goat") in 69.8 is a thinly-veiled reference to L. Calpurnius Bestia would make the Rufus in the poem our M. Caelius Rufus; this identification is supported by *aemulus* ("rival") at 71.3 but made difficult by poem 71's addition of *podagra* ("gout") to Rufus's maladies—not a disease one would expect of the youthful, hale-and-hearty Caelius.

Poem 49 is addressed to Cicero:

Dīsertissime Romulī nepōtum,
Quot sunt quotque fuēre, Marce Tullī,
Quotque post aliīs erunt in annīs,
Grātiās tibi maximās Catullus
Agit pessimus omnium poēta,
Tantō pessimus omnium poēta
Quantō tū optimus omnium patrōnus.

Most eloquent of the descendants of Romulus,
however many there are and however many there have been, Marcus Tullius,
and however many there will be in other years,
Catullus gives you the greatest thanks,
he the worst poet of all.
By as much as he is the worst poet of all,
so you are the best advocate of / for all.

Scholars are divided on the poem's sincerity or cynicism; also, attention has tended to focus on the ambiguity in the final *omnium,* without a whole lot of success. Tatum has argued persuasively that the poem mocks Cicero's social pretensions, and that we should focus less on *omnium* than on the extravagant phrasing (especially in the first half), on the superlatives, and on the word *patrōnus* (significantly in strong last position).

Catullus 79 concerns P. Clodius Pulcher:

> Lesbius est pulcher; quid nī? quem Lesbia mālit
>   quam tē cum tōtā gente, Catulle, tuā.
> sed tamen hic pulcher vendat cum gente Catullum
>   sī tria nōtōrum suāvia reppererit.

> Lesbius is a Pulcher; what of it? Lesbia prefers him
>   to you with your whole *gēns,* Catullus.
> Nevertheless, this Pulcher would sell Catullus with his/your *gēns,*
>   if he could find three kisses from his relatives.

The jokes are as follows: (1) Clodius is a pretty boy (*pulcher*) whom (2) his sister Clodia would rather sleep with (*mālit* in a sexual sense) than with (now former?) boyfriend Catullus; (3) *cum tōtā gente...tuā* (after *mālit* in a non-sexual sense) prepares us for the second couplet by suggesting that Clodia would rather be around one member of her superior family to *all* of Catullus's inferior family. (4) *Vendat* is colloquially similar to our "he would buy and sell [you]" = "he is way richer and more important than [you]," but (5) *vendere* + a proper name X = "to discharge X's estate" (here Catullus conceives of himself as bankrupt even with his whole *gēns* thrown in). The final and biggest jokes: (6) it is implied that Clodius cannot carry out line 3 because no relatives associate with him (now line 3 *cum gente* may go with Clodius) due to (7) his mouth, unclean because of oral sex with his sister. The final joke involves incest but also the notion that impotent men were forced to resort to oral sex.

Catullus 83 almost certainly refers to C. Metellus Celer, and must therefore be one of Catullus's earliest poems (written during or before 59 B.C.):

> Lesbia mī praesente virō mala plūrima dīcit:
>   haec illī fatuō maxima laetitia est.

Mūle, nihil sentīs? Sī nostrī oblīta tacēret,
  sāna esset: nunc quod gannit et obloquitur,
nōn sōlum meminit, sed—quae multō acrior est rēs—,
  īrāta est; hoc est, ūritur et loquitur.

Lesbia says very many bad things to me when her husband is around:
  this is the source of greatest joy to that moron.
Idiot, do you understand nothing? If, forgetful of me, she were silent,
  she would be okay; but the fact that now she yacks on and on and
    interrupts
shows not only that she remembers me but—the thing which is much
    more acute—,
  she is all fired-up; this is the thing, she's ablaze with passion and she
    talks!

Two final poems deserve some mention. Poem 59 concerns a Rufa and
a Rufus (or perhaps Rufulus, its diminutive), but the context and abusive
language appear to make connection with our M. Caelius Rufus impossible.
Poem 98 is addressed to some Victius (or Viccius, or Vittius); insufficient context and textual problems make it impossible to justify conclusively an emendation to Vettius, in order to connect poem 98 to the Vettius of *prō Caelio* ch. 71.

APPENDIX B

TESTIMONIA TO, AND FRAGMENTS
FROM CAELIUS' SPEECHES, AND COMMENTS
OF LATER WRITERS

Appendix B contains the Latin text and English translations of the extant testimonia to and fragments from the speeches of M. Caelius Rufus; the numbering is as in Malcovati, *Oratōrum Rōmānōrum Fragmenta*. For the sake of brevity
and clarity, I have included only those fragments whose sense is clear—I have
excluded a number of small or bland fragments (specifically *ORF* orator #162
[pp. 480–489], M. Caelius Rufus, entries 5, 16, 18, 38) and some fragments that
neither apply to the early part of Caelius's career nor shed light on his character or oratorical style (fragments 29, 30, 31, 32, 33, 35, first part of 39). I have also
excluded testimonia from *ORF* that would repeat what is already in this text
in other places (specifically, fragments 1, 3, 13, 14, 15, 19, 20, 21, and 23 simply
reference passages in *prō Caeliō*, and fragment 17 is given at 178n.). Passages 22
and 25 contain more of the text than that found in *ORF*.

It is worth noting the correspondence between Caelius and Cicero (*ad
Fam.* 8) will be of even more concern to those interested in this material.

2. This passage is from one of Cicero's oratorical treatises, Brūtus, ch. 273,
   written a few years after Caelius's death:

   Nec vērō M. Caelium praetereundum arbitror, quaecumque ēius in exitū
   vel fortūna vel mēns fuit. Quī quamdiu auctōritātī meae paruit, tālis
   tribūnus plēbis fuit ut nēmō contrā cīvium perditōrum populārem turbu-
   lentamque dēmentiam ā senātū et ā bonōrum causā steterit cōnstantius.
   Quam ēius actiōnem multum tamen et splendida et grandis et eadem in
   primīs facēta et perurbāna commendābat orātiō. Gravēs eius contiōnēs aliquot fuērunt, acrēs accūsātiōnēs trēs (*in Antōnium, in Calpurniam Bestiam,
   in Pompēium Rūfum*) eaeque omnēs ex reī publicae contentiōne susceptae;
   defensiōnēs, etsi illa erant in eō meliōra quae dīxī, nōn contemnendae
   tamen sānēque tolerābilēs. Hic cum summā voluntāte bonōrum aedīlis
   curūlis factus esset, nescio quo modō discessū meō discessit ā sēsē ceci-
   ditque, posteāquam eōs imitārī coepit quōs ipse perverterat.

"But I think M. Caelius Rufus should not be excluded from consideration, whether his death was by accident or design. So long as he looked to and followed my leadership, he was such a tribune of the people that no one could protect more steadfastly the senate and the position of the *bonī* (see 105n.) against the base and wild craziness of wicked citizens. His delivery was most commendable—it was ornate and powerful, and yet at the same time he was second to none in wit and sophistication. His several addresses to public assemblies were sober, and his three prosecutions ("Against Caius Antonius Hybrida," "Against Lucius Calpurnius Bestia," "Against Pompeius Rufus") were fierce, and all these were undertaken out of republican political competition; although his defense speeches were not quite as good, they cannot be condemned and were completely acceptable. After Caelius had become curule aedile, with complete *bonī* support, after my exile he somehow fell away from his true self and lost his way; later he began to model those whom he himself had turned away from."

4. Vellēius Paterculus 2.68.1: M. Caelius vir ēloquiō animōque Cūriōnī simillimus sed in utrōque perfectior nec minus ingeniōsē nēquam.

    "Marcus Caelius was a man of eloquence and in his intellect very similar to Curio, but in each man there was rather exquisite taste and a certain amount of delinquency."

The following four fragments are from Quintilian's work on oratory, *institūtiō ōrātōria* (*The Conventions of Oratory*):

6. Quint. 6.3.69: [Cicero] per allēgoriam M. Caelium, melius obicientem crīmina quam dēfendentem, bonam dextram, malam sinistram habēre dīcēbat.

    "[Cicero] used to use Marcus Caelius as an example: he was bettter at prosecuting cases than at defending them, and so he had a good right and a bad left." (Roman soldiers held swords in their right hands and shields in their left.)

7. Quint. 10.1.115: multum ingeniī in Caeliō et praecipuē in accūsandō multa urbānitās, dignusque vir cuī et mēns melior et vīta longior contigisset.

    "There was much genius in Caelius and, especially in his prosecutorial style, much sophistication; he was a worthy man who should have had both better judgment and a longer life."

8 and 9. Quintilian refers to Caelius' *asperitātem* ("oratorical ferocity") and his *indolem* ("innate talents").

The next three fragments come from Tacitus, *dialogus dē ōrātōribus (Discussion Concerning the Orators):*

10. Sunt enim [ōrātōrēs antīquī] horridī et impolītī et rudēs et informēs, et quōs—utinam nullā parte imitātus esset Calvus vester aut Caelius aut ipse Cicero.

"For there are ancient orators who are blunt and unrefined and clumsy and disorganized, and those whom—oh, thank heavens that neither your Calvus nor Caelius nor Cicero himself had ever used them as models in any way!"

11. Ex Caeliānīs ōrātiōnibus nempe eae placent, sīve ūniversae <sīve> partēs eārum, in quibus nitōrem et altitūdinem hōrum temporum agnōscimus. Sordēs autem [rēgulae] verbōrum et hiāns compositiō et inconditī sēnsūs redolent antīquitātem; nec quemquam adeō antīquārium putō, ut Caelium ex eā parte laudet quā antīquus est.

"To be sure some of the orations by Caelius are pleasing, whether in full or in certain sections, in which we well recognize the elegant style and the loftiness of those times. But the misconstrued order of words and badly connected sections and mish-mash of emotions reek of antiquity; and I do not suppose that anyone is so much of an antiquarian that he would praise Caelius except to the extent that he is old.

12. ...amārior Caelius...: "Caelius is caustic."

22. Pliny, *historia natūrālis* 27.2.4: Sed antīquōrum cūram dīligentiamque quis possit satis venerārī? Cōnstat omnium venenōrum ōcissimum esse aconītum et tactīs quoque genitālibus fēminīnī sexūs animalium eōdem diē īnferre mortem. Hoc fuit venēnum quō interemptās dormientēs ā Calpurniō Bestiā uxōrēs M. Caelius accūsātor obiēcit. Hinc illa atrox perōrātiō ēius *in digitum.*

"But who could sufficiently praise the care and diligence of the ancients? Everyone agrees that wolfsbane is the quickest-acting of poisons, and also that if it just touches the female animal's genitals, it will cause death that very same day. This was the poison which Caelius Rufus as prosecutor claimed Calpurnius Bestia had used to dispatch his sleeping wives. From this came that fierce speech of his, entitled "The Oration Against the Finger."

24. Suētōnius, *dē rhētoribus* (*Concerning Orators*): [L. Plōtium Gallum] M. Caelius in ōrātiōne, quam prō sē dē vī habuit, significat dictāsse Atratinō, accūsātōrī suō, actiōnem; subtractōque nōmine, hordeārium eum rhētorem appellat, dērīdēns ut inflātum ac levem et sordidum.

"In the speech which he delivered in his own defense on the charge of vīs, Marcus Caelius declares that Lucius Plotius Gallus had prepared Atratinus's speech; and, without mentioning his name, Caelius calls Plotius a 'rhetorician like puffed wheat,' deriding him as 'a turgid windbag of a yokel.'"

25. Quint. 11.1.51: Hoc adhūc adiciendum aliquās etiam, quae sunt ēgregiae dīcendī virtūtēs, quō minus deceant, efficī condiciōne causārum. An quisquam tulerit reum in discrīmine capitis, praecipuēque sī apud victōrem et principem prō sē ipse dīcat, frequentī trānslātiōne, fictīs aut repetītīs ex vetustāte verbīs, compositiōne quae sit maxime ā vulgārī ūsū remōta, dēcurrentibus periodīs, quam laetissimīs locīs sententiīsque dīcentem? Nōn perdant haec omnia necessārium perīclitantī sollicitūdinis colōrem, petendumque etiam innocentibus mīsericordiae auxilium? Moveāturne quisquam ēius fortūna, quem tumidum ac suī iactantem et ambitiōsum institōrem ēloquentiae in ancipitī sorte videat? Nōn immo ōderit reum verba aucupantem et ānxium dē fāmā ingeniī, et cuī esse disertō vacet? Quod mīrē M. Caelius in dēfēnsiōne causae, quā reus dē vī fuit, comprehendisse vidētur mihī: 'Nē cuī vestrum atque etiam omnium, quī ad rem agendam adsunt, meus aut vultus molestior aut vōx immoderātior aliqua aut dēnique, quod minimum est, iactantior gestus fuisse videātur.'

"Moreover, it must also be said that some oratorical techniques, which are themselves outstanding features in speaking, are less appropriate in certain categories of cases. For who could brook a defendant in a capital case, especially if he is speaking for himself before a conqueror or sovereign, who uses metaphors constantly, new coinages or words derived from antiquity, with a composition that is very much removed from common usage, with long and flowing periods, and with as blissful a state as possible? Would not all these things destroy the necessary impression of nervousness for a man in danger, and destroy the help of pity that must be sought even by the innocent? Would anybody be moved by the fate of him whom he sees is pompous and boastful and fond of parading around his eloquence for all to see even in a moment of great personal uncertainty? No, would he not hate the defendant who was chasing after his words and was anxious concerning the fame of his genius and who felt himself free to be eloquent? When Marcus Caelius was a defendant under the violence law, he seems to me to have grasped this perfectly, saying: 'I hope that none of you, who are here to decide this case, find my expression troublesome, or any aspect of my voice inappropriate, or finally, what is least important, my gesture arrogant.'"

26. Quint. 8.6.53: …quadrantāriam Clytaemestram…: "a Clytaimestra whose price is a farthing"; Caelius used this phrase of Clodia in his defense speech, see 205–216n.

27. …in trīclīniō Cōam, in cubiculō nōlam…: "In the dining room a woman from Cos, but in the bedroom totally frigid"; another one of Caelius's jests. Evidently women from Cos were considered promiscuous. *Nōlam* is probably an invented word, from *nōlle*, "to be unwilling."

28. Quint. 1.6.29: Haec habet aliquando ūsum necessārium, quotiēns interpretātiōne rēs, dē quā quaeritur, eget, ut M. Caelius sē esse hominem *frūgī* vult probāre, nōn quia abstinēns sit—nam id nē ēmentīrī quidem poterat—, sed quia ūtilis multīs, id est *fructuōsus*, unde sit ducta *frūgālitās*.

"[Etymology] can sometimes be indispensable, when the matter under discussion needs explication, as when Marcus Caelius wants to show that he is a *homo frugi*, not because he is temperate and virtuous—for he could not even pretend that—, but because he is 'useful' to many, that is, *fructuōsus*, from which *frūgālitās* ("temperance," "virtue") is derived."

34. Sextus Julius Frontinus, *dē aquīs* ("On the Aqueducts") 2.76: Ac dē vitiīs ēius modī nec plūra nec melius dīcī possunt, quam ā Caeliō Rūfō dicta sunt in ea contiōne, cuī titulus est *dē aquīs*.

"As for illicit behavior of this sort (water fraud!), nothing more nor better can be said beyond what Caelius said in the public assembly in his speech 'On the Water Supply.'"

36. ...perpetuum salientem...: Caelius was "perpetually dancing."

37. Pelias cincinnātus: "Pelias in ringlets," see 205–216n.

39. Quint. 6.3.41: Et Caelius cum omnia venustissimē finxit tum illud ultimum: 'hic subsecūtus quō modo transierit, utrum ratī an piscātōriō
nāvigiō, nēmo sciēbat: Siculī quidem, ut sunt lascīvī atque dicācēs, āiēbant
in delphīnō sēdisse et sīc tamquam Arīona trānsvectum.'

"And after Caelius had most charmingly fashioned everything, then he
said this final statement: 'Just how the second man followed, whether by
a raft or by a fisherman's boat, nobody had any idea. But the Sicilians,
who are playful and witty, used to say that he had sat on a dolphin and so
had been carried across the sea just like Arion.'" (In Greek mythology, the
cithara-playing Arion was cast overboard by evil pirates, but rescued by a
dolphin.)

40. Pliny, *Natūrālis Historia* 35.165: Mātris deum sacerdōtēs quī Gallī vocantur
virīlitātem amputāre, nec aliter citra perniciem, M. Caeliō crēdāmus, quī
linguam sīc amputandam obiēcit gravī probrō.

"The priests of the Mother of the gods, who are called Galli, cut off their
genitalia, and in a parallel situation except for the possibility of death let
us believe Marcus Caelius, who similarly claimed that a tongue had to be
cut off because of a serious perversion.

APPENDIX C

FRAGMENTS OF *IN CLODIUM ET CURIONEM*

Appendix C contains the Latin text and English translations of fragments from the invective *In Clōdium et Cūriōnem,* delivered just prior to *prō Caeliō* and with some thematic resemblances (see esp. fragments 5, 20–25, and Geffcken [1973]).

1. Statueram, patrēs cōnscriptī, quoad reus esset P. Clōdius, nihil dē illō neque apud vōs neque aliō ullō in locō dīcere.

   "O senators, I had decided that, since the defendant was Publius Clodius Pulcher, I would say nothing about him either to you or in any other place."

2. ac furiōsīs contiōnibus indīxerat = "and Clodius had held raving-mad public assemblies"

3. quod simul ab eō mihī et reī publicae dēnuntiabatur = "because at the same time he was threatening me and the nation"

4. nihil mē addere ad alterīus perīculum = "that I add nothing to another man's predicament"

5. sīn esset iūdicātum nōn vidērī virum vēnisse quō iste vēnisset = "but if it had been ruled that a man did not seem to have come where that man (Clodius) had come"

6. ut illō ē iūdiciō tamquam ē naufragiō nūdus ēmersit = "when he emerged from that trial completely bereft, as a naked man from a shipwreck"

6b. Crawford. quō ex iūdiciō velut ex incendiō nūdus ēffūgit = "when he emerged from that trial completely bereft, as a naked man from a conflagration"

7. ac vidē, an facile fiērī tū potuerīs, cum is factus nōn sit cuī tū concessistī = "and so consider whether you could have appointed that man easily, after he was not appointed—to whom you have (otherwise) given in"

8. Syriam sibī nōs extrā ordinem pollicērī = "that we promise him Syria as an extraordinary province"

9. crēditōribus suīs spem ostentāre prōvinciae vidērētur = "he apparently showed his creditors the expectation of a province"

10. ingemuit gravius timidior quīdam crēditor = "A certain rather jittery creditor groaned all the more despairingly."

11. confirmat sē comitiīs cōnsulāribus Rōmae futūrum = "He confirms that he will be in Rome for the consular elections."

12. tantō prius ad aerārium vēnit, ut ibi nē scrībam quidem quemquam offenderet = "He came to the treasury earlier, so that he would not run into anybody there—not even a clerk."

13. quibus iste, quī omnia sacrificia nōsset, facile ab sē deōs placārī posse arbitrābātur = "And by these means that rogue of a man, who knew *all* the sacred rites, reckoned that he could pacify the gods easily."

14. cum sē ad plēbem trānsīre velle dīceret, sed mīserē frētum trānsīre cuperet = "although he said that he wanted to transfer to the plebeians; but he wretchedly wished to cross a strait"

15. hanc loquācem Siciliam nōn adspēxit = "He did not look down on gossipy Sicily."

16. accessērunt ita paucī, ut eum nōn ad contiōnem, sed spōnsum dīcerēs advocāsse = "So few men came that you could say he had summoned everybody not to an assembly, but to a loan settlement."

17. cūius satisdatiōnēs semper indūcuntur = "[he] whose credit guarantees are always being brought up"

18. intellegō quam in absentem esse dīcenda = "I understand how it is that I have to speak these things against a man who is not here."

19. prīmum homo dūrus ac priscus invectus est in eōs quī mēnse Aprīlī apud Bāiās essent et aquīs calidīs ūterentur. quid cum hōc homine nōbis tam tristī ac sēverō? nōn possunt hī mōrēs ferre hunc tam austērum et tam vehementem magistrum, per quem hominibus maiōribus nātū nē in suīs quidem praediīs inpūne tum, cum Rōmae nihil agitur, liceat esse valētūdinīque servīre. verum tamen cēterīs licitum sit ignōscere, eī vērō quī praedium habeat in illō locō, nūllō modō. 'quid hominī' inquit 'Arpīnātī cum Bāiīs, agrestī ac rusticō?'

"First a tough and old-fashioned man attacked those who were at Baiae in April using the warm waters there. What are we to do with this man, who is so dour and censorious? Modern fashion cannot bear a taskmaster who is as full of rectitude and invective as he is: according to him older people cannot even be on their own estates tending to their health without criticism—when nothing is happening in Rome. Actually, it does seem that it is okay to overlook everybody except a man who has an estate in that place. He said, 'How could this man from Arpinum, a farmer and a yokel, have any interest in Baiae?' "

20. quō locō ita fuit caecus, ut facile appārēret vīdisse eum quod fās nōn fuisset. nec enim respēxit illum ipsum patrōnum libīdinis suae—nōn modo apud Bāiās esse, vērum eās ipsās aquās habēre, quae ē gustū tamen Arpīnātis fuissent. sed vidēte metuendam inimīcī et hostis bīlem et licentiam. is mē dīxit aedificāre ubi nihil habeō, <ubi habeō> ibi fuisse. quid ego enim nōn admīrer inpatientem adversārium, quī id obiciat quod vel honestē confitērī vel manifestō redarguere possīs?

"And at this point was he so blind that it easily seemed to him that he saw what he should not have seen? For he did not look back at the very patron of his recklessness, not only the fact that he was at Baiae, but also the fact that he was trying the very waters themselves—waters which had nevertheless been to the taste of a man from Arpinum. But look at the frightful temper and random behavior of this personal and political enemy. He said that I am building where I have no property, and where I have some, that I had been there. But why should I not admire this impatient adversary, who slings statements that you could either honestly admit or plainly deny?"

21. nam rūsticōs eī nōs vidērī minus est mīrandum, quī manicātam tunicam et mitram et purpureās fasciās habēre nōn possumus. tū vērō festīvus, tū ēlegāns, tū sōlus urbānus, quem decet muliebris ornātus, quem incessus psaltriae, quī effemināre vultum, attenuāre vōcem, lavāre corpus potes. o singulāre prōdigium atque mōnstrum! nōnne tē hūius templī, nōn urbis, nōn vītae, nōn lūcis pudet?

"For we should not marvel at the fact that we seem like yokels to him, we who cannot have a sleeved tunic and a fancy hat and purple garlands. But you are very witty; you are refined; you alone are sophisticated. For you female adornments are appropriate; for you the gait of a showgirl is appropriate; you can make your face look like a woman's; you can lower your voice to a whisper; you can make the skin of your body silky-smooth. O you amazing portent, you strange terror! Does not this temple shame you? Does not this city shame you? Does not this life shame you? Does not the light of day shame you?"

22. tū, quī indūtus muliebrī veste fuerīs, virīlem vōcem audēs ēmittere, cūius inportūnam libīdinem et stuprum cum scelere coniunctum nē subornandī quidem mora retardāvit?

"Did you, who wore women's clothes, dare to utter a male voice, you whose relentless lust and scandal, joined with crime, not even a necessarily clandestine delay could restrain?"

23. tūne, cum vincīrentur pedēs fasciīs, cum calautica capitī accommodārētur, cum vix manicātam tunicam in lacertōs indūcerēs, cum strophiō accūrātē praecingerēre, in tam longō spatiō numquam tē Appī Claudī nepotem esse recordātus es? nōnne, etiamsi omnem mentem libīdo āverterat, tamen ex...

"Did you, when your feet were being wrapped in linen stockings, when a turban was being fitted to your head, when with difficulty you were getting your arms into the sleeved tunic, when you were fastidiously putting on a bra, in all this time did you remember that you are a descendant of Appius Claudius? Didn't you, even if your wildness had taken away all your wits, nonetheless..."

24. sed, crēdō, postquam speculum tibi adlātum est, longē tē ā Pulchrīs abesse sēnsistī = "but, I believe, after a mirror was brought to you, you realized that you were a long way from being a Pulcher"

25. 'at sum' inquit 'absolūtus.' novō quidem hercle mōre, cuī ūnī absolūtō lītēs aestimātae sunt = " 'But I was acquitted,' he said. Indeed, by a new custom, damages are assessed against the acquitted!"

26. quasi ego nōn contentus sim, quod mihī quinque et vīgintī iūdicēs crēdidērunt, <XXXI tibī nihil crēdidērunt, quī ab senātū praesidium petierint,> quī sequestrēs abs tē locuplētēs accēperint.

"as if I were not happy, because twenty-five jurors believed me, and thirty-one did not believe you and sought out the senate's protection—they received lavish bribes from you"

27. dīvortium pontificis maximī = "the divorce of the Pontifex Maximus"

28. dē stuprō scelerātō = "concerning this crime-ridden immoral act"

29. integritās tua tē purgāvit, mihī crēde, pudor ēripuit, vīta ante acta servāvit = "Your respectability has acquitted you—trust me on that; your sense of propriety has saved you; the life you once led has kept you safe."

30. quattuor tibī sententiās solās ad perniciem dēfuisse = "that just four votes acquitted you"

31. nam L. quidem Cotta = "for Lucius Cotta indeed"

32. ut posthāc lēge Aurēlia iūdex esse nōn possit = "so that later he could not be a judge under the *lex Aurelia*"

33. errās, Clodī: nōn tē iūdicēs urbī, sed carcerī reservārunt neque tē retinēre in cīvitāte, sed exsiliō prīvāre voluērunt. quam ob rem, patrēs cōnscriptī, ērigite animōs, retinēte vestram dignitātem: manet illa in rē publicā bonōrum consensiō; dolor accessit bonīs virīs, virtūs nōn est imminūta; nihil est damnī factum novī, sed quod erat inventum est: in ūnīus hominis perditī iūdiciō plūrēs similēs repertī sunt.

"You are wrong, Clodius: the jurymen did not preserve you for the city, but for the prison; and they didn't so much want to keep you in the commonwealth as deprive you of exile. For which reason, O senators, embolden your spirits and remember your distinguished station. That common thought of patriots remains fixed on the Republic. Grief has afflicted all patriots, but their courage is undiminished; no new loss has happened, but what was there has been discovered, and in this trial of one depraved man, more just like him have been exposed."

APPENDIX D

WHY *PRO CAELIO*?

Much of the popularity of this speech, both in antiquity and today, derives (1) from Cicero's brilliant use throughout of purposeful wit and personal dynamism in the service of a complex strategy, and (2) from the sheer, timeless fascination with Clodia Metelli and her world.

Pro Caelio's special attractiveness today, over the more traditional speeches (e.g., the *Verrines*, *de imperio Cn. Pompei*, the *Catilinarians*, *pro Murena*, etc.), has much to do with contemporary emphasis on both teaching and research in social history and on hitherto ignored or excluded aspects of the ancient world.[1] The attention paid by both scholars and teachers to political and military history and even to what might be called the monuments of high culture has consequently diminished;[2] the same forces have altered other parts of the modern curriculum and of research agenda.[3] The *Zeitgeist* will, I suspect, prompt teachers and students to read the speech as primarily a document about late-Republican upper-class society.[4] The existence of an indispensible Oxford commentary whose author approaches the speech in this manner, and of an AP* program that is deliberately structured in such a way that we cannot help compare Clodia Metelli with Catullus's Lesbia, will strengthen that tendency.[5]

There is no question that *pro Caelio* is valuable as a purely social document that has much to tell us about the manners and mores of the Roman upper classes. The private and public roles of women; the overall relationship between the sexes; the Roman conception of the past and of the *mos maiorum*;

---

[1] The extent of which, in the area of scholarship, may be seen most easily by comparing the topics and entries of the third edition of the *Oxford Classical Dictionary* (1996) with the topics and entries of the second (1970) or of the first (1949).

[2] See W. Robert Connor, "The New Classical Humanities and the Old," *CJ* 81 (1985–86): 337–347. See also my comment on Buller, "Cicero's *Pro Caelio*: Text and Context," at footnote 4.

[3] Anecdotal evidence is what it is, but I offer the following for thought. I have informally compared secondary school political science and American history texts from earlier generations with those of today, and it is instructive how much more the civic, public, and legal (constitutional, statutory, and common law) traditions of the United States are stressed in the former over the latter. For an interesting consideration of trends in political science research, see Jeremy Rabkin, "Cornell's Public Law Tradition in Political Science," *Cornell University Arts and Sciences Newsletter* 16.2 (1995): 1.

[4] Buller's fine article "Cicero's *Pro Caelio*: Text and Context," *CO* 71 (1994): 121–128, suggests three ways of asking students to approach the speech: through a character study, a sociological study, and/or a rhetorical study; a political study is tellingly missing from his suggestions.

[5] Note, however, that the speech's roots in the politics of the mid-50's b.c. are treated carefully and comprehensively by Gruen and Wiseman.

[*] AP is a registered trademark of the College Entrance Examination Board, which was not involved in the production of, and does not endorse, this product.

ancient slavery; the role of drama, festival, and spectacle; and a dozen other topics can be examined profitably. But over and above all the laughter, beyond Clodia and her salons, and yet just under the surface, *pro Caelio* is every bit as much about politics as the aforementioned speeches of state.

The naked politicization of the judicial system; politicians' currying of favor with the Forum crowd generally and with the *corona* rabble at the trial; the tremendous *auctoritas* and overarching private power of the magnates and great houses like the Claudii; the utter weakness of the magistracy; the complete disconnect between the theory of the constitution and its practice; the ability of sensible decisions of state to become targets of criminal litigation; the fact that this case was tried at all in the way it was tried—all provide a view of the corrosive rot at the heart of Roman law, politics, and public life.

Caelius's political leanings coupled with the internal evidence of the case— not to mention his later involvement with Milo and his aberrations during the Civil War—suggest that he was probably guilty of at least some of the charges; Cicero likely knew this and that fact suggests the political and moral ambiguity of late-republican politics. Cicero's complete social destruction of Clodia, who may have been hardly the wanton sex maniac Cicero claims,[6] is as vicious as it is funny, even taking into account the norms of Republican invective and the gulf between Roman and modern sensibilities. For all his eloquence and wit, and despite what we know about his intelligence, sensitivity, and sense of fair play in so many other areas of his life, Cicero's involvement in this case must bring him down a notch or two in our judgment of his character. So we have come full circle: there is no better way to do a primarily sociological study of ancient Rome than to examine the capacity of the late-republican political system to be morally and ethically destructive—even to men (and no doubt to women) of principle. *Pro Caelio* is an ideal vehicle for such a study.

The Roman Republic was the first large-scale political entity governed not through the personal rule of a monarch, but by an admixture of aristocratic deliberation and popular consent.[7] Its ultimate failure to solve its problems in constitutional law, public administration, applied political theory, economic policy, and foreign affairs, and the relationship among these matters and the social climate of the first century b.c., are themes not to be ignored. I hope that teachers and students will take the opportunity the speech offers to examine such questions, and I have tried in my introduction and notes to point the way whenever possible.[8]

---

[6] The view is espoused by Skinner (1983) and Hillard.

[7] Hence the frequent comparisons to 18C Britain; see Stockton or Haskell.

[8] If students know little about the political traditions of their own country, it might be a reasonable question to ask whether we can expect them to be interested in the political structure and assumptions of the ancient world. But that does not mean we should not try to explore both with them.

APPENDIX E

RELATED HISTORICAL FICTION: BENITA KANE JARO'S *THE LOCK, THE KEY,* AND *THE DOOR IN THE WALL*

Teachers and students will be happy to know that three works of historical fiction that cover aspects of the 50s B.C. have appeared under the imprint of Bolchazy-Carducci Publishers: Benita Kane Jaro's *The Lock, The Key,* and *The Door in the Wall.* Much in these books is speculative, as is inevitable since effective historical fiction must stand on its own as art, which means more fiction than history. It is always a precarious balance between fidelity to history and the creation of plot, theme, and the active involvement of the reader.[1] As history, Jaro's books *are* entirely plausible because her hypotheses rest on impeccable research. The degree of accuracy is such that for the professional classicist there is not a lot of suspense in them. As with Greek tragedy when it was performed before its original audience, we read to see how transmitted, usually familiar material (texts, including fragments; and Roman topography and archeology) is handled in the situations and conversations Jaro creates, and it is treated with agility, verve, thoroughness, and emotional content. And her scholarly notes at the back of each volume conclusively show her as apt a scholar and historian as she is a novelist.

Depending on the instructor's syllabus and approach, these books can be assigned concurrently with the course; AP* teachers could also consider one or more as summer reading or during the weeks after the AP* examination. Each volume is self-contained, yet consistent with the other two.

The Lock covers 62–52 B.C., that is, the period from Rome's holding of its collective breath upon Pompey's landing in Italy to the chaos of the tumultuous year that set the stage for the Civil War. Cicero is the central character, and the book is largely about his handling of the central problems of the 50s: Caesar's and Crassus's conflicting ambitions; Pompeius's awkward, semi-hegemonic position; acerbic politics in the senate; quagmires in foreign policy to confound a Metternich; and control of the Roman street. A considerable

---

[1] Professor Allen Ward's preface, common to all three books, is an excellent statement of the issues; Jaro discusses her approach in appendixes entitled "History in this Book" (*The Lock* 267–268; *The Key* 203–204; *The Door in the Wall* 245–246). These appendixes are useful not only as a primer in methodology for this genre, but also for distinguishing fact, fiction, and the various shades of grey in between.

* AP is a registered trademark of the College Entrance Examination Board, which was not involved in the production of, and does not endorse, this product.

amount of background on the Catilinarian conspiracy is told in flashback in order to explain the politics of the 50s and in particular Cicero's exile in 58 B.C. The youthful Caelius appears: callow and surprisingly charming, even likable; and pp. 191–198 are a detailed treatment of the background to *Pro Caelio* and the speech itself. *The Lock* includes appendices on Jaro's treatment of history; on Cicero's letters; on the words *res publica* (in relation to "constitution") and *boni* (regarding which I would note that "Tories," with its eighteenth-century ring, is an even better translation of this difficult word than "conservative," but would confuse American students); on the meetings of the Senate; on Roman political careers; on time, dates, and weather; on Roman legal procedure; on Caelius's puns *"in triclinium Coam, in cubiculum Noam"* and *"quadrantaria Clytemnestra"*; and on Roman names. A final appendix, "Did Cicero deliver a speech at Milo's trial?" handles a scholarly question in a most competent fashion; I might suggest more explicitly that *Pro Milone* is certainly not the only extant speech of Cicero's that is different from what he actually delivered, a topic that is a prime subject of current scholarship.

The Key covers the literary life of Catullus from 59 to 54 B.C. through the eyes of Caelius Rufus, and of the three books may be the most relevant to AP* teachers. The first-person narration cleverly begins after Catullus's death; Gaius Valerius Catullus senior has arrived at Caelius's house to retrieve his deceased son's remains, and gently requests of Caelius: "Explain him to me." The ensuing first-person narration is at once a biography and a meditation on Catullus's short, intense, and (to Jaro, with whom my AP* students would agree) unhappy life. The appendixes include an original translation of Catullus 63;[2] on Roman names, time, dates, and weather; on the cult of Cybele the great mother, on the poetry of Catullus; and on the words *glubit* and *nostra* in poem 58.

The Door in the Wall covers the life of Julius Caesar through the eyes of Caelius Rufus in the period 61–48 B.C., and features appendices on Jaro's approach to "History in this Book"; on the words "cohort" and "decimate"; and on "What Happened After." In this last appendix, I think it is worth noting here that Cicero's comment that Caelius deserved *vita longior et fatum melius*, "a longer life and a better fate," shows how much he was taken in by Caelius's magnetism and oratory—in my view a slip in judgment that Jaro shares. I find Caelius to be an oily operator.

---

[2] Of which Wilamowitz wrote, "perhaps the most remarkable poem in Latin"; this is a poem that really should be on the AP* syllabus, and whose continued absence is a mystery to me.

* AP is a registered trademark of the College Entrance Examination Board, which was not involved in the production of, and does not endorse, this product.

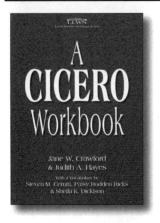
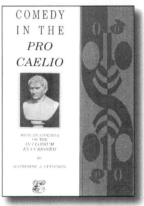